DATE DUE

Demco, Inc. 38-293

DEC 0 1 2011

KAIJA SAARIAHO: VISIONS, NARRATIVES, DIALOGUES

Kaija Saariaho: Visions, Narratives, Dialogues

Edited by
TIM HOWELL
University of York, UK
with
JON HARGREAVES
Independent Scholar, UK
and
MICHAEL ROFE
University College Falmouth, UK

ASHGATE

Bach musicological font developed by © Yo Tomita

Published by
Ashgate Publishing Limited
Wey Court East
Union Road
Farnham
Surrey, GU9 7PT
England

Ashgate Publishing Company
Suite 420
101 Cherry Street
Burlington
VT 05401-4405
USA

www.ashgate.com

British Library Cataloguing in Publication Data
Kaija Saariaho : visions, narratives, dialogues.
  1. Saariaho, Kaija–Criticism and interpretation.
  I. Howell, Tim. II. Hargreaves, Jon. III. Rofe, Michael.
  780.9'2-dc22

Library of Congress Cataloging-in-Publication Data
Kaija Saariaho : visions, narratives, dialogues / [edited by] Tim Howell, Jon Hargreaves, and Michael Rofe.
    p. cm.
  Includes bibliographical references and index.
  ISBN 978-1-4094-2116-0 (hardcover) 1. Saariaho, Kaija–Criticism and interpretation.
I. Howell, Tim. II. Hargreaves, Jon. III. Rofe, Michael.

  ML410.S114K37 2011
  780.92–dc22

2011010615

ISBN 9781409421160

MIX
Paper from
responsible sources
FSC
www.fsc.org   FSC® C013056

Printed and bound in Great Britain by
TJ International Ltd, Padstow, Cornwall.

Contents

List of Examples

Notes on Contributors

Jon Hargreaves is a freelance researcher, conductor, composer, arranger and musician. He completed his PhD in 2008 at the University of York and his thesis, *Music as Communication: Networks of Composition*, investigated issues of communication between composers and listeners in twentieth-century music. Since finishing his PhD he has taught freelance at the University of York, York St John University, and in the junior school of Trinity College of Music in London. In 2009 he worked as Research Associate for Heriot-Watt University, composing music for an experiment investigating the effects of music on dairy cattle. Currently, he is the Research Consultant for the *Changing Key* project, a study of the potential for the role of music in school transition, funded by the Paul Hamlyn Foundation. He now lives and works in London, where he has recently co-founded The Octandre Ensemble.

Liisamaija Hautsalo works as a Post-Doctoral Researcher at the Sibelius Academy, Helsinki, where she also teaches the history of Finnish opera. Her current research project involves the development of online material for teaching Finnish opera in schools. Hautsalo completed her doctoral dissertation '*L'Amour de loin*: The Semantics of the Unattainable in Kaija Saariaho's Opera' at the University of Helsinki in 2008. Her specialist fields are Finnish opera, history of opera, contemporary opera and semiotic theory of musical topics; she also works as a music critic and writer.

Tim Howell is a Senior Lecturer in the Department of Music at the University of York, where he specializes in the analysis of new music. From the publication of his PhD thesis onwards, he has become an internationally recognized authority on the music of Sibelius, which has led to numerous publications, conference contributions and visiting lectures – most notably at the Sibelius Academy in Helsinki. His research has now broadened to encompass contemporary Finnish music. *After Sibelius: Studies in Finnish Music* (Ashgate, 2006) provides an engaging investigation into Finnish music and combines elements of composer biography and detailed analysis within the broader context of cultural and national identity. This study of Finnish musical modernism, the first in English, has been highly acclaimed: 'An elegant, concise and penetrating work that places this music within a larger European context while addressing the difficult question of what is "Finnishness" in music' [*Music Research Forum*].

Vesa Kankaanpää has been a Senior Lecturer at the Turku Arts Academy, Finland, since 1999. He teaches research methods and supervises the academic writing of students working in animation, film, media management, advertising and music. Kankaanpää studied musicology at the University of Turku, music technology at the University of York (UK) and was a visiting scholar at the City University, London. He has published research on Kaija Saariaho's music in Finnish (for example, in *Musiikki*, 1995, and in *Elektronisia unelmia*, 2005), as well as in English (*Organized Sound*, 1996) and in German (*Musiktexte*, 2006).

Daniel March is a Lecturer in the Music Department at the University of York where he specializes in the teaching of music analysis. His research focuses upon music of the late twentieth and early twenty-first centuries. His doctoral thesis, 'Beyond Simplicity: Analytical Strategies for Contemporary Music', provided analytical readings of works by Reich, Feldman, Nyman and others, and a framework for the analysis of music that escapes traditional models. Recent research involves an examination of the work concept in relation to twentieth-century 're-compositions', and analytical approaches to the music of György Ligeti and Louis Andriessen.

Anni Oskala completed a DPhil at Oxford University in 2007 with a thesis that focused on the vocal works of Kaija Saariaho, particularly her first opera, *L'Amour de loin*. After her doctorate, she pursued a research career in the UK public and charity sectors, initially working as a researcher for the Arts Council of England and authoring a number of reports including *From Indifference to Enthusiasm* (2008). Her current post is that of Senior Researcher at NatCen, working on a project called 'Understanding Society', a major new longitudinal study of UK society.

Taina Riikonen is a Post-Doctoral Researcher (funded by the Academy of Finland) in the Department of Doctoral Studies at the Sibelius Academy in Helsinki. Her research project, 'Sonic Interaction', explores the processes of 'encountering' in the context of contemporary sound-making, focusing particularly on the interaction between acoustic instrumentalists and electronics. This process of interaction is evidenced through three different case studies: the chamber ensemble 'Avanti!' (Finland), the free-improvisation group 'Automatic Writing Circle' (London, UK) and the Experimental Studio of Finnish Radio Broadcasting Company.

Michael Rofe is a Senior Lecturer in Music at University College Falmouth, where he specializes in teaching contemporary music. He previously worked as a Lecturer in Music at York St John University, a visiting Lecturer at the University of York and a Course Developer at Canterbury Christ Church University. His research interests centre on musical energetics, particularly as applied to twentieth and twenty-first century repertoire. Having taken his PhD at the University of York, he has recently completed a monograph, *Dimensions of Energy in Shostakovich's*

Symphonies (Ashgate, 2012), in which he offers historical, philosophical and psychological perspectives on the nature of musical energy, analyzing repertoire from a time when energeticist metaphors were widely used in Russian musicology. Other research projects include articles on the work of Russian theorist Boleslav Yavorsky, physical models of time and their application to music theory, and the origins and effects of temporal proportion in music.

Tom Service completed a doctorate at the University of Southampton on the music of John Zorn. He writes about music for *The Guardian*, and is a regular contributor to *BBC Music Magazine*, *Opera* and *Tempo*. His articles have appeared in books and music dictionaries, and in journals in France and Germany. He has given pre-concert talks and written programme notes for many of the festivals, orchestras and opera companies in the UK. He began broadcasting on Radio 3 on *Hear and Now* in 2001, becoming one of the show's regular presenters, and has presented *Music Matters* since the autumn of 2003. Additional work for the BBC includes introducing Proms concerts (on radio and TV), appearances on *Newsnight Review* (BBC 2) and Radio 5 Live.

Preludes and Codas

Kaija Saariaho is internationally recognized as a leading figure in contemporary music, enjoying a well-deserved reputation for works that are both creatively original and of considerable appeal. Her music communicates widely, reaching a refreshingly broad audience, and this special achievement merits careful consideration. In the first symposium book in English to be dedicated exclusively to this single figure, scholars from both the UK and Saariaho's native Finland bring a range of perspectives to her richly varied output. Uncovering the compositional, historical, cultural and sociological issues that have engendered such critical acclaim lies at the heart of this collection of essays. Saariaho's approach to composition is an inter-disciplinary one; it embraces a number of art forms – visual, literary and musical – in works that explore a creative dialogue between image, continuity and time. The content and structure of this volume reflect that breadth of aesthetic, drawing on a variety of approaches to reveal common perceptions of musical creativity.

While such diversity is readily accommodated in a multi-authored collection, the consistency of an underlying compositional identity is also a significant trait. To achieve this degree of unity has involved some important decisions, and it is useful to share these as a prelude to the book itself. Any notion of 'Saariaho studies' is only in its infancy given a lack of well-established experts in this area, so selecting contributors was something of a challenge. A positive sense of freedom of choice had to be offset against its potentially fragmentary nature; there could be a rather more diffuse range of contributions than might easily be assimilated into a coherent volume. Above all, there was never the intention to produce a compendium, as so often that can amount to little more than a miscellany; instead, the aim is to offer something far tighter, more concentrated and carefully structured: a symposium. To that end, the choice of authors became focused on scholars from the UK and Finland, as this provided a meaningful balance between two centres of research within what is effectively a new discipline.

It is perhaps worth noting that while the idea of a 'research group' is standard practice within scientific communities (and indeed is very common in the social sciences), it is still something of a rarity in the arts. The Department of Music at the University of York is an internationally renowned centre for the study of contemporary music, with specialist expertise in the area of (new) music from Finland. To varying degrees, the four UK authors are all connected to this central point of reference; their collaboration provides both a unity of purpose and a variety of approach: a research group, in effect. Another crucial facet in this enterprise concerns Saariaho's Finnish roots. Although a truly cosmopolitan figure, she acknowledges the significance of her national identity: the notion of 'Finnishness' is deeply embedded in her compositional psyche, even though she has lived in Paris since the 1980s. Indeed, this Finnish connection is not simply a part of the origin of this music – it also filters into its reception. Most obviously, there is a relevant body of scholarship and critical study that is only available in its native language. (Finnish is, of course, completely unrelated to other European languages, making this valuable resource stubbornly inaccessible to many – if not most – readers.) The inclusion of four researchers from Finland, all of whom have previously published writings on this composer (in their own language), gives a symbiotic relationship to the whole enterprise. They are able to absorb and comment upon a whole range of thinking and writing that their UK counterparts cannot easily assimilate, while an English-based editorial team can ensure that these materials reach as wide a readership as possible, given the ubiquity of their language.

With the contributor rationale growing out of a York–Helsinki axis, the book needed to be carefully structured if these contrasting views were to be fashioned into a coherent whole. A symposium of nine chapters offering individual perspectives on a single composer, *Kaija Saariaho: Visions, Narratives, Dialogues* reflects the preoccupations of this thought-provoking figure. The grouping of these contributions under three main headings outlines the breadth of Saariaho's creative concerns while subscribing to a carefully formed succession of commentaries. These larger conceptual domains are sufficiently flexible to absorb a number of interpretative approaches, yet distinctive enough to articulate a logical sequence overall. Within this framework, a blend of informed technical discussion and interpretative critical contexts illuminates the composer's choice of subjects that inspire her. But what about her personal voice in all of this? An in-depth interview forms the opening chapter, inviting the reader to 'meet the composer' before engaging with her music. And, of course, music (her truly personal voice) is absolutely central to all of these contributions which, collectively, offer a wide coverage of this repertoire. Consequently, the sheer variety of Saariaho's work and its considerable appeal – features that provided the initial impetus for this book – form the guiding principle behind its construction.

The concept of 'visions' is far-sighted enough to embrace issues that range from Saariaho's compositional manifesto – her formative experiences and aesthetic values – to an interest in the subconscious as portrayed, for instance, through dreams. For Saariaho, the inspirational effects of visual stimuli on her compositional process cannot be overestimated. Earlier interests in electronic media, and continued preoccupations with blurring the distinctions between timbre and harmony, contribute to a desire to 'sculpt' sound into fluid forms. A student of art and design as well as music, gifted with synaesthetic abilities that enable her to see music as colours, many of her pieces are reflective of a visual imagery that was the catalyst for their inception. *Lichtbogen* (1986), a pivotal work within the composer's stylistic development and her growing international reputation, is a case in point. A creative reaction to the ghostly forms of the *aurora borealis*, the choice of title – 'Arches of Light' – is a strikingly visual clue to both the external imagery that prompted its conception and the temporal and formal processes that govern its composition. One feature of the Northern Lights is a sense of infinity – of timelessness. Yet their flickering rays have energy and speed – light in motion. Typically, Saariaho is preoccupied here with all-embracing, slow transformations, generating a sense of stasis on the largest scale: 'arches'. Set against this is a musical surface that is full of life, with its energetic repetition patterns and constant timbral variation: 'light'. Saariaho's music readily invites such interpretations. Connections between extra-musical image and musical realization result in an imaginative interplay of visual and aural responses: *Lichtbogen* reaches out to its audience in a number of different ways.

Saariaho's commitment to literary-inspired musical forms stems from a number of perspectives on the idea of 'narrative'. From the most basic definition of storytelling (as distinct from dialogue), through issues of history, memoir, legend, fortune and experience, various potential ways of generating musical continuity form a crucial strand in her aesthetic. At its most technical, Saariaho's absorption of spectralist thinking, with its inherent composing-out of fundamental acoustic phenomena – their temporal transformation – is essentially a narrative process. This collision of interests, both literary and technical, originates from a formative stage in her career. As a composition student in Finland in the 1970s, she had to come to terms with a music history that was uniquely dominated by a single, patriarchal figure: the so-called 'shadow' of Sibelius, as previous generations termed it. The effect of this legacy was wide-ranging, as Saariaho explains:

> In Finland we have an odd situation: on the one hand, we are equal; on the other, a completely patriarchal system governs. Every area must have some kind of father figure, Kekkonen [the former president of Finland for 25 years], or Kokkonen [one of the most prominent composers in Finland from the 1950s to the 1980s] – there is something inbuilt in it, the whole system of upbringing leads to that. All the important Finns are men, including musicians. It comes from Finnish mythology (in Moisala, 2009: 17).

From this position, it was hardly surprising that while searching for her compositional identity she notes that 'many women writers were important: Edith Södergran, Virginia Woolf, Sylvia Plath, Anaïs Nin. I was interested in how women writers [and painters] had been able to do this creative work, of which I didn't find any satisfying examples in music' (in Beyer, 2000b: 4). This strongly felt literary influence is deeply ingrained and has had long-lasting, positive effects. Not only did it initially manifest itself in an exclusive preoccupation with vocal music, establishing a productive relationship between (literary) text and (musical) form, it eventually resulted in an enormous commitment to writing opera. Saariaho is on record as seeing her compositional output from about 1983 onwards as directly connected to her first opera, *L'Amour de loin* ('Love from Afar'), completed in 2000 (see Beyer, 2000b: 6). With its renewed interest in dramatic discourse and attendant musical continuity, this opera is the culmination of a number of earlier trends. It is also part of an ongoing narrative. This particular focus continues in her later operatic and stage works, and represents a deep-rooted, inter-disciplinary approach.

Consequently, while visual elements most directly contribute to a formal shaping that is broadly architectural and therefore spatial, literary concerns are conveyed through a narrative impulse that is more organic and temporal. These contrasting yet complementary ways of shaping material are the result of a meaningful dialogue between different structural forces. Usefully, this brings us to the last stage of the book. 'Dialogues' is perhaps the most over-arching category here, with the potential to draw upon both visual and narrative elements and hold them in a creative synthesis. An exchange of ideas is a fundamental trait. On the broadest level, given how this music communicates with its audience and how positively they respond to it, there is a genuine dialogue between composer and listener. Internal debates about modernism, and its degree of challenge to tradition, form an aesthetic dialogue applicable to both parties. More locally, the setting up of oppositional strategies to generate tensions that unfold over time conditions much of Saariaho's approach. The complementary process of mitigating between these conflicting impulses – especially in the search for resolution and closure – is essentially one of dialogue. A good example is *Aile du songe*, 'Wing of Dreams' (2001) which, as Saariaho's first major composition after the groundbreaking *L'Amour de loin*, is a work of dramatic oppositions: a concerto (for flute and orchestra). Its overall structure is in two parts, 'Aérienne' ('Ethereal') and 'Terrestre' ('Terrestrial'), titles taken from the Saint-John Perse collection of poems that inspired it. Consequently, dialogues emerge from these extra-musical influences – both visual and literary – and are conveyed through the inherent duality of the concerto genre itself. This fundamental idea of a pairing of opposites operates on a number of perceptual levels: dreams/realities; ethereal/terrestrial; air/land; sky/earth; flute/orchestra; variation/repetition; improvised/controlled; dynamic/static. Musical processes emanate from external impulses, offering a wide range of listening strategies to a variety of audiences.

So much for the composer, the contributors and the construction of this book: what about the reader? In the urgency of a technological age, with its instant communication that seems so reductionist – consider the cull of vowels (in text messaging), the length of tweets (on Twitter) and the single-letter adjective (from the e-book to the iPad) – most people are unlikely to read this volume sequentially, let alone from cover to cover. Flexibility is key. Consequently, each contribution forms a self-contained unit, while their succession may be approached in any order: you are encouraged to browse. Also, in terms of both length and focus, every chapter is designed to be readable at a single sitting (though, in some cases, you may need a lie-down afterwards). For those with greater stamina, the placing of these contributions into groups of three may offer another logical route, should that appeal. For now though, as a further prelude to the book, the ensuing synopsis provides an additional overview; together with a coda that draws together a number of common threads from across the volume, the reader should find different ways to approach its diverse contents. With music that is so successful at reaching out to its audience, this book hopes to communicate with its readership in an equivalent manner.

Starting from the broadest perspective, 'Visions' sets out by recording the composer's own viewpoint; in an extensive interview with Tom Service, Kaija Saariaho explains her aesthetic values and discusses the formative experiences that have shaped her development as a creative artist. She emerges as an intensely private person who is nonetheless all too aware of her hugely public profile, thereby setting the scene for a number of such contradictory elements that surround her music. In the following study, 'From the Air to the Earth: Reading the Ashes', Daniel March outlines the evocation of the nebulous, extra-musical, visual stimuli that have inspired Saariaho's works. This encapsulates a significant characteristic of the sonic world she seeks to portray, as expressive atmospheres are transformed into precisely imagined structures. That dream-like quality of creative inspiration is explored further by Anni Oskala; 'Dreams about Music, Music about Dreams' uncovers the structures and symbolism of a recurrent theme in this music, and locates its findings with reference to Freudian dream theory. Visual stimuli and their potential for psychoanalysis are brought into alignment and offer particular insights into her artistic imagination, especially when read in conjunction with Saariaho's earlier biographical comments.

Literary influences and the close relationship between title and soundscape – the complex inter-connection of words and music – provide a backdrop to the concept of 'Narratives'. Taina Riikonen approaches this issue from a performer's perspective, and 'Stories from the Mouth' considers the projections of speech and music in relation to Saariaho's highly individual flute writing. The questioning of boundaries, more typically applied to compositional parameters (like timbre and harmony), finds a new direction in the context of human characteristics: 'bodily presence and intimacy' – whispering, breathing, speaking, playing. Narratives that are the product of a distinctive type of musical continuity, one that stems from organic growth and the creative recycling of materials, are discerned by Michael Rofe. Adopting Saariaho's comment on her compositional process, 'Capturing Time and Giving it Form' (in Moisala 2009: 54), he uncovers the idea of temporal narrative as evidenced through an analytical reading of *Nymphéa*; the implications arising from this are suitably organic, given their wide-ranging significance. Saariaho's commitment to writing opera is a major element in her oeuvre, and the relationship between these groundbreaking works and a broader operatic tradition forms the starting point of Liisamaija Hautsalo's study: 'Whispers from the Past'. A semiotic approach to the concept of musical topics within *L'Amour de loin* and *Adriana Mater* provides both a literary slant and a more historical outlook on the narrative theme.

Finally, with Saariaho's music being acclaimed for its ability to communicate with audiences, the third phase of this volume involves a range of 'Dialogues'. The clearest genre to focus on oppositions and combinations, 'Dualities and Dialogues'

– the concerto – forms the basis of an analytical investigation of selected works. My intention here is to demonstrate how competing formal impulses – architectural and spatial versus organic and temporal – are directly conveyed through the concerto, a medium that Saariaho particularly values. This is offset by Vesa Kankaanpää's 'Dichotomies, Relationships: Timbre and Harmony in Revolution' in its more technical consideration of spectral methods and their musical results, at a formative stage in her career. A creative dichotomy emerges from Saariaho's individual engagement with the blurred relationship between timbre and harmony. As this issue is the focus of Saariaho's first theoretical essay about her own music, Kankaanpää's chapter is an important exploration of the implications of her (self-)analysis. A closing investigation of how Saariaho constructs such highly effective 'Networks of Communication', and their significance for our perception of her music, helps to open up new debates and synthesize fundamental issues in a thought-provoking discussion. A number of elements crystallize here as Jon Hargreaves, in an individual blend of philosophical, psychological and analytical approaches, uncovers a range of listening strategies evoked through the metaphor of *Du cristal ...à la fumée.*

Ending in a cloud of smoke, which is where Chapter 2 began, suggests a kind of cyclic quality to the book as a whole – though it is really just one of many coincidental crosscurrents that reside amongst this collection. A variety of perspectives within self-contained chapters amounts to a succession of individual viewpoints: this is the strength and appeal of any multi-authored volume. With authors given free rein to choose the issues, approaches and musical contexts that best illustrate their personal topics for discussion, observing underlying threads that run throughout the book is of interest. Certainly these themes offer a number of signposts for the reader, but they are also indicative of shared concerns which, in turn, may point to some fundamental qualities in Saariaho's music. While these chapters subscribe to the logic of a precisely formed framework, individually they offer freely imagined discussions. Although this is by no means accidental, it nonetheless does involve aspects of speculation, chance – a degree of randomness. Coincidence is a powerful force. Of course, all of this is perfectly appropriate to the study of a composer who deliberately and creatively synthesizes such contrary impulses within her musical narratives. Indeed, it is a notable feature of any engagement with modernism – let alone with the twentieth century itself, which still remains the most untidy period in (musical) history.

Historical context may be a useful starting point for these codas of common themes; finding a 'place' for Saariaho's music, how it might 'fit' in a post-serialist, post-spectralist – even post-modernist – world is of interest or concern (depending on your standpoint) to several authors. Focusing in a stage raises the spectre of contemporary music in general and Finnish new music in particular – though Saariaho's prolonged (and by now permanent) residence in Paris positively forces us to adopt a more cosmopolitan stance. The extraordinary nature of the Finnish phenomenon, this small country seemingly on the fringes of Europe that is such a big player on the international stage of current musical creativity, is not to be underestimated though. Finland has well and truly emerged from the shadows and come into the spotlight by now. Wherever we seek to position Saariaho's achievements in the competing demands of globalized, twenty-first century composition, we must acknowledge (as she does herself) an indebtedness to the highly educated, open-minded and supportive attitudes to artistic endeavour that characterize her homeland. The cultural values of Finland embrace all artistic creativity – and music in particular – in an enviably enlightened way. Interestingly, though, few commentators here feel it necessary to investigate Saariaho's position in relation, say, to Sibelius, whose shadow cast light on subsequent generations of composers. It seems as if her distance from tradition, coupled with the lack of a single chronological route of musical development, has proved to be more relevant: less 'after' Sibelius, more 'beyond' him. Fragmentation and diversity are crucial. We are no longer content (if, indeed, we ever were) to view history as merely one thing after another: cross-currents and contradictions along with discontinuities and interruptions seem to interest us more.

The pioneering spirit associated with Kaija Saariaho – as the first woman composer from Finland to achieve international recognition – has somehow retreated into the distance as well. What remains so surprising is the time it took for a woman to achieve this status in the first place. Finland was, after all, the first country in Europe to give equal voting rights to women in national elections (in 1906) and this has resulted in an impressive degree of equal opportunities, reflected through a social democracy that values fairness. But, once again, Saariaho has chosen to maintain a discrete and considered distance: she claims to have no gender agenda. As Pirkko Moisala explains:

> She frequently emphasised that she did not want her gender to be an issue and that she did not want to be called a 'woman composer' any more that she wanted to be labelled a 'computer composer'. She wanted people to experience her music as music, instead of as music composed by a woman (Moisala, 2009: 16).

Issues about the role of women composers are correspondingly embedded (rather than highlighted) in the chapters of this book, with the operas providing the most direct comment here. The subject matter of *L'Amour de loin* and especially that of *Adriana Mater* perhaps offer the clearest insight into any feminist thinking on the composer's part – though only to the extent that individual listeners seek to relate to it. Performance issues arising from Saariaho's personal engagement with writing for the flute provide a further, refreshingly novel perspective on this topic. Any relevance to the formative stages of her composing career emerges with both frankness and self-awareness during the interview which opens this book. All of this conveys a notably human, personal quality that lies behind the artistic remove of the concert-hall.

It appears that different degrees of 'distance' collectively form an ongoing strand amongst various chapters, crystallizing in the idea that Saariaho has an individual – distinctive – voice within current musical styles. Part of that

Kaija Saariaho: Visions, Narratives, Dialogues

uniqueness stems from a very special attitude to musical timescale, though it is possible to locate this attribute within typically Finnish preoccupations (see Howell, 2010); few composers today write music that has such slow-moving, background transformations. A number of perspectives on the projection of musical time, especially in conjunction with the positioning of formal space, recur in several studies that are otherwise quite different. Whether or not such approaches are analytical, psychological, philosophical or historical, or even if they are geared (respectively) towards compositional intention, listener perception, aesthetic value or scholarly reception, time and motion are fundamental traits. This issue almost amounts to a leitmotif within the book as a whole. Indeed, the sheer variety of ways in which temporal concerns are manifest within such contrasting genres becomes a compositional fingerprint in itself. Any composer working in this post-tonal world, who defines their craft as 'capturing time and giving it a form', is likely to prompt investigations of how this might be achieved: Saariaho is always prepared to address true essentials. Consequently, this gives rise to a number of related topics of which musical continuity, temporal narrative, formal perception and structural perspective seem the most prevalent. Saariaho's economy – deploying a minimum of material to maximum effect – is a significant common denominator in this regard.

But what about the distinctive sound-world that her music inhabits? 'Harmony', 'timbre', 'texture' are perhaps the most frequently used terms in this book, especially in relation to the whole notion of 'spectral composition'. Fortunately this is not the place to steal the thunder of fellow contributors, so most of the technical, analytical and perceptual characteristics of Saariaho's (spectral) soundscapes can only appear in the fullness of time – over the course of this volume. On the broadest scale, stylistic 'placing' of this music becomes relevant again, providing a useful context. As a student in Helsinki in the late 1970s, the emergence of musical modernism through the achievements of Erik Bergman (1911–2006), the earlier works of Einojuhani Rautavaara (b. 1928) and, above all, in the compositions and teaching of Paavo Heininen (b. 1938) enabled Saariaho to engage with current trends. But with something of the prevailing post-serial mentality proving to be a limitation, she became a founding member of the 'Ears Open!' society, *Korvat auki* – a vanguard of modernist developments that proactively sought to challenge the establishment. Characteristic of this group was its interest in compositional developments outside their native Finland, especially in continental Europe; coming into contact with the spectralist music of Gérard Grisey (1946–98) and Tristan Murail (b. 1947), was a notably formative experience. Looking back, it seems somehow inevitable that Saariaho, along with her colleague Magnus Lindberg, would end up studying at IRCAM – though her settling in Paris thereafter was a more measured decision.

The deliberate blurring and re-defining of traditionally discrete parameters, seen by many as a stock-in-trade feature of Saariaho's sound-world, can be traced back to this period. (For more details, see Howell, 2006; Moisala, 2009.) Engagements with electronic media, computer-generated materials and a preoccupation with spectral analysis form an ongoing, developmental thread within Saariaho's oeuvre. The idea of 'composer as theorist' is also relevant here. Saariaho is someone who researches and theorizes what she does, applying those findings to her music and establishing underlying principles. But this rational, compositional approach is offset by expressive, aesthetic concerns. This music never sounds like some kind of technical exercise: it is frequently praised for its sensual beauty.

By now, Saariaho's reservoir of technique is so fully integrated into a process of 'sculpting' sound into fluid narratives that any separating out of its constituent elements is almost a contradiction in terms. 'Almost' is important here. Markedly differing views on this common issue arise during the chapters that follow, with a range of perspectives on how far harmony and timbre, for instance, may be assimilated as separate/distinctive or integrated/unified entities. Additionally, there is much debate about how this may be perceived by audiences, understood by analysts, evaluated by psychologists. In turn, the larger-scale ramifications of this sonic flexibility and its structural shaping – how the listener comes to process form, or whether form is actually just a process – creates a range of potentially conflicting, contradictory, even paradoxical viewpoints. 'Contradiction' therefore becomes a theme in its own right. It encompasses widely differing critical opinions, a range of oppositional strategies within the compositional frameworks that Saariaho adopts, and a creative aesthetic that combines expressive sensuality with discipline and rigour.

The fact that there is no single way to assimilate or appreciate this music is confirmed by these chapters. Such diversity should be warmly welcomed, as it is surely a strength that so much variety exists within a truly distinctive compositional voice. Therefore, as we come to conclude that Saariaho's artistry reaches out to a refreshingly broad audience, it seems as if this particular Coda has returned to the opening Prelude: so it must be time to stop. Personally, *Kaija Saariaho: Visions, Narratives, Dialogues* is the culmination of a long-term project that has moved from my championing the cause of Finnish new music within the international arena to our celebrating the remarkable success of one of its leading exponents. The collaboration that follows is between authors who share a sincere commitment to uncover their emotional experience and intellectual understanding of this highly imaginative sound-world. Ideally, something of their collective enthusiasm for Saariaho's sheer inventiveness will emerge from these writings; our aim is simply to encourage you to engage further with Saariaho's creative individuality and, hopefully, to add to your enjoyment of her music.

Tim Howell
University of York, September 2010

Acknowledgements

For me, the initial impetus for this project was quite a simple one: a question of balance. *After Sibelius: Studies in Finnish Music* (2006) was a single-authored volume that considered the music of eight composers; *Kaija Saariaho: Visions, Narratives, Dialogues* is a book about a single composer, written by eight authors. Symmetry is a pleasing concept. Consequently, given the collaborative nature of this enterprise, there are a number of individuals and institutions whose contributions and support have been particularly invaluable. Without their commitment and assistance, this book would never have become a reality: I am extremely grateful to all concerned. With the composer herself at the centre of this project, I extend my warmest thanks to Kaija Saariaho – for agreeing to be interviewed about her life and work and for being so candid and insightful about her formative experiences – and to Tom Service for facilitating this process.

The Department of Music at the University of York has provided me with research leave and financial support to allow the requisite time and resources to bring this book to fruition. It also has proved to be something of a creative focus for a number of shared values and approaches common to the English contributors in this volume. To some degree (and as *alumni* this is quite literally the case), Jon Hargreaves, Daniel March, Michael Rofe and Tom Service have long-standing connections to this central reference point. Correspondingly, our Finnish counterparts have their own links as they were all contributors to another multi-authored study, *Elektronisia unelmia: kirjoituksia Kaija Saariahon musiikista* [*Electronic Dreams: Writings on Kaija Saariaho's Music*], edited by Anne Sivuoja-Gunaratnam (2005). I am grateful to Helsinki University Press (now Gaudeamus HUP) for granting permission to Liisamaija Hautsalo, Vesa Kankaanpää, Anni Oskala and Taina Riikonen to draw upon some of the materials outlined in that anthology. Moreover, all these authors were refreshingly open to the idea of expanding and developing their thoughts, given this new context for their work, and I warmly commend their willingness to do so.

Elsewhere in Finland, special thanks are due to the staff at the Finnish Music Information Centre for all their help and advice. Their website (<www.fimic. fi>) gives far more detailed and up-to-date biographical information than a book like this could ever provide, especially as Saariaho continues to be so active. I am especially grateful to Andrew Bentley, Founding Head of the Department of Music and Technology at the Sibelius Academy in Helsinki, for his crucial input to this project – especially during its early stages. His exceptional linguistic skills gave me unprecedented access to a body of scholarship that would otherwise be beyond my reach, while his thoughtful reading, measured consideration and lively discussions have been enormously helpful. Special thanks are also due to Anna Krohn at the Sibelius Academy for her practical support during my various research trips to Helsinki.

Closer to home, I greatly value the commitment, enthusiasm, insight and creativity of my two co-editors, Jon Hargreaves and Michael Rofe, with whom I have enjoyed such a productive and enlightening working relationship – and friendship – for some years now. Having completed their doctoral studies and embarked on the early stages of truly promising careers, I wish them every success in the future, especially in these straitened times. Despite the best of intentions, competing demands and time constraints have resulted in differing levels of availability; I know that Jon will agree that Mike's editorial role has been particularly demanding, and join me in expressing our gratitude for all his extra work. Finally, I am indebted to my partner, Cathy Denford, for her unfailing encouragement throughout this lengthy project. Her contribution extends far beyond the creation of the image on this book jacket – even if that threatens to overturn the old maxim that you 'shouldn't judge a book by its cover' – and I am eternally grateful for her constant support.

The Music Sales Group, London has kindly granted permission for the following extracts: CENDRES Music by Kaija Saariaho (© Copyright 1998 Chester Music Limited). All Rights Reserved. International Copyright Secured. Reprinted by Permission. TERRA MEMORIA Music by Kaija Saariaho (© Copyright 2007 Chester Music Limited). All Rights Reserved. International Copyright Secured. Reprinted by Permission. L'AMOUR DE LOIN Music by Kaija Saariaho; Libretto by Amin Maalouf (Music © Copyright 2002 Chester Music Limited). (Libretto © Copyright 2002 Amin Maalouf). Exclusively licensed to Chester Music Limited. All Rights Reserved. International Copyright Secured. Reprinted by Permission. FROM THE GRAMMAR OF DREAMS Music by Kaija Saariaho; Words by Sylvia Plath (© Copyright 1988 Edition Wilhelm Hansen Helsinki OY). All Rights Reserved. International Copyright Secured. Reprinted by Permission. NOANOA Music by Kaija Saariaho (© Copyright 2000 Chester Music Limited). All Rights Reserved. International Copyright Secured. Reprinted by Permission. LACONISME DE L'AILE Music by Kaija Saariaho (© Copyright 1983 Edition Wilhelm Hansen Helsinki OY). All Rights Reserved. International Copyright Secured. Reprinted by Permission. NYMPHEA Music by Kaija Saariaho (© Copyright 1988 Edition Wilhelm Hansen Helsinki OY). All Rights Reserved. International Copyright Secured. Reprinted by Permission. ADRIANA MATER Music by Kaija Saariaho; Libretto by Amin Maalouf (Music © Copyright 2006 Chester Music Limited). (Libretto © Copyright 2006 Amin Maalouf). Exclusively licensed to Chester Music Limited. All Rights Reserved. International Copyright Secured. Reprinted by Permission. GRAAL THEATRE Music by Kaija Saariaho (© Copyright 1998 Chester Music Limited). All Rights Reserved. International Copyright Secured. Reprinted by Permission. NOTES ON LIGHT Music by Kaija Saariaho (© Copyright 2007 Chester Music Limited). All Rights Reserved. International Copyright Secured. Reprinted by Permission. LICHTBOGEN Music by Kaija Saariaho (© Copyright 1986 Edition Wilhelm Hansen Helsinki OY). All Rights Reserved. International Copyright Secured. Reprinted by Permission. DU CRISTAL Music by Kaija Saariaho (© Copyright 1990 Edition Wilhelm Hansen Helsinki OY). All Rights Reserved. International Copyright Secured. Reprinted by Permission.

Oxford University Press has kindly granted permission for the following: *Phoenix* by Richard Causton © Oxford University Press 2006. Extract reproduced by permission. All rights reserved.

Tim Howell
University of York, September 2010

Visions

Chapter 1
Meet the Composer

Kaija Saariaho in Conversation with Tom Service

Encounters with composers are always richly strange experiences. It is impossible not to carry an image of what you think the person who wrote this music might be like in person, as if a composer's character, behaviour and personality ought to mirror the qualities of their music. With Kaija Saariaho, the distinction between the persona and the music is especially fascinating. She is one of the most famous living composers in the world, yet she is an intensely private person; she writes music of sometimes voluptuous warmth and sensuality, yet, in real life, she shares that clichéd characteristic of her fellow Finns in not exactly being the last word in loquaciousness: she seems to weigh her spoken thoughts as analytically as her music is intuitive and apparently unsystematic. And yet there are points of contact. Saariaho has a tangible ethereality when you meet her – which is so often the paradoxical impression of her music. Her work has the vivid evanescence of a dream, it conjures a weightless physicality, it shimmers with invisible light. In our conversation, she reveals the biographical origins of her private creative universe, the internal and external struggles she endured growing up in Finland in order to fulfil what she instinctively felt as her destiny to be a composer, and how her musical voice was formed on the continent once she left her homeland for good in the 1980s, making her home in Paris, where she still lives.

****

Did you come from a musical family in Helsinki?

I didn't come from musical circles at all. My father was a kind of inventor who created his own business in the metal industry. When the business started taking off, my mother was just at home with the children; with me, the oldest, my sister and my brother. My parents didn't have any real education. They came from very poor families from the eastern part of Finland. So it was a family without any kind of cultural background. Music, from the start, was completely my own thing. Music was my own universe, but I had nobody to guide me. It was quite haphazard, what I learnt and what I didn't learn.

So how did you first really discover music?

When I was really a little child. I was very sensitive. There was some music that frightened me, and some that I liked. We had an old-fashioned radio at home, so I listened to music on that. But I also heard music when I was a girl that didn't come from a radio. It was music that was in my mind. I imagined that it came from my pillow. My mother remembered me asking her to turn the pillow off at night when I couldn't sleep; to turn off the music that I imagined inside my head.

We had a beautiful summer house in Karelia, in my mother's village. I still own the house, in fact, but I don't have time to go there very much. I remember when I was six or seven that I heard Bach's music on the radio there. It was fantastic to hear that music in the midst of nature. I remembered his name, and because I went to a Rudolf Steiner school, I studied German. I learnt that 'Bach' meant 'little river'. And I thought that was wonderful – it really corresponded to what I imagined from hearing his music.

So you must have wanted to play that music, to perform the music you felt so connected to?

Well, I started to play the violin at school. But it was so badly organized: my parents had no idea what should happen, and I had a terrible teacher who never even taught me how to tune the instrument. I was completely lost. But good things did happen. At that time in Finland, children could be quite independent and go out on their own, so when I was 12 or 13 I started to go to concerts in Helsinki on my own. It was all my own adventure.

And what did you see? Were there concerts or pieces that made a special impression on you?

I went to anything I happened to hear about. I still have enormous holes in my musical culture, you know, because it was all so haphazard. But I heard great Russian musicians, who were allowed to play in Finland in the sixties – Gilels, Richter, [David] Oistrakh and Rostropovich. I think I was impressed, but I didn't feel cultured enough to be able to really put them in context. I started to buy vinyl LPs at the same time: whatever I happened to find. I remember I found one big package of Dieter Schnebel's music – I picked up whatever there was in the music stores in Helsinki!

Were you playing the piano by this time?

Yes, but I really had a feeling that I didn't know anything. I was a lousy pianist. I was a very shy person, and my lack of culture made me even more shy. And having to do all these music exams: well, they went more or less OK, but it was never anything brilliant, never anything great. I became even more uncertain of myself. I knew I had this imagination and a real need to express myself musically – I had a horrible need to do it – but because I was such a lousy instrumentalist, I thought as a composer I would be even more lousy. I remember reading about Mozart when I was 11, and realizing all the things he could do at my age, and I thought I cannot do this music thing. I always had the feeling that music is so important, I should not dirty it with my small person. I had all the time the feeling that I didn't have enough talent – and yet I had this very big need to express myself musically.

But you must have had ways of at least trying to express that musical necessity, maybe even some early attempts at composition?

I wouldn't have dared to show my compositions to anyone at that age. But the first things I tried when I was nine or ten, I played on the piano in our living room. My mother loved me playing when she was lying there on the couch, but she didn't like it when I tried out my music, which was not smooth music. I was trying out chords and sounds. She was really irritated by that and said, 'Why don't you play the music you're supposed to play?' So I learnt the guitar when I was 13, because I could play it on my own in my room. And I started to compose a piece called *Yellow and Nervous*. It's interesting: that title has two things, the character – because I'm always looking for some character in my music – and this colour perception I have always had. I don't know where it is now, but that was a piece I tried to write down. And as time went on, I began to express myself by setting poems, and writing songs.

The shyness you talk about – that was a personal thing as well as a musical thing?

Yes. Because shyness is part of being insecure – and I was very insecure. As a teenager you have other problems. I was a very pretty girl, so I tried to get more confident by being beautiful, by being the object of admiration. That was what I was looking for, to get more confidence. In fact it didn't help me at all, because, of course, instead of outer confidence, I needed inner confidence to do what I wanted to do. But there was no one to help with that. Musically, I had no chance to discuss composition with anyone, or someone to test my skills. When I spoke to my parents about wanting to be a composer, my father was very angry. Even when I got into the Sibelius Academy, he wouldn't speak to me. He thought it was crazy, that I was ruining my life. I had visual talents, for drawing, etching, sketching – I would spend Sundays at his office drawing plans for houses, for buildings – and he thought I should be an architect. That made sense for him. It was craziness instead to try something that there was no proof I was any good at.

So I escaped. When I was 18, I got married, because I wanted to get away from my parents. His name was Saariaho, and he was an architect. I'm sure I thought I loved him. He loved me: he was a wonderful person. He was an architect, maybe four or five years older than me. But when I married him, I found myself in another prison. I was not even married for one year before I fell in love with a painter. But I kept my husband's name, deliberately. I didn't want to have my father's name [Laakkonen]. I never asked what my husband thought about that! At that age, when you are in so much pain yourself, you hurt other people without properly understanding what you're doing. I ended up living with this painter, a very famous Finnish artist, Olli Lyytikäinen, for seven years. I thought when I met Olli that I had never met anyone so free, and I wanted to be as free, as independent, as he was. But he was an alcoholic, and he became jealous when my career as a composer started to get going and I started to become stronger and stronger. And when things went badly with him, I had a nervous breakdown. I still had enormous problems.

And yet during that time, and that relationship, you did finally make it to the Sibelius Academy, and become a composer as you had always wanted to. What was your route there, to Paavo Heininen's composition class?

It was a long journey. Originally I thought about applying to the church music course, because I thought I could become an organist in a church somewhere. I would play Bach; I would play an instrument I loved. But that isn't what happened. When the exam came for the course, you had to sing, and for some reason there was no voice coming out of my head. I just couldn't sing. I don't know if it was because I was so nervous, or if it was some psychological thing telling me this is not what I should be doing; whatever it was, I didn't get on that course. Instead, I was taken to the art school and the university, so I continued my musical studies at the Conservatory of Helsinki [a separate institution from the Sibelius Academy]. And I was composing. I played piano for a student theatre, and that brought me back to composition when I was 19 or 20. I started to write songs again, and this feeling of necessity grew – I must, I must; I just need to compose.

Although I got some kind of degree, I did not complete those courses. I knew – somehow – that I had to study with Paavo Heininen. I don't remember what I had heard of his music by then; of course I must have known some of his pieces, but this was another feeling of necessity. But there were no places available in his class. So I called him up. He asked me, 'Is composition so important to you?' and said that there was no room for me. I told him that I just really needed to study with him. So one Thursday I went to see him. I was still incredibly shy. He asked me questions to find out how much I knew about music, which I answered shyly; like singing the opening of the *Sacre de Printemps*, and other things. But however shy I was, I had decided that I would not leave the room until he had taken me on his course. It was crazy, but I knew I could not leave the room. All of the strength I had, I put into the fact that I would not get up from my seat before he allowed me to study with him. He tried to say many times there was no room for me – but finally he had no choice. I became his pupil.

Underneath your shyness, it seems you had an astonishing stubbornness and strength!

It's more that feeling of necessity. It's not strength, because it's something you feel you have to do, so there is no other choice. The thing is, studying with Paavo was very hard. He was very tough. And I knew so little! Thankfully I made friends like

Magnus [Lindberg] and Esa-Pekka [Salonen] who supported me and didn't think I was ridiculous. But I was so poor analytically that Paavo asked me to go to the library of the Sibelius Academy and study this and this score. I mean, he told that to everybody, but someone like Magnus had all those scores at home! However, I was very advanced in music theory, and by then I had done all the degrees in harmony and counterpoint that could be done. I had even done piano studies to the necessary level. But I was still not a good instrumentalist like Magnus, who was a very good pianist – and still is. Sometimes Paavo would say to me that my music was too much in my imagination, and for the next lesson I would have to write music just for the piano, and write nothing down. I still felt inferior because of my lack of instrumental skills.

But your inner confidence must have been growing at the same time?

It came little by little through my work. One week, Paavo told me to look in the mirror ten times a day and say to myself, 'I can, I can do it'. He saw there was so much energy in me that was lost to this lack of confidence. It was a difficult time, but I was so excited, because I was so desperate to compose. And I advanced very quickly. I started so much later than most people, but there are some pieces from around that time that can still stand. I had things to express, but I just didn't have any kind of technical means to express them.

One turning point was when Paavo told me not to write any more vocal pieces – 'it's too easy for you – now you'll concentrate on instrumental music'. And it was very difficult, like telling an alcoholic not to drink any more. Even when I read the telephone book, I started to hear music! But transferring that energy to instrumental music, it actually brought me back to my childhood perception of music, which was so full of smells and colours. And that really opened up my music enormously.

Did this fulfilment of your creative impulse improve your relationships too – with your family?

Yes. My father was extremely touched when he came to a big concert when my music was played. He never got really interested in my music, but he at least started to see the reality of where I was. My mother tried to follow me, too – even if she never really understood the music, she enjoyed the success I started to have.

You must have been a distinctive presence in the composition department then – not least because you were the only woman studying there.

It was really a very patriarchal system back then. There were some teachers who actually would not teach me, because they thought it was a waste of time. 'You're a pretty girl, what are you doing here?' That sort of thing. It's funny. I was a really fragile, nice-looking girl, not this kind of determined, bossy person. My femininity was so apparent, so unavoidable.

So what were the things that Heininen made you write? Were you influenced by the new things you heard and experienced?

There was not much that we heard in performance, but of course there were influences from Ligeti, who I loved, from Nono, some of whose music I liked a lot, and from Messiaen, whose work Paavo made me analyse. And Berio, too. The library was very good at the Sibelius Academy, but it wasn't really before I went to Darmstadt in 1978 that I heard new music in performance.

Did Paavo encourage you to go to Darmstadt?

Paavo was completely unusual in Finland because of the internationalism of his training. He had studied with Bernd Alois Zimmermann, and with Persichetti in New York, so it came from him, the idea to know the whole scene of contemporary music. It seemed natural, the only thing to do, to go to Darmstadt and see what was going on. And I found many really interesting things. For example, the first time I heard Tristan Murail's and Gérard Grisey's music – that was fantastic! I will never forget the effect it had on me. Their music was not played in Scandinavia and it was not even recorded – well, there was one record, but it had not reached us up there. It sounded so fresh, it was just unbelievable. We had had this post-serial education, where octaves are forbidden even in an orchestral context, and Grisey's and Murail's music just sounded so good. Gérard had already articulated certain things in writing about his approach to the overtone series, which helped me a lot.

Their music gave me confidence, and that was true of all the music I was attracted to: it was music that gave me confidence for my own work. Much later, it was the same with Messiaen's opera [*St François d'Assise*] which gave me confidence to write my first opera, *L'Amour de loin*. The there were many other French composers we heard, and Italian composers, like Salvatore Sciarrino who was not known so well then, and I loved his string music. There were also neo-romantics like Detlev Müller-Siemens, who was some kind of a star at that time, but whom we [Lindberg, Salonen, and Saariaho, who travelled to Darmstadt together a couple of times] couldn't take seriously at all. It was fantastic to have all this polemic around new music. I also got to know [flautist] Camilla Hoitenga at that time, and Pascale Crition, a French composer living in Paris; visiting her was the reason I first got to know Paris.

You haven't mentioned Boulez or Stockhausen or Xenakis as composers who gave you confidence.

I knew that music already, and I admired it. But I did not like it very much, although *Le Marteau sans maître* I respected very much, and Xenakis's *Kokkos* for solo cello was helpful when I was trying to find solutions for my notation. But I didn't find myself in their music.

You also met your next teacher, Brian Ferneyhough, in Darmstadt.

I showed Brian a few things because he wanted to be in touch with as many composers as possible. Grisey said, 'Don't come to show me your score if you don't think it's got something to do with my music, I cannot give you general advice', but with Brian, it was the opposite. New, different music was like fresh meat to him! I showed him one piece and he read it through and said, 'OK, I see that your heart is there but your brain is over here, they are not together'. And this was a fantastic lesson to give me. It was exactly what I felt at the time: that I had some technique now, and still this enormous need to express, but they still did not match. I think it was the most important thing he ever told me.

Despite the fact that you went to study with him in Freiburg for two years, from 1980?

My idea was to leave originally just for one year, because I still hadn't finished my diploma at the Sibelius Academy. I had the feeling that I should be there with Paavo for the rest of my life, that I had so much to learn from him. It was a kind of agony, when they said I had to do a two-year course in Germany. My idea was always to go back to Paavo and study with him. He was like a father figure for me, even if it was not an easy relationship. He could be very terse and even rude: that was his way of teaching. He never said anything positive, ever. Very often, Magnus and I had lessons with him on Thursday one after another. Then we would have lunch together, and very often I cried, and we tried together to solve my problems.

Yet you wanted to go back to him?

I felt that I owed him everything: all that I knew about music came from him. And he encouraged me to go my own way – as did Brian.

So what happened in the Ferneyhough class when you got to Freiburg?

I was immediately in this extremely post-serial school. And I realized – well, I knew already – that this was not what I wanted. These guys were drawing these unbelievable diagrams on the blackboard, systems, and interactions, and all of that – and what did you hear of it in the music? All of that complexity, for what aural result? It was kind of a crash course to get me out of that whole thing. Perception, hearing what's happening in music, had been so important with Gérard's music and Tristan's music. I remember I met Tristan when I visited Pascale around that time in Paris, and I told her I was going to Freiburg. She said, 'For me, those people are not musicians!'

It sounds like you didn't get much out of those Freiburg years…

I got a lot, because I got out of Finland. It was similar, in the end, to getting rid
of the prison of my parents. In Finland, I started very quickly to be seen as the
woman composer. Even as a student that started to happen, because the musical
circles are so small there. People heard of this pretty girl who was hanging around
composition classes, and word got around very quickly. I felt they wanted to put
me in some kind of drawer where I really didn't fit. I felt it was such a uniform
culture, and I needed more space to move, to breathe. And then to see Finland from
the outside, like seeing your parents' home after you move out, was so refreshing.
And I started to take distance from Paavo too. I realized that I had advanced a lot,
but that maybe he had taught me the most important thing, which was how to keep
on constructing my music. I knew I would never go back to study with him – even
if I thought at that time that I would definitely return to Finland.

*So Freiburg and Ferneyhough opened up new horizons to you – and the direction
of your life changed.*

I started to visit Paris and my friend Pascale Crition while I was living in Freiburg,
and she knew Tristan and Gérard. Because I was so interested in their music, I
became enmeshed in the Parisian musical scene. And I learned about IRCAM,
the chance to learn about computer technology in music, and I was accepted on
the course in January 1982. I liked Paris a lot, I met my husband, Jean-Baptiste
Barrière at IRCAM, and I did very well on the course. We learnt about physics,
acoustics, as well as the programmes used at IRCAM. I was especially interested
in CHANT, the synthetic voice programme. All of that meant that by 1983, when I
had finished in Freiburg, it was quite clear that I would move to Paris. But it took
a while to settle into Parisian musical life. I didn't yet have many commissions,
because nobody knew me there. I managed to get small things like an exchange
grant from the French Culture Ministry, but my music was not much played. It was
a really frustrating time.

   I was working on my first piece for large ensemble, *Verblendungen*, which
was premiered in 1984 by the Finnish Radio Symphony Orchestra and Esa-Pekka.
This was the first piece I composed without any teachers. I worked on the tape
part in the INA-GRM Studio in Paris, and it was later played at a computer music
conference in the city. It was an enormous success: my first on an international
stage. As a result, the conductor of the Paris performance, Paul Mefano, wanted
to commission an ensemble piece, which became *Lichtbogen*, so that was the first
important commission that did not come from Finland.

*How important were these two works, Verblendungen and Lichtbogen? Were they
the first pieces you wrote in which you felt that technique and expression – or brain
and heart, to use Ferneyhough's terms – were properly fused?*

Things changed enormously even between the two pieces. I think that *Verblendungen* is still very stiff. It was very consciously planned, and I carefully stuck to my plans, so there is a stiffness in its expression. With *Lichtbogen*, the key was my relationship with cellist Anssi Karttunen. I went to see him because I needed to make some cello recordings for the piece, and to learn about some aspects of string technique I still didn't know about. And in that process of working together, something happened to the music. I feel that *Lichtbogen* is a piece I can approve. It's breathing music, where *Verblendungen* is not.

But how do you make a piece like Lichtbogen *breathe? I mean in the combination between live performers and electronics.*

It took several years to learn. But I started to learn about how sounds behave in space, and how I could use my knowledge of the physical properties of sound in my orchestration, how I could realize my dream spaces. All of these things started to come together. From 1982, I did nothing else but compose – or try to compose. It was incredibly hard work, and very frustrating. I was so angry that my music was not played more, but at the same time, that frustration made me think a lot, and I heard a lot of concerts. One of the most interesting things for a young composer is to go to a concert and hear a piece that you hate, and try to understand, why is it bad? Why doesn't it work? What would I have done instead? I always work much more with my ears rather than analysing other people's scores.

But what about your relationship with Boulez and his music? You can't have avoided that in Paris in the early 1980s.

Boulez's music didn't touch me at all. And coming from Finland, I didn't have very developed social behaviour. So I didn't immediately go and meet Boulez. I only realized much later that I should have gone and shown him my scores. I didn't, because his music didn't interest me that much. And I think I paid an expensive price for that: he has never conducted my music. Never. He must have felt my behaviour was strange, but there was nothing malicious in it. It was only because I was very timid, and interested in other people's music more.

Grisey's, especially ...

But Grisey's approach did not match mine. I became his friend, but he had a very systematic way of analysing his sonograms; his orchestration was mathematical, and my work is not at all systematic or mathematical. It comes back to what I learnt from the technology at IRCAM and elsewhere. The technology, the machine, only gives you what you put into it, what you ask it. There are no wonders with it. The machine cannot compose for you, cannot make you better. And I don't want the machine to compose for me – I like composing! I didn't have any ambition to create a programme that would do something complex and wonderful, because I want to do the complex and wonderful myself.

Complex and wonderful: a good description of the pieces that began to define your voice, your musical identity – and your fame, in the late eighties and early nineties, like Du cristal ...à la fumée, your violin concerto, Graal théâtre, and the vocal music you started to write towards the end of the 1990s, for soprano Dawn Upshaw especially. What characterizes this period of your music for you?

Harmony, texture, and timbre: those things were then, and still are, at the heart of my musical thinking. The challenge was to find enough craft and experience to translate all of that thinking, those ideas, into my music, into musical notation. It was a very big effort, a result of working hard on my compositional process – which is really a complex interaction between my intellect and my whole being. And when I had found the basic intellectual tools to open myself up to music, I was ripe for writing the kind of music I wanted to.

Du cristal ...à la fumée was very important for me, because it was my first piece for large orchestra. It crystallized my ideas concerning musical form, evolution, and transformation. It was a really large-scale work [Saariaho thinks of the two parts of *Du cristal ...à la fumée*, for solo cello and orchestra, as a single entity], and it finished a certain period in my compositional life, I feel, and started another one. After it, I stopped thinking only in terms of linear transformation and started looking for more dramatic solutions and situations for my music.

One catalyst for that change was that I was starting to work with important soloists. I composed my violin concerto for Gidon Kremer, for example, and I got to know Dawn Upshaw. And having to think about these important musicians and writing music specifically for them was a new challenge in my music. I could no longer construct compositional tools for myself alone: I had to make them work for other musicians. All of the pieces I have written for soloists have something to do with the personalities of the musicians themselves. They become, more or less, portraits of these people. It's strange to say, but writing these concertos and solo pieces for these brilliant musicians was the first time that I was really aware that composition is a public job! It was always so extremely private an expression before for me.

That publicity wasn't just about composing concertante works, though: by the mid-1990s, you had become a famous composer! And you were thrust into the limelight even more when you won the Grawemeyer Award in 2003 for your first opera, L'Amour de loin. Did all of this public recognition have any impact on your musical life?

It was all a little bit shocking, and it took a certain time to understand this public role, because I had been so much concerned only by my music in the past. But I don't think it has changed my working methods. Maybe, though, it has taught me to try to keep my privacy, and not to let people's expectations of who I am and what I do really bother me. Because, in fact, what can anyone 'expect' of my music? Only something that they have heard already. People just want the same thing – but better. But inside, as a composer, I am already somewhere completely different. There are always pressures in the rest of life, but somehow I keep them outside of me. My work will always be, in essence, very private work, and the most important thing is that I have enough time and the right conditions to do it.

L'Amour de loin *was a hard-won prize for you, creatively speaking.*

I felt when I wrote it that everything I had written up to that moment was somehow in that piece. All the material, my approach to harmony, to texture – all of it was there. And so after the opera, I somehow felt that I was starting again. Not from scratch, of course, but on a new basis. That explains the clarity, the formal freedom, and also the new expressiveness of the flute concerto, *Aile du songe*, the piece I wrote just after the opera. I give the soloist more freedom in that concerto than in my others, because I was no longer working with electronics, which force the performer in some way to be limited in time.

So what then, more generally, is the relationship between your pieces that use electronics, and those that don't?

Each piece has a different starting point. Let's take *Nymphéa*, for string quartet. I wrote that piece around the time that the first digital mixer came out: this was the first time you could physically do complex sound processing without having ten people to do the mixing. So that's why that piece uses the electronics it does. If I look at the pieces of mine that use electronics, it's often solo pieces because I'm interested in extending the instrument or finding a partner for it. In my new opera, *Emilie* [composed for Karita Mattila – and no one else; the piece is a 90-minute solo for soprano], I have some very specific reasons to use electronics. But if I didn't have those reasons, I would not use technology. That was always the case, in reality. The electronics are there because there is an expressive necessity for them to be there. And in any case, the gear gets old and out of date so quickly. We have enormous problems updating my older pieces all the time.

Mentioning Emilie *brings us back to opera: you are now an opera composer, one of the most successful and performed anywhere, with three full-length pieces, all to librettos by Amin Maalouf –* L'Amour de loin, Adriana Mater *and* Emilie. *What was your journey towards large-scale music theatre?*

It's so strange to me, because I don't feel like an operatic composer. The pieces have been big successes in France, but on the other hand, I've had the nastiest reviews I have ever received from the French critics about my operas. It's a very interesting contradiction, because, in general, I am very appreciated here and there is a lot of warmth and respect towards me from the musical world. But I think some French people – or French critics – have problems with opera. And they cannot stand it if you do something that is touching. They want opera to stay very intellectual and modernistic.

And your operas are deliberately, unselfconsciously touching, dealing with the big themes of love, of war, of existence. Is that a brave thing to do, in the context of a culture that wants opera to be modernistic rather than moving?

I don't feel that it's brave, because I don't want to do superficial things. And I think that the only interesting thing in opera is when a composer writes something real, which is touching for all of us. So it's not brave, it's just: why would I do anything else? For example, in *Emilie* – why did I want to do it? I wanted to create something for Karita that was a real challenge for her, to push her to her musical limits. I only realize now what an enormous thing it is, to be alone on an opera stage for one and a half hours!

I wonder whether your attraction to opera isn't a version of the same impulse that made you compose Yellow and Nervous *all those years ago: for all that they are grand operatic pieces, there's something private, interior, intimate about all three of them. Are they really still your private dreamscapes brought into public life?*

It's always the inner space that interests me. And in a way that makes my operas very difficult to stage. In *Emilie*, this woman is writing a letter for 90 minutes – so what do you do with that? It's very private: everything is happening in this woman's mind during one night when she's working. Like all of my operas, it should have the effect of being fundamentally private music, music that I want to communicate with the inner world of my listeners, just as it expresses my inner imagination.

How completely does it express your inner world, though? Is there a precise correlation between what you imagine in a new work, and what you hear at the première?

I don't think that any of my pieces are able to express completely what I would like to express. Maybe that's the reason I continue to write new pieces. I think it's an unreachable utopia you know. I don't know about my colleagues, but I cannot be very happy about the music I have written before. I am never sitting down and listening to it and thinking, 'Oh, this is wonderful'. Some pieces survive better than others, of course. The operas are the pieces in which I have put most of my energy. They are enormous works every time, and they take a huge effort not only from me, but also from everybody around me. I hope that some of that energy is in the music, and I hope I'm able to communicate some of the ideas I have been trying to communicate. But I also see and hear my weaknesses in these pieces. Even if I am not somebody who goes back and revises pieces very easily. For all their problems, I respect the moment in which I wrote these works.

Chapter 2

From the Air to the Earth: Reading the Ashes

Daniel March

'Light', 'Rainbows', 'Smoke' – names for events that are, quite literally, impossible to pin down, which are experienced only fleetingly, which drift into our senses and then recede, leaving remainders, memories, cinders. The evocation of the nebulous, of things that, like music itself, leave little trace, which continue to exist only in the recollection of their many occurrences, has been a touchstone for composers through the ages; the ability of music to draw out such ideas, self-reflexively almost, is clearly acknowledged in Kaija Saariaho's compositions. One need only examine the titles of many of her works to see this resonance, and the critical response to her music has often been to draw parallels to evanescent experiences in the natural world.[1] Whilst the limited – finite – duration of most music we encounter means that such parallels are not unique to Saariaho's work (the essence of musical experience is, as John Paynter expressed it, 'how it is made to go on in time, and – most significantly – how it is made to stop' (Paynter, 1992: 26)), her compositional language involves a particularly explicit exploration of time and scale, and thereby how music is perceived, and how it is remembered.

The following discussion presents a cluster, a constellation, a network of music – a network suggested initially by congruencies of titles – in an attempt to articulate, if only tangentially, some of that exploration and of the intertext in which it might productively be placed. It will be unsurprising that Jacques Derrida's exploration of supplementarity plays an important role here; over the course of the last forty years, there has indeed been much reading of the ashes – the tendency to examine texts in relation to their exclusions, their supplements, their blindnesses, their remainders, has become well-established, and this way of thinking about music informs much of the following discussion, even when not directly invoked.[2] More

---

[1] Saariaho herself has written of the possibilities of both the natural and the social world being progenitors of music: 'Sometimes I ask myself whether music is brought about by the friction between the musician and the surrounding world, or rather from the energy tapped from nature and other arts. In my specific case, maybe the latter, maybe both. I also feel that smells, light and colours are a wellspring of musical ideas' (Saariaho, 2000: 114); in her discussion of Saariaho's compositional process, Pirkko Moisala explores how the sensory world acts as an inspiration and how those ideas are translated into musical works (Moisala, 2009: 55–9).

[2] These ideas have become so well entrenched into musicological discourse that the list of secondary texts is perhaps at last superfluous – for Derrida's own discussion of

explicit, and central here, is the trope of the cinder, which, in Derrida's writing, represents another attempt to name, to illuminate, the trace. In *Cinders*, Derrida describes how one particular phrase continually returned to him: '*il y a là cendre*' ('cinders there are'). 'Cinder remains, cinder there is, which we can translate: the cinder is not, is not what is. It remains *from* what is not, in order to recall at the delicate, charred bottom of itself only non-being or non-presence' (Derrida, 1991: 39). To oversimplify, the image of remainders without weight, that cannot be held, that crumble as we reach out to grasp them, is a potent one.[3]

Equally potent, of course, is the inevitable association to be made with human mortality and the ashes of cremation, and from there to the holocaust – the *shoah*, certainly – but Derrida also observes how 'there is a holocaust for every date, and somewhere in the world at every hour' (Derrida, 2005: 46). Derrida makes these connections explicit in his discussion of Paul Celan in *Shibboleth*, but the trace of Celan also runs through *Cinders* – these texts forming part of the work of mourning that marks Derrida's later writing. All these are, self-evidently, topics far beyond the scope of the present discussion, but evoked here as part of the wider meaning into which some of the much more circumscribed – and, by comparison, trivial – detail that follows might be placed. They are part of the current chapter's aim to read *in* (and to read in*to*) the music some of those deeper questions which it might be able to address – they could usefully be considered as ghosts, which remain present even when not observed.[4] If, when reading (the music, and the words that follow), one continues to hear what Derrida calls the 'terrifying echo' of Celan's invocation of ashes and of night in *Engführung* (Derrida, 2005: 47), then this music has a marker, a rule, against which any invocation of similar themes might be tested – and thereby be brought into a process of critical exchange. By recalling the way in which both writers have considered loss, mourning and remembering, the music might also begin to resonate with these traces – they might become, as cinders, part of a new constellation forming around this network of music.

Cendres, Cinders

Saariaho's 1998 composition *Cendres* is not a major work – in two senses. Firstly, scale: scored for alto flute, cello and piano and only nine minutes long, it obviously lacks the scope of the large orchestral works and, more recently, operas, for which Saariaho is particularly renowned. It also seems like a work of consolidation, growing from earlier concerns rather than exploring a new range of expression or

---

supplementarity, see Derrida, 1976: 141–64.

[3]   Lawrence Kramer evokes *Cinders* in his discussion of the autonomous artwork in *Classical Music and Postmodern Knowledge* (Kramer, 1995); my own use of Derrida's text is much more circumscribed.

[4]   I refer self-consciously to Derrida's own writing around ghosts, spectres, in particular *Specters of Marx* (Derrida, 1994).

meaning. Secondly, and more interestingly, *Cendres* sits in a particular relationship to the much larger orchestral diptych *Du cristal ...à la fumée* ('From Crystal ... into Smoke') (1989–90). As Saariaho explains in her programme note, 'I found the basis of the musical material for this piece [*Cendres*] in my double concerto *...à la fumée*. ... The name of the piece also derives from this' (Saariaho, 2010). Thus, immediately, we are invited to hear this work as a remainder: a remainder of the fire that gave genesis to *...à la fumée*, as the airborne cinders which have continued to drift and which only now come within our sensory field, as a bringing together of fragmentary remains into a new frame, as the earlier work's supplement.[5]

The use of common material is clearest at the opening. Both pieces begin from the low E♭ that also forms the starting-point for other music by Saariaho (and must be one of the most-discussed single pitches in recent musicological literature): it is this note that, performed on a cello with varied bowing and articulation and analysed by Fourier transform, is used as the basis for the pitch material of works such as *Amers* (1992) and *Près* (1992).[6] In both *Cendres* and *...à la fumée*, this initial sonority evolves in a broadly similar way. *Cendres* precedes the cello oscillation between E♭$_2$ and its fourth harmonic on G♮$_4$ by a plucked piano note, whereas *...à la fumée* enriches and extends that initial oscillating gesture by additional orchestral sonorities, but both pieces use what is fundamentally the same piano gesture (in *...à la fumée*, shared with the synthesizer) gradually to introduce new pitches, starting with F♯$_3$, and then B♭$_5$ (see Example 2.1 overleaf), before reaching an initial climax of chromaticism.

When directly compared, however, the differing trajectories are more pronounced: the timescale is altered (*Cendres* evolves more quickly), as is the sense of direction – each piece moves from this opening gesture in its own particular way. One might consider this effect as a similar initial seed giving rise to different organisms, or perhaps as changing lights cast on the same object (a crystal, a prism?) creating shifting reflections or refractions – images evoked in other works. How each piece concludes is suggestive here. For *...à la fumée* this ending comes after a series of exchanges where the flute and cello soloists have moved more obviously to the fore (rather than being embedded within the orchestral texture), and there is a clear sense of return to the E♭ centricity of the opening of the work, reinforced *sff* by lower strings in the penultimate bar. In *Cendres*, nearly the same material is employed to

---

[5]   *Du cristal* and *...à la fumée* – and their interrelationship – have already been the subject of some discussion, see, for example, Stoianova 1991, Pousset 1994, and Brech 1999.

[6]   Detailed analysis of *Amers* has been undertaken by Stoianova (1994 and 2000) and Lorieux (2004). One could speculate on the choice of this particular pitch as the starting point of a number of compositions: in particular it is tempting to make an (unauthenticated) link to the opening of Wagner's *Das Rheingold*, with all the attendant imagery of flowing water. More prosaically, Saariaho herself has explained how she was unsatisfied with the cello writing in *...à la fumée*, and how she welcomed the opportunity of a 'second chance' to explore that instrument with *Amers*, which she began with the same trill (Michel, 1994: 18–19).

Example 2.1 ***Cendres* – opening material**

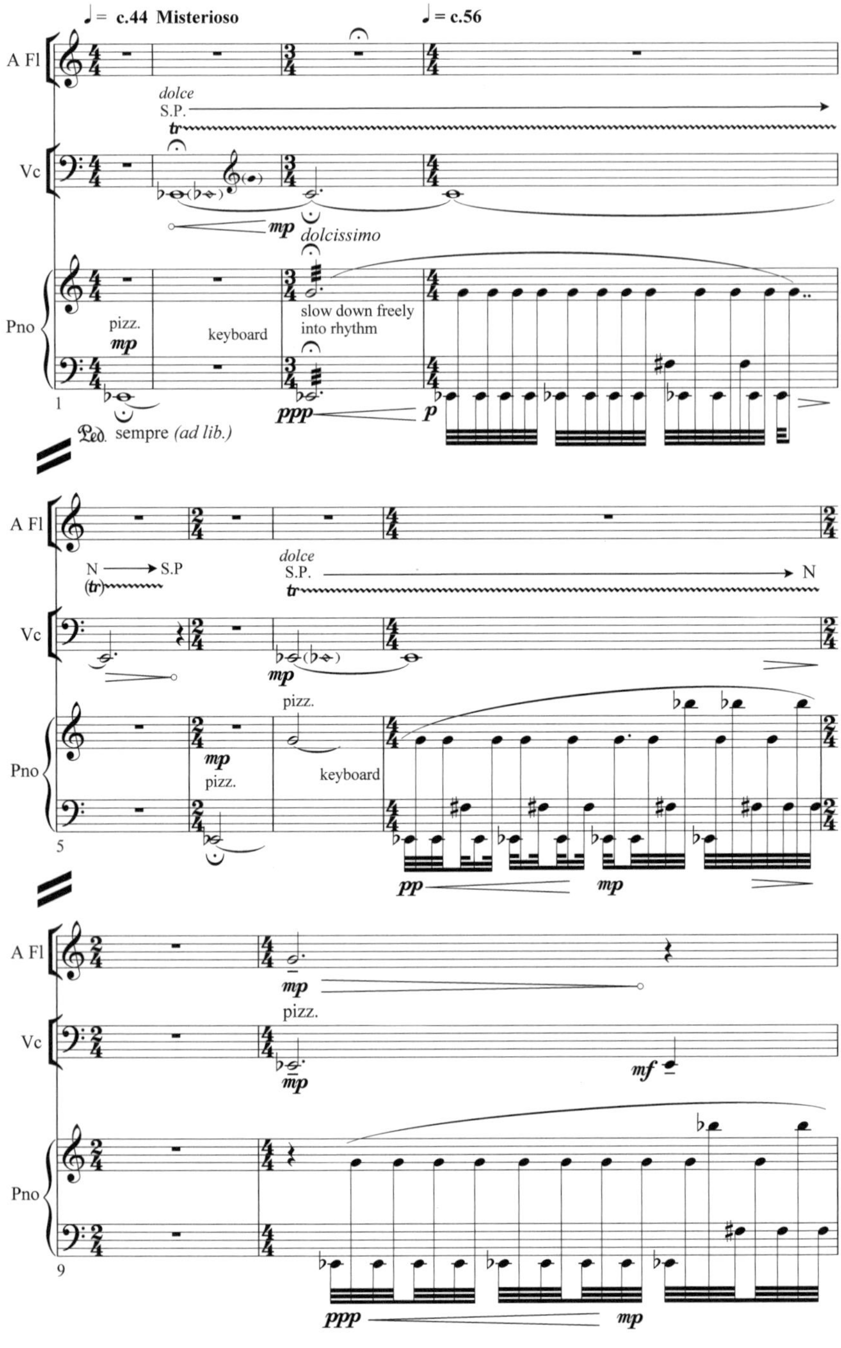

A Fl
mf
Vc
mf
poco a poco più energico ma sempre dolce
Pno
11
7
A Fl
Vc
arco
N
S.P.
mp
mf
Pno
6
12
mp
5
poco agitato
A Fl
N
S.P.
Vc
mf
f
gliss.
Pno
3
mf
f
6
7
13
5

a rather different effect. In bar 155, the penultimate flute–cello exchange from *...à la fumée* is re-used, but now underpinned by a piano harmony built on a low G♮ and using a modified form of the subsequent flute and cello gesture (Example 2.2a). This material is then used as the basis for what is in effect a seven-bar interpolation in the later work, before arriving at its 'original' form in bar 165 (Example 2.2b). The E♭ centricity seems initially to be reinforced, with a *fermata* E♭$_2$ in bar 157 (*...à la fumée* has a G♭$_4$ here),[7] but in bar 166 the emphasis seems to shift back towards G♮$_3$ – with the G♭ of *...à la fumée* finally turning up as part of the final piano right-hand gesture. These changes mean that the 'aftershock' in the following bar becomes in this work more clearly connected to the gesture that it follows – and to an inverted form with which the first part of the piece ended (bars 63–5); also suggestive is the addition of a final bar's rest.

Other direct connections between the works are fragmentary, with transplantations of material from the earlier into the later piece varying in how recognizable they remain. For example, the alto flute's spinning breath-tone, bars 17–18, is taken from bar 79 (now *agitato* rather than *intenso*), where it also comes after a comparable process of pitch-filtering. Similarly, bars 41–2 of *Cendres* – which form a characteristic rotation of a fixed pitch collection – use bars 154–5 of the earlier work, with the synthesizer part moved to piano (those bars themselves revisit the gesture of bars 33–4). The striking *dolente* figure towards the end of the work (bars 136–7) is taken from bars 400–401, where it is equally prominent. In a longer passage near the beginning of the second part of the piece there is a more complex process of quotation and allusion at work: the flute and cello at bar 75 take a single bar from a longer soloistic passage of *...à la fumée* (a passage that later also makes its way into *Cendres*, bars 125–30), whilst the cello material at bar 76 derives from the constant semiquaver movement of the orchestra that surrounds it. Finally, bars 78–80 repeat, in reverse order, the soloists' and harp's lines.

This partial listing of interconnections indicates the kinds of reworking to be found here. Material is revisited, sometimes directly, but also taken in a changed direction, so that, as with the opening of both works, the process of growth remains distinct. The atomization and re-use of this earlier material might reinforce the idea that *Cendres* can be viewed, literally, as 'cinders', fragments, remnants – one might even be tempted to identify these as Derridean 'revenants'. However, the work also places these musical ideas in a new framework: they are not just collected, but brought together – fused – into a new dynamic process, a new context.[8]

---

[7] The *visual* equivalence between E♭ and G♭ when switching between treble and bass clef may be significant in this context.

[8] Saariaho explains this process from the composer's perspective: 'Even if I were to use similar structural solutions in several pieces I would need to find them again each time. I can never look at something that I did in an earlier piece, and say, well, I could do the same thing here, it would do just fine. Even if I end up doing something similar, I need to feel the necessity again' (Beyer, 2000a: 308–9).

Example 2.2 *Cendres* – ending

a) Bars 155-9

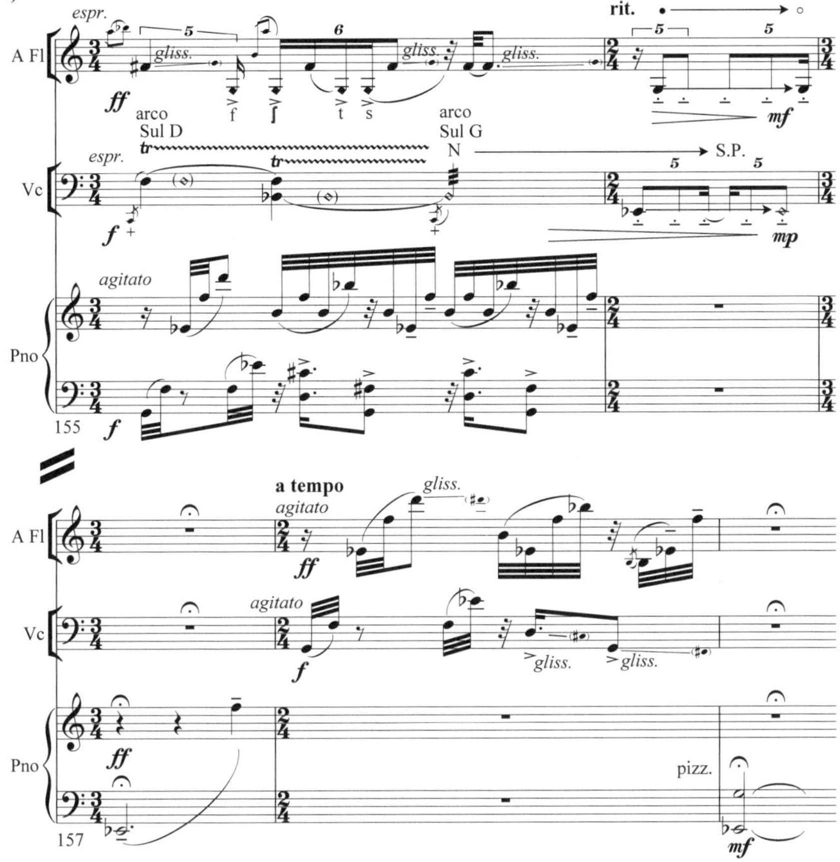

b) Bars 165-8

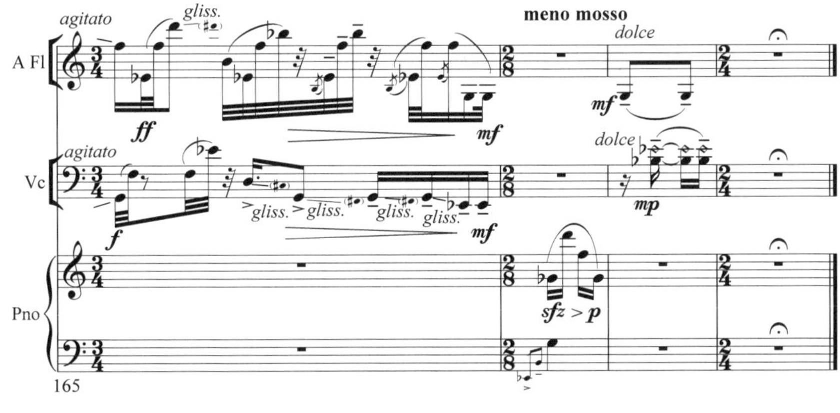

Dérive, Drift

Part of that context, and an important aspect in our understanding of the work, is the image of 'drift'. The music often appears to be in a state of flux, of motion, and one seems naturally encouraged to hear it in this kind of metaphorical way. Certainly, the idea of Saariaho's music as a representation of a gradual temporal process – a music of transition – has been a common thread in appreciation of her works, not least, as observed above, because of their titles. Playing with words a little further, I would like to make a connection between this piece and a work that, in titular terms at least, adopts this idea of drift – Pierre Boulez's 1984 composition for flute, clarinet, violin, cello, vibraphone and piano.

There is more to this, of course, than a simple process of word association. The IRCAM connection is the most obvious link between the two composers, but the wider positioning of Saariaho's music in terms of geography has also been an issue of some discussion (see, in particular, Mäkelä, 2007).[9] Whilst Saariaho's relationship with Boulez and IRCAM deserves an extended examination, there are some more immediate intersections to be found between these two particular pieces. The title '*Dérive*' not only connects with 'drift' (in particular, the French word is used for deviation from a sailing ship's original course), but also with the verb *dériver* (to divert, or to derive) – and Boulez has commented how the titles of this and the later *Dérive II* acknowledge their shared derivation from material originally conceived for *Répons* (*The Ensemble Sospeso – Pierre Boulez*, 1993). The way in which *Dérive I* uses the SACHER matrix has been well documented (for instance Bradshaw, 1986, and Bösche, 1997) and it is not so much the process of composition that is the focus here, but rather a number of features of that work that overlap with the concerns of *Cendres* – indeed, which might be viewed as progenitors for the type of expression to be found there.

Most significant here is the way in which *Dérive* articulates a series of harmonies through a filigree surface; the primary palette of six, fixed-octave hexachords is used throughout, and the concentration on this very limited amount of material in part gives the work its poise. The harmonies are articulated in two primary ways: in the first part of the piece decorated by flurries of grace notes and trills, which give each sonority a sense of inner movement, as if one were seeing the molecular vibration within a series of crystals; the second part turns them sideways, and creates a series of initially slow-moving, but increasingly complex and evocative linear strands, which culminate in what Susan Bradshaw has described as the 'uninhibited expressiveness' (Bradshaw, 1986: 223) of melodies such as that given to the flute towards the end of the work. This sense of line emerging from a series

---

[9]   Being British, and based somewhat to the west of this Franco-Finnish axis, I am further disqualified by a lack of linguistic competence from commenting on such connections. Throughout this discussion I would wish to emphasize those aspects of the works that can be understood as a part of the broader, 'internationalized' repertoire of 'new music', rather than being indicative of national identity, or of natural language.

of static objects seems an important way in which 'drift' might be interpreted, along with a larger-scale sense of the music moving past – a sense created by the increasing density of the proliferation, the individual shaping through dynamics and speed of motion given to each line, counterpointed by the cutting between one harmonic object and the next.

These modes of articulation are also important within the repertoire of *Cendres*. To take illustrative examples: the passage at bar 95 articulates a fixed harmonic field through trills and tremolandi (Example 2.3a overleaf), whereas that at bar 143 elaborates the harmony heterophonically (Example 2.3b). Also significant in the music is a gesture that again involves a retracing of fixed pitch-spaces – though in a more dynamic and repetitive way than *Dérive* – the most extended example of which is found beginning at bar 50 (Example 2.3c).

There are further connections. Both works fall broadly into two parts and involve a more energized, linear mode of presentation in their second halves: *Dérive* finishes with a coda marking another return to the initial tempo and revisiting the type of gesture found at the opening; *Cendres*, although involving more of an overlap of material between its two halves, also returns to its opening E♭ sonority just before the final passage. Both works display evidence of their composer's experience with electronics, and both partially represent ways of imitating electronic processing through acoustic instruments. This is clearest with the use of resonance – resonances that evolve or that modify the sonority thrown into it – and in the use of gradual transformation, parameter by parameter. These transformation processes, on a harmonic level, however, also mark a clear distinction between the two works. Whereas in *Dérive* the changes from one harmony to the next are generally clear-cut (notwithstanding a process of 'bleeding' between them), in *Cendres* there is a much more self-conscious manipulation of harmonic fields in order to create a particular sense of motion. It is this dynamic process that needs to be examined further.

Taking Form

The predominant approach to the discussion of the details of Saariaho's music has been what must broadly be called 'spectral'.[10] This is, of course, unsurprising, as it is from a particular way of thinking about composition that the impetus for much of her music originates. In these terms, many gestures can be understood as 'composings out' of simpler acoustic phenomena or electronic transformations, and it is in this way that much of *Cendres* asks to be heard. The situation is complicated in this case by the piano, which pushes the music into adopting equal temperament – though the cello writing in particular plays with the ways in which that too can be manipulated.

---

[10] Although an old joke, the punning potential of 'spectral' (of a spectrum or of a spectre) is, in the current context of ghosts, perhaps more suggestive than usual.

Example 2.3 *Cendres* – **examples of characteristic material**

a) Bars 95-7

b) Bars 143-5

c) Bars 50-51

As Vesa Kankaanpää has shown, and as the composer herself has articulated, harmony and timbre in Saariaho's work have a particular relationship (Kankaanpää, 2006; Saariaho, 1987). In what follows, the emphasis will be on how one might re-imagine this work's processes of transformation – first from a technical perspective, and then in terms of trajectory and direction. As has already been outlined, *Cendres* begins from the low E♭ which forms the starting point of a number of Saariaho's works. For *Amers*, this cello note was analysed to establish the structure and intensity of the partials involved when moving between *sul tasto* and *sul ponticello* position; in his discussion, Grégoire Lorieux reprints an example of the spectra that result (Lorieux, 2004: 3). Even without the detailed information of that analysis, however, one can clearly perceive how Saariaho uses this way of understanding timbre to control the opening of *Cendres*. The thin, metallic sound of the plucked piano E♭$_2$ blends easily with the opening cello *sul ponticello* E♭$_2$ and the G♮$_4$ with which it alternates. This reinforcement might be considered 'harmonic' – in the sense of belonging to the natural series of overtones – as is the addition of B♭$_5$ in bar 8. By this point, however, F♯$_3$ has also been 'energized' by the piano, and additional pitches rapidly propel the sound towards an inharmonic spectrum, reaching an initial climax in bar 13, shown above in Example 2.1. Thus this passage may be heard metaphorically as the playing of a single pitch, E♭$_2$, with a transformation from a spectrally pure mode of articulation (*sul tasto*) to one that is much 'dirtier' (*sul ponticello*). The dynamism this process creates is released at the arrival point of a new 'tonic', C♯$_2$ in bar 14, initially overlaid with a new harmonic cloud, then gradually thinned back to a semitone F♯–G$_4$. Here, the process of gradually removing pitches from the top and bottom of the initial harmony is an analogue of using a variable band-pass filter – a clear example of an instrumental re-imagining of an electronic process.

Other passages may be heard as presenting different analogues. The quickly rising, gapped scalic passages in bars 44–50 could be interpreted as mimicking a rapid equalizer sweep of the spectrum; bars 56–8, where an attenuated run of this kind is initially presented in fragmentary form before being gradually revealed, might suggest a process of intercutting or of interpolation of two types of material. The music between bars 35 and 37 presents another type of filtering process. Starting from F♯–G$_4$ once again, the music divides into two streams. The upper stream 'widens' the filter, to the interval of a major seventh, before closing it back down to the two pitches with which the process started. The lower stream of music articulates a move downward from B♭$_3$ to C♮$_2$: C$_4$ is initially established as the upper boundary of the pitch-band before lower pitches are introduced; these are given prominence simply through how much they are 'energized' – here the number of times each one is sounded in a given timespan.

So far, so familiar. What this means is that this music can fairly straightforwardly be described as a series of transformation processes, for example:

Bars 1–13 Gradual accrual of pitches across the registers
Bars 14–18 Filtering from wide to narrow pitch-band
Bars 18–24 Pitch sweeps from low to high and back; gradual descent of
upper voices
Bars 25–32 Filtering from densely to thinly filled pitch-band

Hearing the music in this way obviously invites images of movement and of gradual change through time. This becomes even more pronounced if this passage is presented in graphic form: in Example 2.4, thin lines represent pitch-gestures, whereas thicker lines indicate filtering processes. Particularly clear here is the way in which the music, for example the passage in bars 35–40, may be thought of in geometric terms – this use of two-dimensional graphics to think about process is a part of Saariaho's own vocabulary (see for example, Saariaho, 1987: 107). Also apparent is how the music alternates between passages of what might most easily be called tonal clarity – where a bass note is accompanied by a spectral aura ($E\flat_2$ and G_2 are the clearest 'fundamentals' in this case) – and much denser passages of chromaticism.

Example 2.4   *Cendres* **– reduction of opening**

Such a reading of *Cendres* in terms of processes derived from a spectral understanding of sound is easily persuasive. Hearing the music in this way requires, in part, a knowledge of the types of processes used by Saariaho (and others) to generate and control material, and also of the origin, for example, of the harmonies which overlay the opening E♭ sonority. What this means, however, is that the music *enacts* an acoustic process; however one may attempt to match pitches and amplitude, it is clearly impossible to re-synthesize a cello pitch by playing the piano – one can, however, point towards it.[11]

But it is possible to propose another, supplementary, reading. This is to reinstate the significance of pitch, or rather, of a pitch-based way of hearing this music. The timbre–harmony relationship is indeed complex, with Saariaho's work representing different explorations of how they interact – in what follows I do not wish to suggest that one way of listening is necessarily more appropriate throughout, but rather that we can experience both, drawing one or the other into focus in certain contexts. Example 2.4, above, acts as the starting point here. As can readily be observed, there is a significant pitch relationship in this music between E♭ and G♮. This is most obvious right at the outset (the E♭$_2$–G$_4$ opening), but is also recalled at the very end of the work, where the piano, bar 166, reinforces G$_3$ – this change of octave serves to emphasize the importance of pitch *class* in this relationship (an importance already suggested by the plucked E♭$_2$–G$_3$ dyad in bars 64 and 159, and the way that, in the previous bar, the cello glissandos from G$_2$ to E♭$_2$). As a bass note, G$_2$ also plays a significant role. Introduced in bar 12, where it initiates a stepwise, directed motion towards C♯$_2$, it is given extra weight by its role in underpinning the first harmony-rotation of the piece, bar 41 – further reinforced by the *f* marking. The rapid movement back to E♭ immediately afterward re-emphasizes this close relationship. The G pedal here is approached via an emphasis on C♮$_2$, a 'plagal' movement that is mirrored in the second part of the work by a 'perfect' G–C motion in bars 130–9 (see Example 2.5 overleaf). Whilst one can overstate these examples of tonal residue in this piece, their presence suggests a more complex frame of reference than might at first emerge – and, of course, these particular tonal ghosts also return to haunt the more recent music, as we shall shortly see.

But what of the effect here? These ghostly presences might suggest a return to the trope of ashes, of mourning, of cremation, and there are other features that this could unlock. The music is partly an interplay between music in a state of transformation and music that stays in the same place – the harmonically

---

[11]   It may legitimately be objected that this re-synthesis is not what is being attempted here – analysing the sound is not the first step to recreating it, but rather is a way of unlocking ways of imagining *new* sounds and how they might be controlled. In what follows, I am not arguing with the validity of such an approach from a composer's point of view, but would like to consider the music from a listener's multivalent perspective, where it is one possibility amongst several. Interestingly, this kind of 'spectral' hearing does not seem to be indicated for a work such as *Dérive*.

Example 2.5 *Cendres* – 'mirroring' of bass-note movement

stable passages of looped material that recur throughout. Their appearance is marked firstly *disperato*, then *dolce*, before finally, in the negative climax of the work, *dolente*. Coupled with the use of glissandi, which give the figuration an unmistakably dolorous character, this trajectory is one of loss. The second part of the work may also be interpreted in these terms. It begins with a clear sense of energy – freed from the more overtly spectral concerns of the first part, there is a greater emphasis on line and its expressive potential. The use of uniform note values here, of repetition, of the flute finding its 'voice' (through the use of whispered phonemes) and the cello being given greater autonomy, all underscore the *furioso* marking. This energy gradually dissipates, however, with the *dolente* material coming increasingly to the fore. Whilst much of the music seems to want to return to that initial sense of energy, this is not achievable, nor is it possible to settle on the clarity of harmony that characterized the first part – the return to an E♭ centricity is suggested, but only approached through short mementos, keepsakes. The final passages, *agitato*, are once again wisps, fragments, ashes.

To the Earth

As Saariaho points out in her note, the title of her second string quartet, *Terra Memoria* (2007) – 'for those departed' – refers to (and plays with) 'two words which are full of rich associations: to earth and memory'. The earth in which we are buried, the ground to which ashes fall, the sites of mourning – all these senses are bound up here. This work might, then, be read as the coming to rest of cinders after their airborne journey; it is a place of rootedness, of repose, but also a record of, the evidence for, that transience. As Saariaho explains, the music not only seeks to be some kind of memorial, but also sets out to invoke the apparatus of memory:

> We continue remembering the people who are no longer with us; the material – their life – is 'complete', nothing will be added to it. Those of us who are left behind are constantly reminded of our experiences together: our feelings continue to change about different aspects of their personality, certain memories keep on haunting us in our dreams. Even after many years, some of these memories change, some remain clear flashes which we can relive (Saariaho, 2010).

Given this apparent clarity of purpose, this work seems to ask to be read and interpreted in a rather different manner than *Cendres*.[12] Saariaho goes on to indicate that there are technical aspects of the music that illuminate her themes metaphorically: 'These thoughts brought me to treat the musical material in a certain manner; some aspects of it go through several distinctive transformations, whereas some remain nearly unchanged, clearly recognizable. … Here earth refers to my material, and memory to the way I'm working on it.' Of course, the relationship between earth and memory, as that between material and compositional process, is much more complex than any simple binary opposition; the web of memories experienced in visiting a gravesite illustrates the way in which the two are intimately connected. This perhaps suggests that material is always-already bound up with memory, and, certainly in *Terra Memoria*, the invocation of the musical past takes on a much more significant role. Thus ghosts, spectres, revenants are here again.

Within the context established by *Cendres*, it is tempting to hear the more obvious tonal residue, the passages of more conventional counterpoint, and of the working out of musical ideas within *Terra Memoria* as illustrative of the groundedness evoked by the title – to imagine the harmony in particular, as having more weight, of being earthbound. There are clearly, though, a number of common features, and reading one work in the light of the other might also serve to illuminate what appears a change of emphasis, rather than of essence.

At the level of the musical language, of the repertoire of gesture and technique, there are many points of contact. Most obviously, the trills and small glissandi, the oscillation between natural and harmonic tones, and the continual shifting between normal and *sul ponticello* playing remain much in evidence, as does the larger-scale sense of a slow-moving music articulated through a detailed, filigree surface. There are again passages where a harmonic field is presented through a regular foreground motion: the material at bar 40ff (Example 2.6a overleaf) is the first instance of a gesture which is repeated, varied, and transposed during the following passage – the sense of a 'fixed' harmony so prevalent in *Cendres* recurs, as does a dramaturgically appropriate 'weeping figure' some bars later (Example 2.6b). Further connections also suggest themselves: the work begins and ends with harmonies emphasizing D$\sharp_4$ (it is the highest pitch of the opening, eight-bar sonority, and becomes embedded within the return to this gesture which characterizes the closing eight bars), and what is arguably the climax of the work is also created through a sustained, *ff* unison E$\flat$ and its decoration and manipulation – although this is the E$\flat_4$ of *Dérive* rather than the E$\flat_2$ of *Cendres*.

The range of gesture is, however, much wider, more varied, richer in association and interconnection; much of this is due to what appears a more conventional approach to motivic working. A pervasive presence in this work is a four-note motif, gradually revealed by the second violin at the outset of the piece – this

---

[12]   In passing, it is interesting to note the prevalence of the string quartet when twentieth- and twenty-first-century composers seek to evoke what is past, or to memorialize – examples include music by Crumb, Reich, Andriessen, Birtwistle, Riley and Górecki.

Example 2.6   *Terra Memoria* – opening section: characteristic material

a) Bars 40-41

b) Bars 62-3

circling idea, A♯-B-A♭-G keeps reappearing in different forms, with the middle interval variously widened and contracted.[13] This approach is at its clearest in the creation of the long melody which appears twice: first towards the very beginning of the piece on first violin; later, in the last two minutes, transferred to the viola,

---

[13]   Here are two more spectres: in their most compressed form, these four notes become B-A-C-H (see also Kramer, 1995, in this context); when widened they transform into Bartók's Z-cell (0,1,6,7) – to whom the type of expression to be found within this work would not perhaps be wholly alien.

Example 2.7 *Terra Memoria* – **violin/viola melody**

a) Violin I, bars 15-21

b) Viola, bars 314-21

placed within a much more active surrounding texture, and expanded and varied timbrally (Example 2.7 shows both passages). The expressiveness attained through this very restricted pitch material is reminiscent of György Ligeti's later works, specifically music such as the 'Hora lungă' of his *Viola Sonata* (1994) – there is a similar sense of poise, of exploring a series of pitches in detail, and of an expressiveness found through a refusal to come fully to rest. That this melody is heard twice might be connected with Saariaho's characterization of how memories can be clearly retained or metamorphose over time; Pirkko Moisala suggests a clearer anthropomorphism for this type of motivic working: 'Even though the musical gestures are constantly varied, they provide consistency. They are like people: they gather new experiences and remember the past differently than before; nevertheless, they maintain their recognizable identity' (Moisala, 2009: 92). The effect in *Terra Memoria* is rather more ambiguous, however. Certainly, the material is now heard anew: placed within a changed context, both in the architecture of the piece and in its immediate sonic envelope, that is inevitable. However, the link created to the opening of the work, particularly given the close interconnection between beginning and ending passages, also gives the piece a cyclic quality – it returns, grounded, to the point from which it began.

Within that large-scale return, the piece as a whole falls into four main sections, but through the widespread use of similar or related material a more complicated process of referring to past events emerges. For example, whilst the *misterioso* opening of the work charts a gradual increase in intensity before the long violin melody finally appears (which leads into a contrasting passage characterized by the *agitato* articulation of clear harmonic fields), there is a sudden return to the opening sound-world to end this section – a number of bars are repeated, but are now simplified, clarified. The 'weeping' figure with which this first section concludes goes on to permeate the third section of the work – a process that might legitimately be called 'developmental': presented *fff con violenza, impetuoso*, there is a sense of anger, of violence coupled with sadness, the kind of expression which, to evoke Ligeti's *Viola Sonata* again, Arnold Whittall has associated with that work (Whittall, 2003: 204–7). *Doloroso* or *lamentoso* passages are interspersed with double-stopped outbursts – making use of the primary four-note motif, these linear gestures clearly connect with the rest of the work – and this section is again cyclic: we arrive at almost the same place, with another six closely related chordal gestures – but these now mark a decrescendo into the *molto calmo* of the final section.

Example 2.8   *Terra Memoria* – contrasted material of second section

The second section of the work most clearly illustrates the process of transforming or alluding to already-heard material: it initially sets up a contrast between an upwards *espressivo* gesture, which begins as a de-energized extension of the *agitato* from earlier, and a series of harmonies, trilled, *delicato* (Example 2.8). Whilst these remain calm, reposed, the interspersed music becomes increasingly animated, reaching at bar 106 a sense of clarity which seems to act as a development. This, however, clearly refers back to the opening of the work and in particular the cellular repetition found there – and it again goes through a gradual process of increasing animation before suddenly reappearing in its baldest form at bar 132. Even this reappearance is transformed, however – the use of harmonics makes for a more delicate, glassy timbre – and this material eventually splinters into a tremolando shimmer. The passage that follows – a rapid, descending figuration that, eventually, forms a kind of pre-echo of the *più giocoso*, scherzo passage towards the end of the work – also connects backwards: here, to the *agitato* music first heard at bar 40.

Counterpoints and Unison

It is not just internally that this music can be heard as making reference to the past – it also recalls styles and techniques associated with earlier periods. If approached in a manner that focuses on the tonal implications of some of the material and its transformation – the kind of pitch-based approach suggested earlier for *Cendres* – then these become increasingly apparent. There is an attention throughout the work to questions of implication, direction and combination of pitch class – 'voice leading' and 'counterpoint', one might call them – and listening to these with attention can also clarify the overall shape of the music.

The two outer sections of the work illustrate this process quite clearly. In the approach to the long violin melody in the opening section, an $F\sharp_4$ is unexpectedly introduced on the final semiquaver of bar 15 (see Example 2.7, above). The effect here is quite pronounced: this sudden sharpening of $F\natural$ – the highest pitch in the texture for the previous three bars – does, literally, lead the first violin into the $G\natural$ that follows. Furthermore, this movement is underpinned by a bass-line descent F–E♭, thus forming a compound major third in the outer voices – despite the chromaticism within that span, the tonal implication is hard to resist. This interval, $E\flat_2$–G_4, is, of course, also the starting point for *Cendres*, but its effect here is quite different. Rather than being presented as a self-standing object from which the music starts, to be explored, transformed, it is here heard in a longer-range context – as part of the articulation of a directed process. This process is shown in the reduction of Example 2.9a overleaf; the first 34 bars of the piece present a gradual semitonal bass descent from F_2 to C_2, coupled with a treble ascent. This semitonal bass movement, along with several instances of parallel motion, can be found throughout this first section; interestingly, the passage that follows, bars 34–64, returns to the same point after following its own, different trajectory: the cyclic quality of this music again reasserts itself.

At the end of the work, a comparable, though somewhat more complex, structure can be observed (Example 2.9b). Bars 325 to the end present, more quickly, the same bass motion as bars 1–34, but the ambiguity between the minor and major tenth here is suggestive given the dramaturgy of the work – a conventional coding would give the major a 'redemptive' quality, but this piece seems to refuse to end with any such positive commitment. The remainder of this section appears concerned with containing – contextualizing – the second moment of clear unison in the piece: the sustained, **pp** multi-octave C♯ in bar 304. The passage begins with two slow-moving melodic strands – the first presented by first violin and viola six octaves apart. This idea of a chromatic line doubled some octaves distant is again a gesture very typical of Ligeti's late style (for discussion, see, for example,

Example 2.9   *Terra Memoria* – **reduction of opening and closing passages**

a) Bars 1-64

b) Bars 293-end

Floros, 1996: 59–63); into this 'vacuum', second violin and viola weave their own melody, doubled two octaves distant. The sense of loss here is palpable, particularly coming after the *furioso* chordal passage – this is the aftershock of that trauma. The relationship between the two melodic strands again emphasizes the interval of a tenth at points of rest and, in bar 300, slips once again between major and minor. The point of unison itself is approached through glissandi in the outer parts, and the effect here is truly one of arrival – not only gesturally, but also in terms of pitch class.

What was described earlier as the climactic point of unison, the $E\flat_4$ in bar 234, is also reached through a directed process: filtering a pitch field down to only a few notes – the type of technique observed repeatedly in *Cendres*. The ending of this process is shown in Example 2.10: at the very last moment, the music arrives on a unison D, which then leads conventionally into the $E\flat$. The passage that follows is remarkable for its undecorated quality, in particular the starkness of the motif in

Example 2.10 *Terra Memoria* – bars 229–39

bars 234–5. The longest sustained E♭ comes a few bars later, where, subjected to gradual transformation between *sul ponticello* and normal position, coupled with the *fff* marking and the inevitable fluctuations of intonation that playing at this dynamic creates, this note fizzes with energy – it is grainy, dirty, rich in expressive potential. A comparison with the techniques of *Cendres* suggests itself here. In that earlier work, it was suggested that some of the gradual accruals of pitches could be heard as analogues, representations, of timbral transformations – during the process of pitch-addition at the outset, one can imaginatively recreate the (recorded and analysed) change in cello tone to *sul ponticello*. At this climactic moment in *Terra Memoria*, this process is presented to us directly. Rather than a representation, we hear the change itself; rather than being modelled through other sounds, we hear the sound as it is; rather than imagining a gesture that took place in the past, we are confronted with it now. Rather than hearing wisps, shards, cinders, we are given something solid, tangible, earth-bound. From the image to the reality, from the air to the earth.

Epilogues

And yet, and yet. Objections to this way of reading immediately suggest themselves. Most obvious perhaps are questions of specificity. What of the many other works displaying similar processes as *Cendres* – are these passages also to be perceived 'metaphorically', as tokens of something not present? Can all such works therefore be considered as cinders in this way? What of the listener who does not wish to hear (any) music as a mirroring of spectral processes? What of comparable passages to the unisons of *Terra Memoria* in other works – are these always indicative of 'groundedness'? What gives it that quality here? In both pieces, what of the surrounding music, the context of the work, and the overall sense of drama?

More broadly, the reading presented here sets up a number of dualities that immediately open themselves up to deconstruction, most obviously that between 'air' and 'earth' – ideas that are invoked but hardly interrogated. In the first instance, listeners may not make the associations with different types of material that has been insisted upon here – or may not consider the distinction to be as straightforward as has been suggested. On a wider level, the two types of listening that have been outlined are again not wholly distinct, and the intention here has certainly not been to suggest an 'either/or' way of proceeding. Further, to move from that duality to a consideration of possible meanings is perhaps an interpretative leap too far.

However, even with these objections held firmly in place, the interpretative lever that has been suggested above might provide a way of thinking through the pronounced change of sense between the two works. *Cendres* presents a mode of articulation that is rarefied, crystalline, hard to penetrate, whereas *Terra Memoria* is less obviously polished, rougher, and more clearly expressive. Aspects of their construction reinforce this characterization, as has been observed. The earlier work is also more straightforwardly self-standing – notwithstanding its interconnections with *...à la fumée*, the mode of expression is more clearly internalized – whereas the latter makes a wider range of reference to familiar, more conventional expressive and technical models.

On a slightly different level, *Terra Memoria* could be said to be an answer to the type of musical expression found in *Cendres*, in that it suggests a move towards a music that is given shape, necessity and direction through a re-imagining of conventional pitch-based movement. A similar approach may also be found in one further composition with which, as a supplement, it seems appropriate to end this discussion, a work that further illuminates the related questions of musical coherence. *Phoenix* (2006), by British composer Richard Causton, fits closely on a titular level with the other music examined here: rising from the ashes of its own funeral pyre, the phoenix is a potent symbol of reinvention and rebirth – which also, of course, 'completes' the trajectory of the network of pieces in this chapter: cinders drift, fall to earth, and from them new life may be born.[14]

Beyond this simple narrative, however, the differences of 'vision' that these works reflect (evidenced through the music that results) also cast light on one other – when placed into this context, *Phoenix* opens up a number of new interpretative possibilities. The connection between Causton's and Saariaho's music is an indirect one – certainly, both composers have been influenced by works most commonly included within the category of 'spectral music', as Julian Anderson observed some years ago (Anderson, 2000: 20–21). However, in Causton's more recent works, any direct lineage is harder to identify, but there remains a continuing attention to detail of sonority and the ways in which sounds can evolve. An example of the type of timbral animation he favours is found right at the opening of *Phoenix*: here, using *bariolage* and timbral trills, the gradual entry of pitches in the high treble register is given a strange, otherworldly sense through the fluctuation of pitch that results. In this respect, though not in terms of energy, it resembles the central E♭ of *Terra Memoria*, but here the sound is more tentative, fragile.[15] This gesture is repeated, in shortened form, at the beginning of the second section of the work – like *Dérive* and *Cendres*, the work falls into two parts, here clearly demarcated by the composer – but what is striking here is the sense of note-against-note working. This is continued throughout the piece;

---

[14]   In terms of scoring, there is also a congruence between the four works: *Phoenix* uses the same instrumentation as *Dérive* with the exception of the vibraphone; *Cendres* reduces that ensemble still further (and substitutes alto flute); all pieces use cello; three include violin and cello.

[15]   In correspondence, Causton pointed out that this material refers back to the second of his *Two Pieces* for two clarinets, where a similar type of timbral trill is marked 'incandescent' – the invocation of fire obviously fits within the poetics of *Phoenix*; also suggestive is the fact that the earlier work is entitled 'Song to End Mourning'.

Example 2.11 *Phoenix* – 'Cantilena'

Causton has talked about particular compositional habits he has developed in order to guide his counterpoint,[16] and, without the listener necessarily being aware of what these are, the effect is one of clear direction, giving each gesture a sense of inevitability.

There are moments of disjunction here too, however. Immediately following the glassy opening, the piano introduces a series of chords in a constant quaver motion, underpinned by long-held bass pedals. Some bars later, marked 'deranged', flute and clarinet (and to a lesser extent the strings) play over this material in a different tempo (in the ratio 5:4) – the composer has likened the effect here to scribbling over an existing artwork, graffiti-like. This passage returns in the second section of the piece, where the sense of violence that it projects is more pronounced, and where it foreshadows a passage of *moto perpetuo* – the same tempo, but now moving with a constant semiquaver movement from violin and cello. Beginning from their bottom strings, the instruments ascend – initially in parallel before gradually finding their individual trajectory – through a process of repetition of short cells, with pitches added above as the lowest are gradually removed. Though technically this resembles passages found in *Cendres*, in terms of gesture it is much more aggressive, particularly with its underpinning of *ff* sustained pitches from piano and clarinet – if this piece is indeed a response to ideas of death and rebirth (the dedication is in memory of Joanna Greenfield, whose husband part-commissioned the work), then, as with *Terra Memoria*, part of that response is of

---

[16] Personal correspondence with the author.

Example 2.12 *Phoenix* – 'Epilogue'

anger, of violence, of intense feeling.[17] Between these passages, however, there are also moments of calm and delicacy, in particular at the end of the first section, which disintegrates ('dies') into single notes and disappearing piano chords.

The climactic moment comes with a brief *cantilena* – one might again draw a comparison with the unison passage in *Terra Memoria*, but the effect here is less conventionally expressive. The melody is again made strange through the use of continually fluctuating timbre (Example 2.11) – this song, sung by a new and unfamiliar voice over a punctuation evocative of bells, is to be suddenly cut off as it crescendos to *fff*. If the first section ends with a sense of disintegration, the second seems to be leading towards a reconciliation; the piano – initially distinct from the other instruments, partly because of its inability to sustain pitches – finally joins the ensemble as an equal. But as it does, the music breaks off. Not in this work the sense of return observed in both *Cendres* and *Terra Memoria*, but instead an epilogue, in which the music seems to have been pared back to its

---

[17]   However, the companion piece, *Sleep*, for solo flute, which uses as its inspiration a poem by George Seferis, seems to be the more straightforward 'in memoriam' – *Phoenix* is rather more complicated in its poetics.

essentials (Example 2.12 above). Again, in its sense of counterpoint, in its clarity, it provides an answer to the questions of how to progress musical ideas posed by the very opening of the work, but its dramatic effect is much more significant. Whilst this passage certainly does not offer redemption, or resurrection even, we *are* given a kind of balm to the violence with which the work has confronted us. Rather than music of transcendence, this music is clearly rooted, presenting recognizable chorale-type gestures through familiar – conventional – instrumental articulation. This passage of music both completes and re-energizes the trajectory of the work as a whole – whilst it sounds partly as the coherent outcome of what has gone before, it also opens up new directions, giving rise to fresh implications and expectations. And then it stops. It is not with a straightforward vision of the reintegration of splintered elements, or a re-fusing of cinders back into living form that this music ends: it is, instead, with yet another supplement – musically and dramatically – that continues to resonate even after the final sound has died.

Chapter 3

Dreams about Music, Music about Dreams

Anni Oskala

> I'm someone who remembers many of my dreams. Sometimes I dream music, and sometimes I remember it. Other times it leaves just a memory of an atmosphere, or some instrumental colour. But I don't write dreamy, floaty music. It's more to do with dreams as a gateway to secret existences, like death and love, the basic things that we know nothing about. (Kaija Saariaho, in Kimberley, 2001)

Kaija Saariaho has always been fascinated by dreams and dreaming. She believes that these phenomena act as a gateway to our unconscious, and tries to interpret meanings within her own experiences based on notes kept in a dream diary (Siltanen, 1982; Koskelin, 2002; Oskala, 2005). To this end, she has delved into research literature on dreams, in particular the theories of Sigmund Freud (1856–1939), the founder of psychoanalysis and of the systematic study of dreams. The topic of dreaming recurs in the titles of Saariaho's works throughout her career. We know that she considers the selection of a title to be an important part of the compositional process – it helps her to crystallize her ideas.[1] The recurring dream-related titles suggest, therefore, that dreams are also a long-standing source of compositional inspiration.

This chapter examines five works by Saariaho which refer to dreams or night-time: *Im Traume* ('In a Dream', 1980), an early piece for piano and cello; three vocal works from the late 1980s/early 1990s – *From the Grammar of Dreams* (1988), *Grammaire des rêves* ('Grammar of Dreams', 1989) and *Nuits, adieux* ('Nights, Farewells', 1991); and Saariaho's first opera, *L'Amour de loin* ('Love from Afar', 2000), focusing on its dream scene.[2] These case studies demonstrate different ways in which dreams have inspired Saariaho at various stages of her career, in works spanning two decades.

The analyses show how concepts found in dream theories can help to illustrate specific aspects of musical and textual organization. Connections are drawn at two levels: firstly, instances where musical ideas appear to have been drawn consciously from the theories are highlighted, with reference to the composer's public statements and writings. At this level, dream research literature functions

---

[1]   See Nieminen, 1985: 26; Michel, 1994: 22; Beyer, 2000a: 308; Stearns, 2002; Huter, 2003: 83.

[2]   This chapter does not cover two other pieces by Saariaho whose titles refer to dreams – *Caliban's Dream* (1993) and *Aile du songe* ('Wing of Dreams', 2001) – because, in these cases, the specific features of dreams and dream theories discussed here are less suited as analytical tools.

as an 'extra-musical' source of inspiration, in a similar way to prose, poetry or visual stimuli in other works. Moving beyond issues of biography and inspiration, the works are analysed in more detail at the second level, with reference to Freudian terminology. This is not to suggest that Saariaho herself had specific conceptual or structural parallels with dream theory in mind whilst writing these pieces, or that her psychic processes at the time of composition were connected with those identified in the music (see Spitz, 1985: 98–135). At this level, the approach taken here could be described as 'hermeneutic', as defined by Lawrence Kramer (1990, 1995, 2001), akin to previous analyses of musical works with reference to psychoanalytic concepts.[3] Effectively, parallels are drawn between Saariaho's music and the psychic processes of dream formation and Freudian dream analysis.

From a general perspective, almost all music has elements of development, variation and re-combination that could be related to aspects of dream theory, and much previous scholarship has similarly sought to elucidate musical structures with reference to psychic processes.[4] The focus here is on elucidating specific features of the pieces in question with reference to Freud's ideas about the structure, psychological function and interpretation of dreams.

---

[3]   I refer here to the growing body of musicological studies that seek to examine musical processes with reference to psychoanalytic concepts and terminology, for example those of Sigmund Freud, Jacques Lacan and Julia Kristeva (see Välimäki, 2002 and 2003). Several of these studies use psychoanalytic concepts as an explanatory frame without suggesting that the composer in question had consciously intended such a conceptual parallel (see Johnson, 1994; Schwarz, 1993 and 1997; Cumming, 1997; Lyotard, 1998; Välimäki, 2001). In the context of Saariaho's vocal works, precedents for this approach include Marja Minkkinen's description of the role of text with reference to Kristeva's concepts (the semiotic chora, the symbolic, etc.) (Minkkinen, 2005; as well as her 2003 dissertation). Anne Sivuoja-Gunaratnam's analysis of the text fragmentation in the last section of *Lonh* with reference to Barthes' Lacan-derived concept of *jouissance* also borders on this type of approach (Sivuoja-Gunaratnam, 2003b).

[4]   For example, Friedman compares primary processes to the logic of melodic transformation, and Ehrenzweig considers techniques in serial music and the creative process in general (Friedman, 1960; Ehrenzweig, 2000 [1967]: 33–4, 49–55). Lyotard has more recently suggested that the text treatment in Berio's *Sequenza III* reflects the logic of the unconscious (primary process) (Lyotard, 1998). Musical structures have also been compared with various other formulations of unconscious psychic processes: Julian Johnson has pointed out similarities between the syntactical processes in Mahler's *Ninth Symphony* and Julia Kristeva's conception of the maternal *chora* (Johnson, 1994). In turn, David Schwarz has compared pre-symbolic psychic structures and the music of the minimalist composers Steve Reich and John Adams with reference to Kaja Silverman's Lacan-derived concepts of the 'acoustic mirror' and the 'sonorous envelope' (Schwarz, 1993). Building on Schwarz's work, Naomi Cumming has provided a psychoanalytical interpretation of Reich's *Different Trains* with reference to Kristeva and Lacan (Cumming, 1997).

Freud and Dreams

According to Freud, dreams are not irrational, but they follow a different logic from conscious thought. His seminal work, *The Interpretation of Dreams* (*Die Traumdeutung*, 1900), was the first serious attempt to systematize this structural logic, and thus, as per his title, to arrive at a method for interpreting dreams. The fundamental tenet underlying his work was a belief that dreams provide a uniquely direct access to the unconscious, which is usually suppressed and inaccessible. He coined the umbrella term 'dream-work' to refer to the various unconscious processes that distort the true, 'latent content' of a dream, turning it into 'manifest content', fragments of which are remembered by the dreamer (Freud, 1999 [1900]: 211–329). By virtue of appearing in such a distorted form, unconscious thoughts bypass the 'psychic censorship' – the inner resistance to bringing any repressed wishes to consciousness – and can, therefore, feature in a dream. Freud also suggested that manifest content frequently uses material from the previous day (ibid.: 127–8). Saariaho's views resonate with Freud's theories, and some of his concepts have helped her to analyse her own dreams (Oskala, 2005).

Freud identified four main processes at play in dream-work. The first two are responsible for the seemingly irrational symbolic content, and for the loss of linear time and any ordinary sense of causality. Firstly, 'condensation' refers to multiple ideas, people or elements that are merged into one hybrid, while in the second process, 'displacement', the relative psychic importance of the various dream elements is altered as they are reorganized and/or replaced (so, for example, content might be substituted by something else associated with it, or the recipient/cause of a strong emotion might be changed). The third psychological mechanism at play is the selection of elements for the manifest content that can be expressed visually, caused by the limited means of representation in a dream. The fourth and final process, 'secondary revision', is an attempt to create a more coherent whole by making links and connections between various episodes in the dream. In Freud's own words, 'with its snippets and scraps it [secondary revision] patches the gaps in the dream's structure', and in parts where the revision is successful, the 'dream loses its appearance of absurdity and incoherence' (Freud, 1999 [1900]: 320).

Having developed this theory, Freud proposed a method of interpreting dreams that would penetrate beyond the distorted manifest content, allowing the true, latent content to be gauged. In his view, because dreams result from unconscious processes, their interpretation should be based on individuals' own free associations about their contents (a method he originally formulated with Josef Breuer in their work on hysterical patients). The task of the interpreter is to analyse and search for links between the various, seemingly disparate elements related by the dreamer – the latent dream thoughts (ibid.: 98–105). Further, Freud proposed that all dreams can ultimately be shown to be disguised 'wish-fulfilments' if analysed in this manner, (ibid.: 98–105), expressing, in concealed form, the innermost repressed wishes of the dreamer.

Calculated Unpredictability in *Im Traume*

Saariaho's earliest work explicitly associated with dreams is *Im Traume* ('In a Dream') for cello and piano, completed in 1980. At the time, she was exploring musical structures with sudden switches between materials, yet with static harmonic frames. As she has described,

> Some works resulted in which I tried to fashion a musical dynamic by using abrupt transitions between different materials and thus to compensate for the absence of large-scale tensions within the harmonic material. In these works I used widely differing textures and modes of musical performance – the only common factor between the different materials is harmony which, paradoxically, becomes the most stable element of all. As an example, my piece *Im Traume* (1980) for cello and piano consists of harmonic material which is well-defined and non-dynamic, whilst giving a certain background colour to the ensemble. This material constitutes an 'area' which is modified by differing events at the level of timbre and texture ... The transitions from one texture to another are very abrupt (Saariaho, 1987: 97–8).[5]

It seems that Saariaho drew extra-musical inspiration for such compositional explorations from her study of the structures of dreams (Koskelin, 2002), and she once specified that one of her aims in *Im Traume* was 'to construct a formal whole which progresses as I think our dreams often progress: as fast transitions, seemingly irrational yet meaningful associations. Moods change unexpectedly or gradually, metamorphoses change the familiar into something new.'[6]

Im Traume is indeed characterized by rapid changes of tempo and texture; the slowly moving interludes and piano passages marked *dolce* or *espressivo* give way time and again, without warning, to the percussive core material of the piece. There are also sudden and extreme changes of dynamic: the score contains over 50 *subito f* and *p* markings. Thus, as the various episodes appear unconnected, and the changes are unprepared, one could say that the influence of secondary revision is not felt in this 'musical dream'. However, there is a 'hidden' logic beneath the apparently chaotic musical surface of *Im Traume*. Throughout the piece, the 'cello and piano vary a basic pool of harmonic material, built around the core pitches C, C♯, D, D♯, G, G♯ and A. There are also certain recurring musical gestures: pitch clusters structured around tritones or fifths articulate a number of formal junctures, as do the recurring *sul ponticello* strikes in the cello, notated on their own four-line staff; C and G *pizzicati* permeate the piece, at times underpinning whole sections like a pedal point (see, for example, pages 5–6 of the score). The static harmony and recurrent gestural content create coherence and unity across

---

[5]   See also Saariaho, 1981: 117.

[6]   Saariaho cited in cover text of the LP *Music by Harri Wessman, Usko Meriläinen, Kaija Saariaho, Johannes Brahms* (JASELP 0010, 1987).

the piece; this is perhaps what the composer herself was referring to with her last phrase, 'metamorphoses change the familiar into something new'.

Saariaho's phrase 'seemingly irrational yet meaningful associations' also reflects her belief, in line with Freud, that dreams can be analysed to reveal important psychic truths. In Freudian terms, the harmony in *Im Traume* can be seen as a musical illustration of 'latent dream content', which is the unifying principle behind all the seemingly fragmentary 'manifest dream content' – the various textures and timbres of the piece. While Saariaho herself has not made this connection with explicit reference to *Im Traume*, she has spoken elsewhere of her strong belief, rooted in Freudian principles, that a dream often tries to communicate its central latent dream thoughts by presenting them repeatedly, in different guises. As she has stated, 'When [in a dream] there are some really important things, then the thing comes again and again, tries to get the message across to you, but always in a different way' (Koskelin, 2002).

Recurring Dreams about a Distant Love: *L'Amour de loin*

In *The Interpretation of Dreams*, Freud also commented on the typical relationship between successive (sections of) dreams:

> In the interpretation of dreams consisting of several main sections, or of dreams belonging to the same night, we must not overlook the possibility that these different and successive dreams mean the same thing, expressing the same impulses in different material. That one of these homologous dreams which comes first in time is usually the most distorted and most bashful, while the next dream is bolder and more distinct. (Freud, 1911: 216).

Thus, certain dream thoughts can recur in various guises within a single dream, and a person can also experience similar content during the separate episodes, or across a longer time period. Saariaho is particularly interested in this idea as a result of her personal experience of recurring nightmares (Siltanen, 1982: 49), and she has come to believe that they happen because the dreamer has not yet grasped the unconscious message that the dream is trying to convey:

> In the case of nightmares a nightmare can specifically be repeated always in the same form … These things are really important for me because I am a person who remembers many dreams, and lives in them a long time and writes them and tries to understand them, because I feel that during the night the brain is working at high speed to clear things which have not been cleared during the day (Koskelin, 2002).

Freud also commented on the relationship between daytime fantasies and dreams. The transformation of daydreams to night-time dreams is in itself a fairly common phenomenon, although there is a characteristic 'peculiar to the dream as distinct from the daydream: its content of imagined ideas is not framed as thoughts, but transformed into sensory images which we believe in, and which we think we are actually experiencing' (Freud, 1999 [1900]: 348).

Given this context, it is interesting to examine Saariaho's opera *L'Amour de loin* ('Love from Afar', 2000), because one of its central themes is the protagonist's (troubadour Jaufré Rudel's) incessant dreaming and daydreaming about love. At the start of the opera, he fantasizes and describes an idealized distant lady whom he purports to love. A Pilgrim who has arrived from overseas gives these fantasies a more concrete form, telling him that the Countess of Tripoli, Clémence, fits the description perfectly. From this point on, Jaufré can think of nothing else; she fills his waking thoughts during the day, and he dreams of her at night. Following this, Act IV as a whole takes place at sea: Jaufré has decided to make his dream come true and meet her, embarking on a voyage to Tripoli, accompanied by the Pilgrim. However, unresolved inner conflict takes a toll on Jaufré's physical and psychological condition during the journey, and he arrives dying. Shocked by his death, initially, Clémence revolts against God, but finally accepts what has come to pass and decides to take the veil to cherish the memory of their pure, ideal love forever.

The way Jaufré's dreams are described in *L'Amour de loin* is a perfect illustration of how daydreams might be transformed to become night-time dreams. He seems truly to believe that Clémence is the lady in his dreams, even though he has never seen her. At the start of Act III, he tells the Pilgrim,[7]

> Since you spoke to me of her, nothing else occupies my mind. At night, when I'm asleep, there appears this face so sweet with sea-green eyes that smile at me and tell me that it is she, even though I have never seen her. Then, in the morning, in my bed, I lament that I have not been able to caress her, nor hold her to me. Is that not madness, Pilgrim? And to think that she, over there, far away, suspects nothing of it!

The visual and life-like character of dreams is most explicitly reflected in the dream scene (Act IV, scene 2), which the librettist, Amin Maalouf, included at Saariaho's request (Pennanen, 2000).[8] The calm opening mood – Jaufré and the Pilgrim are sleeping – soon yields to an increasing rhythmic urgency, which reflects the growing turbulence of the sea and of Jaufré's dreaming mind. The texture thickens and the dynamic level mounts, reaching its climax in bars 240–44 whereupon, in the middle of the night, the protagonist wakes and jumps up, noticeably shaken, uttering, 'I have seen her, Pilgrim; I have seen her as I see

---

[7]   All references to the libretto are from a translation by George Hall available at <http://www.tripoli-city.org/amour/index.html> (accessed 25 August 2010).

[8]   From early stages of planning, Saariaho expressed a wish to incorporate dreams into her opera – they were one of the six mentioned libretto 'requirements' noted in an early sketch from 9 August 1995.

you! … She was here, and her body, and her face and her white dress lit up the night.' As Jaufré goes on to describe his dream in more detail, it is enacted on stage. The white-clad Clémence walks towards the sea, singing, first in French and then in the ancient Occitan language, the verse, 'Your love fills my mind / Waking and dreaming / But it's dreaming that I prefer / Because in dreams you're mine!'[9]

The orchestral accompaniment to Clémence's song, which consists of a repetitive triplet figure, distinctive instrumentation (vibraphone, crotales, string harmonics), whispers and birdsong in the opera's electronic part, and vowels and humming in the chorus, distinguishes the dream from the surrounding operatic 'reality'. In addition, the repetition of the verse in Occitan reinforces a sense of spatial and temporary distance. According to Jaufré, the song is one he has composed, and during its visual enactment he joins in for a moment, repeating the line, 'Because in dreams you're mine'. During the Occitan verse, however, he resumes his agitated description of the dream; Clémence moves away, walking on the sea, but he is too scared to follow her.

In line with Freud's theory, the manifest content of Jaufré's dream in Act IV is a concoction of several memories and thoughts of the previous day(s): the Pilgrim's description of Clémence's piousness and long robe (Act I) becomes seamlessly fused with Jaufré's own fantasies of her physical appearance; the dream also evokes Jaufré's earlier fantasy about the lady of his dreams, originally voiced in Act I, scene 2: 'In a passionate voice she will sing my songs.' It is also evident that Jaufré is experiencing recurring dreams of essentially the same content: the dream he recounts in Act III, and the one he has in Act IV, are both about Clémence, and she departs from him in each case.

Saariaho's setting illustrates the recurring dream-thoughts musically. An oboe melody lends musical unity and coherence to the ongoing dramatic narrative (see Example 3.1 overleaf, which transcribes two instances). As shown in Example 3.2, the melody is played on the oboe during Jaufré's description of his dream (Act III), and it reappears in the dream scene as the melody of Clémence's song. The change from an oboe and an oral account of the song (Act III) to singing voice and

---

[9]   The text of the song in the dream scene is based on a *canso* of the twelfth-century troubadour Jaufré Rudel (fl. 1125–48), *Quan lo rossinhols el folhos* (Occitan 'When the Nightingale in the Leafy Wood'). Maalouf has incorporated content from two other verses of this song into the libretto as well: the first verse talks of the nightingale singing his songs, which connects to the opening scene where Jaufré is composing a song about a nightingale, and the content of Jaufré's dream reflects another verse that translates as, 'For this love I am so enflamed / that when I go running toward her, it seems to me that backwards / I turn around and that she goes off there fleeing, / and my horse goes so slowly / I hardly think I will ever get there / if she does not wish to hold herself back.' (Verse 4 in 'Version 3', reproduced from Pickens, 1978: 80–81). Maalouf also incorporates Jaufré's other *canso*, *Lanqand li jorn son lonc en mai* (Occitan 'When the Days are Long in May') into the libretto in Act II, and the libretto of *L'Amour de loin* overall is based on the historical Jaufré's *Vida* (see Lampila, 1997; Hautsalo, 2000: 17; Langlois, 2000: 24).

Example 3.1 *L'Amour de loin* – recurring oboe melody

a) Prologue, bars 64-72

b) Act III, scene 1, bars 118-36

a stage visualization (Act IV) perhaps depicts how the idea of Clémence grows increasingly elaborate and impassioned in Jaufré's mind as time passes, whilst also resonating with Freud's belief that in recurring dreams of similar content, the latter ones are usually 'bolder and more distinct'.

Continuing with the Freudian line of inquiry, what could be the unconscious message that this recurring dream is attempting to convey? At the level of manifest content, it appears to reflect Jaufré's wish to be united with his distant love, but arguably, it reveals a more complicated picture in terms of latent content. His apparent eagerness to meet Clémence is in fact contradicted by his deeper, unconscious desire to keep her as a 'love from afar' – in the future, rather than a concrete, present reality. This desire is transformed by dream-work, and is expressed as a physical inability to keep Clémence near: in the dream that he describes in Act III, Jaufré feels incapable of caressing or holding her, and in the dream scene his fear prevents him from following her over the rail of the ship.[10] The lyrics of Clémence's song (which Jaufré says is one of his own compositions)

---

[10]   See Iliescu, 2003: 35; Hautsalo, 2004: 23; and Hautsalo, 2005: 249 for descriptions of the dream scene as an anticipation of the opera's overall plot: the impossibility of true union between Jaufré and Clémence.

Example 3.2   *L'Amour de loin* – appearances of the 'Love from Afar' theme

Act, scene	Bars	Description	Dramatic context
Prologue 'Traversée'	30–34	1(a), phrases C–D, starting note F_2, oboe solo	
Prologue 'Traversée'	64–72	1(a), oboe solo	
II, 1	157–9	1(a), phrase A, oboe 1	Clémence tells how much she misses her native land of France
II, 1	286–9	F_2–E_2–B_1, variation of phrase A, oboe 1	The Pilgrim tells Clémence about Jaufré
III, 1	118–36	1(b), oboe 1 and 2	Jaufré relates his dreams about Clémence to the Pilgrim
IV, 1	247–50; 253–6	1(a), phrase A, oboe 1	Jaufré tells that he has seen Clémence in his dream
IV, 1	263–79	1(b), soprano	Clémence sings in the materialization of Jaufré's dream
IV, 1	283–314	Variation of 1(b), soprano; melody becomes fragmented, phrase A repeated bars 308–10 and 311–14	Occitan version of the song
V, 1	90–93	1(a), phrase A, oboe 1 (cf. II, 1, bars 157–9)	Clémence is thinking about the forthcoming meeting with Jaufré
V, 3	637–47	1(a), oboe 1 and 2 (cf. 'Traversée', bars 64–72)	Clémence's defiance subsides and turns into deferential longing
V, 4	718–21; 723–32	1(a), phrases C–D, starting note F_2, soprano (cf. 'Traversée', bars 30–34); three variations, bars 723–32	Clémence's prayer to her 'love from afar'

in that scene lend further strength to this interpretation, as the third line explicitly states, 'But it's dreaming that I prefer'.

Jaufré's dreams appear thus to bear witness to the Freudian notion of dreams as a route to the unconscious, as his suppressed wish is expressed in a symbolic, disguised form. To pass the 'psychic censorship', his underlying desire is distorted: it is framed in a poetic context and the song is sung by Clémence, not the dreamer himself. Further, upon its repeat, the wish is also linguistically concealed, presented in Occitan, an ancient language, unfamiliar to the modern audience, as well as to the protagonist.[11] In this instance, it appears that the dream succeeds in bringing Jaufré's unconscious turmoil to the fore, as it is immediately followed by his first desperate admission of his fear and indecision:

> I'm afraid, Pilgrim, I'm afraid. You are the voice of reason, but fear does not heed the voice of reason. I'm afraid of not finding her, and I'm afraid of finding her. I'm afraid of being lost at sea before reaching Tripoli, and I'm afraid of reaching Tripoli. I'm afraid of dying, Pilgrim, and I'm afraid of living. Do you understand me?

As explained above, this inner conflict takes its toll on Jaufré's physical and psychological condition. He is taken to the citadel unconscious, recovering his senses only for a short while during which, driven by the tragedy of the situation, he and Clémence hastily confess their love for each other before he dies in her arms. Their vocal lines meet in unison for a few fleeting moments, but never attain a fully fledged union. The two 'lovers from afar' are brought together, yet their meeting is as short-lived as it is impassioned; their love is to remain an unconsummated ideal. This apparently tragic denouement is at once also a type of wish-fulfilment for Jaufré, however, since his dream never becomes a reality. Indeed, his last words, incited by Clémence's kiss, are: 'In this instant, I have all I wish. Why ask life for more?'

Clémence's initial reaction to Jaufré's death is anger; she revolts against God at first, but, as mentioned earlier, finally accepts what has come to pass and decides to take the veil to cherish the memory of their pure, ideal love. Once her defiance has subsided, the melody heard previously in Jaufré's dreams about his distant love is played on the oboe (bars 637–47), as a reminder of love's power to outlive death. In the final scene of the opera, Clémence's prayer to her 'distant love' brings together her continuing love for Jaufré and her longing for the distant God (see Hautsalo, 2005: 249–51). Her prayer is set once more to the same melody, signalling her acceptance and understanding of the mystery and perfection of ideal, unconsummated love. All in all, then, *L'Amour de loin* is essentially an opera about dreaming of, and loving, the unattainable; indeed, the title of the opera could alternatively be translated into English as 'love *of* distance'. At the start of the opera, Jaufré is content with fantasizing about an indefinite, idealized woman, and the same sense of ambiguity and acceptance is recaptured in Clémence's closing prayer. As the drama unfolds, Jaufré's recurring night-time dreams about Clémence allow us to share in his deepest, unconscious fears and desires, and they express in symbolic form his preference for distance.

---

[11] It appears that the librettist, Maalouf, has diverged from a literal translation for these crucial lines 3–4 in French. A literal English translation of the whole verse reads: 'I am preoccupied with this love / Waking and then dreaming asleep / for there I have marvellous joy / because I rejoice there rejoicing with joy' (Pickens, 1978: 79).

Vocal Works and the Grammar of Dreams

From Dream Theory ...

> During the composition process [of *From the Grammar of Dreams*] I read a
> book by William Foulkes called *A Grammar of Dreams*. That was one source
> of inspiration. It explored how thoughts are arranged and how the linearity of
> a phrase is broken down in dreams. The notion of thoughts bouncing here and
> there yielded musical ideas ... Plath's texts also impressed me as very dream-
> like in their mood (Saariaho, in Komsi, 2001: 20).

Saariaho first came across *A Grammar of Dreams* in the early 1980s (Siltanen,
1982: 49). In addition to her interest in Foulkes's theories in themselves, Saariaho
has related that she also found musical inspiration in the book later that decade
(Saariaho, 1999 [1987]). This is reflected in the titles of her vocal works composed
between 1988 and 1991: *From the Grammar of Dreams* (a cycle of five songs
for soprano and mezzo-soprano), *Grammaire des rêves* (for soprano, alto and a
five-piece ensemble), as well as *Nuits, adieux*, for vocal quartet (SATB) and live
electronics with a title related more broadly to night-time. In this section, it will be
seen that the concepts of dream theory can fruitfully be used to illustrate specific
compositional features of these three vocal compositions, starting with a further
look into Foulkes's work, in order to understand better what Saariaho found so
fascinating, and how his theories might relate to the pieces under study.

(William) David Foulkes is a leading cognitive dream theorist (born 1935).
His monograph, *A Grammar of Dreams*, has Freudian roots – it includes a lengthy
section on Freud (Foulkes, 1978: 27–87) – but it also draws on more recent work on
structuralism, linguistics and neuropsychology (ibid., 1978: 103–90). In Freudian
terms, the 'grammar of dreams' provides a way to describe and understand the
associative paths of the transformative processes of dream-work. At the core of
this theory is the idea that dream thoughts can be conceived of as sentences whose
linearity has been broken up. Taking this as a premise, Foulkes devises a cognitive-
linguistic notational system – the 'grammar' itself – for describing and analysing
the content of dreams, dubbed the 'Scoring System for Latent Structure' or SSLS
(ibid., 1978: 193). By using carefully selected key words (verbs and nouns) and
presenting them with abbreviations and specific signs (for example, $\leftarrow$, $\rightarrow$, $=$,
$+$, $-$), Foulkes argues that SSLS can be used to describe in a reductive manner
the original linearity behind the various apparently unconnected components of a
dream (ibid.: 199–244).

... to Compositional Practice

Saariaho found the idea of dreams as sentences that have been fragmented and
re-ordered particularly inspirational in the late 1980s. This makes sense in the
context of her compositional development. In 1982–86, Saariaho's compositional

focus was on electroacoustic exploration of timbres, with the human voice used as a non-linguistic source of timbral material. In the late 1980s, however, after feeling 'blocked with voice' (Maycock, 1989; Oskala, 2007: 81–9), she found renewed interest in using semantic text in her music and in writing for live singers. In this period, a defining feature of her vocal writing was the use of text as a source of both semantic meaning and of purely sonic content (Oskala, 2007: 85–9); the vocal parts move about lithely along a continuum from full semantic units to fragmented phonetic material.[12] Foulkes's ideas on textual fragmentation in dreams were perfectly suited to offer extra-musical inspiration for Saariaho's vocal idiom in this period of change and exploration.

It seems likely, therefore, that in addition to having derived two titles from his book, Saariaho's approach to text was guided and inspired by Foulkes's ideas in the three 'dream-themed' vocal works composed in this period. In all three, text is presented both in fuller semantic units and in fragmented form, broken up into syllables and individual phonemes. In fact, the selected texts are themselves fragmentary in terms of syntax, and opaque in meaning – this is perhaps what the composer meant by the 'dream-like' mood in Plath's texts in the citation above. Furthermore, all three pieces involve more than one singer and Saariaho takes the opportunity to superimpose the same or different texts in her setting, thus adding to the textual jumble.

In summary, it seems evident that Foulkes's ideas about the structure of dream thoughts influenced Saariaho's text selection and setting in *From the Grammar of Dreams*, *Grammaire des rêves* and *Nuits, adieux*, all composed between 1988 and 1991. While she had been familiar with Foulkes's ideas since the early 1980s, only upon re-reading his work in the later part of the decade did she have the idea of applying some of these concepts in her compositions. Further, in addition to text treatment, it will be seen in the next section that the overall form of these pieces can be illustrated with reference to concepts of dream theory, even though Saariaho herself might not have intended such parallels while composing.

Dream Episodes in Nuits, adieux

First, the somewhat unusual overall structure of *Nuits, adieux* can helpfully be elucidated with reference to the structural principles of dreams. As the title implies, the piece consists of a number of sections entitled '*Nuit*' (night) and '*Adieu*' (farewell). There are a total of five each, presented first in alternation and then three of each are heard in succession. The '*Nuit*' sections are set to four dream-like text passages from Jacques Roubaud's novel, *Echanges de la lumière*, consisting of individual words and textual fragments. In the novel, six people converse about light – its nature and character, its relation to the world and existence – on six evenings. The passages selected by Saariaho are opaque contributions by a

---

[12]   Consider Saariaho's sound/noise axis, and its use in timbral organization (Saariaho, 1987).

Example 3.3	*Nuits, adieux* – **textual material**

Section	Bars	Text
Nuit I	1–24	Roubaud, passage 1
Adieu I	25–58	Balzac, lines 1, 4, 2, 3
Nuit II	59–79	Roubaud, passage 2
Adieu II	80–111	Balzac, fragments of lines 1–6
Nuit III	112–34	Roubaud, passage 3
Nuit IV	135–87	Roubaud, fragments of passages 1–4
Nuit V	188–99	Roubaud, passage 4
Adieux III–V	200–238 (end)	Balzac, fragments and full version of lines 1–6

character named William H., consisting of collections of individual words and text fragments with no clear syntax or semantic progression. The first four lines of the first passage, for example, read, '*Dans l'air / s'arrache / de la terre / au noir la lumière / et la crache*' (In the air / uproots itself / from the ground / into darkness the light / and spits it').[13] The '*Adieu*' sections in turn set text from a six-line fragment of Honoré de Balzac's *Séraphîta*. These texts are used in a particular way across the sections of the piece, as shown in Example 3.3.

There is a progression in the presentation of the Balzac, apparently from fragments towards a complete rendition of a given text: a number of lines are first presented in mixed order ('*Adieu* I'), then in fragments ('*Adieu* II'), and fragments again before a final full rendition ('*Adieux* III–V'). In the meantime, the first three '*Nuit*' sections set each of the Roubaud passages, the fourth being set to fragments from each before a full setting of the final passage in '*Nuit* V'. Notably, however, some key words are present throughout all four Roubaud passages – *lumière, la nuit* –the first and the third in particular, consist largely of the same text material, presented in different order (and in a different page layout in the original novel).

In a Freudian framework, the piece could therefore be understood as a set of dream episodes with recurring content (the '*Nuit*' sections). Although no fixed interpretation is necessary, the intervening '*Adieu*' sections could perhaps be seen as moments of waking between the dream episodes, as the dreamer goes through the content of the dream, the message becoming gradually clearer with each repeat.

Battling with a Nightmare: From the Grammar of Dreams

In *From the Grammar of Dreams*, Saariaho chose to set fragmentary texts by Sylvia Plath (1932–63): the poem 'Paralytic' from the posthumous collection *Ariel* (1965), and three fragments from the author's only novel, *The Bell Jar* (1963).

---

[13]	Roubaud, 1990: 12, 13–14, 47 and 69.

Example 3.4   *From the Grammar of Dreams* (Song I) – intensifying vocalise

'Paralytic' uses few full stops, and semantically connected text portions are consistently divided across different lines and stanzas, giving the impression of a 'stream of consciousness'. Similarly, the first and longest fragment from *The Bell Jar* mostly consists of one long, incoherent, stream-of-consciousness sentence, listing unconnected (traumatic) memories from the protagonist's past (see also Minkkinen, 2005: 68–9). Within an overall musical depiction of dreaming, I would argue that the first song of *From the Grammar of Dreams* also depicts the process of waking up from a dream. At the start of Song I, the mezzo-soprano part is set to a gradually intensifying vocalise (see Example 3.4); this culminates in a sudden declaration of 'A bad dream. I remembered everything'.

The text is first uttered in repeated fragments, then in full form (bars 21 and 25). This creates a very vivid impression of the mezzo-soprano suddenly waking from a bad dream experienced during the first half of the song, and then gradually calming down while thinking of the events in her dream. This impression could have been explicitly intended by Saariaho, who has described the first song as a musical representation of a nightmare (Komsi, 2001: 21). To continue on this line of interpretation, the soprano part of Song I could in turn be interpreted as a musical depiction of the actual nightmare. Against the vocalise, the soprano delivers the poem 'Paralytic' in a fragmented, disjointed and timbrally volatile manner. Despite the apparent disorder, the soprano line is structured as a series of melodic progressions towards an $F\#_5$–G_5 motif, concluding with an $F\#_5$–G_5 trill. This order beneath disorder could be seen as a musical depiction of masked latent content and coherence in this musical dream, similar to the harmony in *Im Traume* explored above.

Going further still, after the 'nightmare' of Song I, the remaining four songs of the cycle can readily be understood as a reflection of the process of *interpreting* the dream using the Freudian method of free association. During this process, the two singers represent the conscious and the unconscious parts of the dreamer's mind.[14] This interpretation begins in Song II, where the mezzo-soprano recites a string of elements she remembers about her bad dream ('I remember[ed] the cadavers and Doreen and the story of the fig-tree and Marco's diamond') and tells of an association of them all to her own life ('Maybe forgetfulness'), as if she were in Freudian dream therapy. Saariaho has changed Plath's text to be in the present tense ('I remembered' to 'I remember') which enhances the psychological immediacy of the account.

In the meantime, the soprano part continues independently, illustrating the vivid unconscious activity that occurs while the dreamer's conscious mind is reflecting on the dream. The interaction of the two vocal parts is also illustrative. In the first half of Song II (bars 1–15), the soprano and mezzo-soprano sing simultaneously, alternating between text delivery in half voice and vocalise, creating between

---

[14]   In the revised version of *From the Grammar of Dreams* (2002) for soprano and electronics, this impression is suggested very strongly, as there are two voices but only one sound source.

Example 3.5 *From the Grammar of Dreams* (Song II) – combined melodic line them a unified melodic line (see Example 3.5). In this way, the musical setting illustrates the constant search for connections between the remembered fragments of manifest dream content and its hidden, true significance, concealed in the unconscious parts of the mind during the interpretation of the dream.

After the mezzo-soprano has finished going through the dream thoughts and associations in Song II, Songs III–V depicts how the protagonist – the dreamer – gradually comes to terms with the unconscious traumas revealed by the nightmare. The solution proposed by the melancholy Song III, set to a fragment from 'Paralytic', is a Buddhist retreat from life – 'ask nothing of life so life will ask nothing of you'. Song IV also begins in an unpromising way: set to fragments from *The Bell Jar* describing the novel's protagonist Esther's suicide attempt, the song offers a vivid musical depiction of drowning with a texture dominated by desperate breath sounds. In bar 26, however, the strong and insistent beat of the heart, depicted musically with repeated iambic rhythms, draws the singers back to life. As pulse is rarely present in Saariaho's music of that period (Otonkoski, 1989: 3), its use here reinforces the musical and narrative effect. By the end of the song, both voices affirm their wish to live on with the repeated phrase 'I am.' The mezzo-soprano's hesitation returns and turns the affirmation to a question, 'Am I?', in bar 37, resolved only in the soprano's final whisper, 'I am' (see Example 3.6 overleaf).

The fifth and final song acts as a final affirmation of the newly found peace of mind – making *From the Grammar of Dreams* comparable in overall progression to *The Bell Jar*, where Esther's mental health and sense of self is finally restored (De Lauretis, 1988: 129–33). Decorative, melismatic, a vocalise in both parts finally turns into the positive closing words, 'I smile', set to a crescendo on a bright major third. According to Saariaho, the wordless melismas of Song V are a depiction of birdsong (Komsi, 2001: 21). Perhaps after going through the traumas of the nightmare, the song's protagonist observes her own life from afar, from a bird's-eye view, before returning back to reality and life, smiling.

A Dream of Love: Grammaire des rêves

For *Grammaire des rêves*, Saariaho created a fragmentary text collage by selecting portions ranging from full verses to individual lines and words from several poems by Paul Eluard (1895–1952) (Saariaho, n.d.).[15] Suitably, the key themes in the selected fragments are dreaming, irrational dream visions and idealized, symbolic descriptions of love. The composer's treatment of the selected texts breaks down the linearity and syntax of the sources. Rather than make a through-composed setting, Saariaho repeats and reorders words,

---

[15]   Most of the material derives from poems IV, VI, VII, VIII, XIV and XXVII of the opening section ('*Premièrement*') of Eluard's collection *L'Amour la poésie* ('Love Poetry', 1929). Individual fragments also derive from the poem '*Le Miroir d'un moment*' from *Capitale de la douleur* ('Capital of Pain', 1926) and the long, prose-like section '*Nuits partagées*' from the collection *La Vie immédiate* ('The Immediate Life', 1932).

Example 3.6 *From the Grammar of Dreams* (Song IV) – depiction of drowning

a) Bars 22-7

b) Bars 34-9

syllables and individual phonemes (see also Minkkinen, 2005: 69–80). Analysis of the textual arrangement and musical setting of the Eluard fragments suggests an overall dramatic progression from dreaming to waking, not wholly dissimilar to *From the Grammar of Dreams*; perhaps herein lies the deeper structural connection between these twin-titled pieces.

To begin with, at a number of structural junctures, there are textual fragments that suggest a temporal frame for the musical events – a night that gradually turns into dawn: 'the night is passing' (*'la nuit se passe'*, bar 49), 'it is dawn' (*'l'aube se passe'*, bar 89), and 'the night ends' (*'la nuit s'éteint'*, bar 140). Indeed, the opening part of the piece gives the impression of being a musical depiction of the dreaming mind during sleep. The fragmentary text treatment, already discussed above, supports this reading, and Saariaho explicitly instructs the singers to 'speak dreamily' in bar 62. Looking at the text fragments, this appears to be a dream about a blue-eyed lover, interspersed with apparently irrational material about stars and assorted childhood memories. The various dream episodes often re-use the same textual material from earlier on, with growing intensity, in line with Freud's notion; subsequent, homologous dream episodes are 'bolder and more distinct'. For example, the passionate stanza 'My love for having fulfilled my desires / Set your lips on the sky of your words like a star' (*'Mon amour pour avoid figurée mes désir / Mis test lèvres au ciel de tes mots comme un astre'*) is first presented in fragmented form in the opening section, with the fragments brought together in a second, passionate rendering of the text in bars 76–88, marked 'ecstatic'.

After this section, the impassioned mood of the dream subsides and the process of waking up begins. The musical flow becomes distinctly more controlled and regular; for the first time in the piece, all members of the ensemble play in synchrony (bars 89–100). The change of mood reflects the text, which now describes elements of the waking world – birds, trees, wind, light – as dawn approaches; the use of birds as a signal of the present, waking world is a point of comparison with the final movement of *From the Grammar of Dreams*. At the end of this section, in bars 101–10, the singers convey, in jerky, accented phrases that the lover in the dream is closing his eyes (*'tu terme tes yeux'*), with the dream starting to fade away. The process of waking up continues, and the musical intensity mounts, finally culminating in bars 184–9 with frantic five-fold repetition of 'it is dawn' (*'l'aube se passe'*) followed by the realization that 'you are not there' (*'tu n'es pas là'*), conveyed in a high, desperate cry in both voice parts.

In the section immediately preceding this moment of awakening (bars 169–88), the text of the singers is a collection of individual fragments and words from the previous sections, and some new words that are associated with the same themes (for example, *'des bois'* ('the wood') and *'les feuilles'* ('the leaves') relate to the earlier fragment *'un arbre'* ('a tree')). It is as if during the process of waking up, the dreamer is going through the material and realizes that the lover has gone – it has all been a dream. Alternatively, however, this section could also depict a process of retrospective reflection about, and interpretation of, the dream, using a method of free association similarly to *From the Grammar of Dreams*. Either way, the musical dream *Grammaire des rêves* is essentially a Freudian wish-fulfilment of love, to be lost upon waking.

Music about Dreams

Saariaho has applied a range of features associated with dreams in her music. At different stages of her career, as her compositional preoccupations have changed, different aspects of dream theories have caught her attention. The abrupt transitions in dreams inspired early works such as *Im Traume*, while in the opera *L'Amour de loin*, completed 20 years later, she re-uses a melody to illustrate the recurring dream of the opera's protagonist. In between, at a time when Saariaho was returning to writing for live human voices, specific ideas about the arrangement and syntax of dream thoughts inspired Saariaho's approach to text selection and treatment.

There are also similarities between these 'dream' pieces. First, the idea of 'hidden logic' – of presenting and repeating similar material in different guises, either within a single dream (piece), or across separate episodes or dreams – has found musical application in several of the works. Second, the musical dreams, in particular in *L'Amour de loin* and *From the Grammar of Dreams*, bear witness to this composer's belief that dreams can act as a gateway into the dreamer's deepest, unconscious conflicts, doubts and wishes. Finally, it has been shown that the principles of Freudian dream interpretation can offer an analytical framework for describing the particular arrangement and treatment of text in Saariaho's three vocal pieces composed between 1988 and 1991.

The 'dream analyses' suggested here are, of course, only one possible interpretive take on these fascinating pieces of music – but they result from an approach that is clearly fruitful for describing and analysing certain characteristic features and structural process of these works. As Freud also reminds us, for dream interpretation:

> The most difficult thing is to persuade the beginner in dream-interpretation to recognize the fact that this task is not over when he has a complete interpretation of a dream in his hands, one that is meaningful and coherent, and enlightens him about all the elements in the dream-content. Besides this, it is possible that there is an overarching interpretation of the dream which has escaped him. It is really not easy to get an idea of the wealth of unconscious trains of thought in our thinking, all struggling for expression, nor to believe how clever the dream-work is in its polysemous mode of expression, killing seven flies at one blow (Freud, 1999 [1900]: 340).

Narratives

Chapter 4

Stories from the Mouth: Flautists, Bodily Presence and Intimacy in Saariaho's Flute Music

Taina Riikonen

The flute is one of Kaija Saariaho's favourite instruments. She has explained part of this attraction in terms of the sound-producing mechanism of flute playing, which allows a combination of breathing, whispering and tone generation. Consequently, speech, whispering and different kinds of breath tones become central sonic elements in Saariaho's flute writing, requiring performers to use a range of sound-producing techniques. Such characteristics are constantly recombined in ways that radically alter the player's sound-controlling mechanisms: the 'classical' pure and dense sonority extends to the seamless layering of breathy hissing, speech and whispering. In very literal terms it also turns the flautist into a speaking subject, a concept that seems to undermine the Western art music ideal of musician transparency (see Goehr, 1998).

This chapter discusses the flautist's bodily presence when using speech and breath techniques, with special reference to the solo flute works *Laconisme de l'aile* ('Laconism of the Wing', 1982) and *NoaNoa* ('Fragrant', 1992). These pieces introduce subtle continua within a sound/breath axis and in order to explore this, particular attention is paid to the intimate flautist–flute relationships that redefine processes of embouchure (the position of the lips). Both works question the existence of borderlines between flute sound and speech, as well as the singular embouchure; these pieces are based on the assumption of flexible relationships between flute and flautist. For instance, *Laconisme de l'aile* begins with the flautist reciting a poem by Saint-John Perse, and when speech gradually turns into whispers and finally breaks down into phonemes, the flute sound production intertwines closely with this transformational process. In a way, the flute texture is a product of speech. In *NoaNoa*, however, various mixtures of speech, flute tones and breath sounds interact with electronic materials (which are both pre-recorded and presented in real time).

The aim here is to explore musical sound production primarily as a bodily process, resulting in an analytical approach that extends beyond conventional dualisms such as mind/body, music/language and expressive/technical. The methodological framework employed represents an intersection between performance studies, the sociology of the body, and gender studies, revealing common narratives. One of the main themes concerns how a particular flautist–flute relationship may generate different meanings and interpretations in the context of performance as a result of interaction with contemporary instrumental techniques (see Hennion and Grenier, 2000).

The epistemological basis of this study is wide-ranging, consisting of interviews with flautists who have premiered Saariaho's works, and discussion of relevant scores and recordings. This combination of approaches and its attendant data is fruitful as it gives rise to multi-dimensional observations: the interactional processes in music can be understood as simultaneously bodily, symbolic and relational (see Burkitt, 1999). Flautists and their bodies are seen not as corporeal containers of pre-determined musical ideas, but as highly productive intermediaries – working between various gestures, habits, spaces, languages and practices. The key focus is on the constructive, socio-material nature of the flute–flautist relationship and the subjectivity of sound production.[1]

The embodied aspects of music and music-making have been of interest for several decades in studies of popular music, ethnomusicology and the sociology of music (see Blacking, 1973; Attali, 1985; Frith, 1996; Whiteley, 1997). These paradigms theorize the body primarily from the perspectives of sociology, cultural studies, feminism, cultural anthropology and philosophy. A recent tendency has been to conceptualize embodiment through an approach drawn from cultural studies, examining identities, bodily experiences and socio-material cultures as particular relationships (see Shilling, 2001: 340; see also Welton, 1998; Burkitt, 1999). Criticism of the Cartesian mind–body dualism is ongoing within the multifaceted fields of feminism, cultural studies and philosophy (see Barker, 1995; Davis, 1997), but in general there has been a slight epistemological shift in the theorizing of socio-material procedures. Cultural contexts are understood more and more as fluid practices rather than fixed matrices (Rawnsley, 2007: 640).

All this questioning of meanings located in the mind–mind[2] reality has come surprisingly late to the study of Western art music. One of the few relevant examples is George Fisher and Judith Lochhead's article, 'Analyzing from the Body' (2002). The writers suggest that it is important to study the embodiment of art music practices, particularly in performance, because music as a sonic art is never exclusively a mental phenomenon. Furthermore, when musical meanings

---

[1]   This emphasis is perhaps the most musician-centred among the wide range of studies on Kaija Saariaho's music. Her work has been considered, for example, from the perspective of music analysis (Iitti, 1993 and 2002; Grabócz, 1993; Kankaanpää, 1995 and 1996; Brech, 1999; Howell, 2006), investigating gender and composer problems (Moisala and Diamond, 2000; Iitti, 2001), exploring electronics as a compositional element (Emmerson, 1998), focusing on her operas (Hautsalo, 2000) and in the context of gestures of desire and love (Sivuoja-Gunaratnam, 2003a and 2003b).

[2]   See Suzanne G. Cusick's seminal article, 'Feminist Theory, Music Theory and the Mind/Body Problem' (1994), which discusses the (assumed) meeting of minds between composer and listener.

are located in bodily actions, the performative aspects of sound-making could be conceptualized more strongly from a practical basis (Fisher and Lochhead, 2002: 39). Fisher and Lochhead emphasize the concept of performativity and its relation to the epistemologically active body, suggesting four themes when theorizing the body in the context of art music: cognition, sexuality, performance and cultural anthropology (ibid.: 44). In this chapter, the intertwining of performativity and sexuality are investigated through an in-depth examination of the flautist–flute relationship in Saariaho's flute music.

The Flautist's Open Lips

The Western transverse flute is played with open embouchure – the mouthpiece is not *inside* the mouth of the player, as is the case with the recorder, ney, kaval, clarinet, saxophone, oboe and bassoon, for example. Consequently, it is quite easy for the flautist to speak, to whisper or to generate a breathing sound at the same time as making actual blowing movements. However, with the emergence of modern woodwind-playing techniques (in the context of Western art music) in the early decades of the twentieth century, the very core of sound-producing techniques remained sacrosanct. It is no coincidence that the use of speech to extend flute techniques came quite late, after developments in flutter-tonguing, key clicks, vibrato changes and various kinds of articulation (see Bartolozzi, 1982 [1967]). As Lydia Goehr remarks, the strong binary divide between music and language, particularly as portrayed in the formalist ideologies of the Romantic period, has had long-lasting effects (Goehr, 1998: 92–3). The existence of words, as well as the use of programmatic ideas, was considered a threat to the 'inner' world of absolute music. However, speech is located in the very same area of the flautist's body as that of flute-sound production. Therefore, actually speaking (or whispering) while playing modifies the instrumental sound quality. Such a break with the predominant classical ideal of a breathless flute sound offers a new perspective on the instrument – the integration of speech and flute sonority. I suggest that the main reason for the inhibited use of breathing sounds in Western flute playing has been the ideal of the transparent, disembodied player (see Goehr, 1998: 142). The loss of that transparency changes the sonic object, the flautist, into a gendered and sexual body, which cannot act separately from the carnal – sometimes symptomatically called 'extra-musical' – realm, with its variety of meanings.

The rupturing of a solid flute sonority through diverse breathy sounds also undermines the ideal of a rigorously mastered embouchure construction. The exclusive body-building of certain facial muscles opens up possibilities of diverse embouchure settings: the embouchure cannot be fixed, but has to be in constant change. Instead of being a strictly controlled construction in the production of a dense flute sound, the flautist's lips become more of a fluid aperture of mixed sonic emanations. This constant half-openness, this potential for creating messy sounds by speaking, whispering and playing simultaneously, is a quality that Saariaho has used in a very particular way in her flute works. The texture is based on the shifting continua of intermingled sounds, and that brings the embouchure – the lips of the flautist – to the nexus of sound production.

French feminist Luce Irigaray also considers lips (in the plural) to be central body parts. In her well-known elaboration of feminine sexuality,[3] she emphasizes the sexuality of woman as multiple and diverse thus:

> As for a woman, she touches herself in and of herself without any need for mediation, and before there is any way to distinguish activity from passivity. A woman 'touches herself' all the time, and moreover no one can forbid her to do so, for her genitals are formed of two lips in continuous contact. Thus, within herself, she is already two – but not divisible into one(s) – that caress each other (Irigaray, 1985 [1977]: 24).

Irigaray's poetic writing often parallels and intertwines 'the two sets of lips' of a woman: the lips of the mouth and the genital lips (Irigaray, 2004 [1977]: 18). Lips are conceptualized as a threshold, as always half-open; they are therefore 'strangers to dichotomy and oppositions' (ibid.: 18), resulting in 'several voices, several ways of speaking resound endlessly, back and forth' (Irigaray, 1985 [1977]: 209). Similarly, the embouchure of the flautist playing *Laconisme de l'aile* and *NoaNoa* cannot be fixed; it is in a constant state of subtle change. The lips form the spatiality for several different encounters: between the flute and the lips, between speech and breath, and between language and flute sound. These different elements and modes of action are not in opposition, but are more like changing stages of sonic continua. These are always already plural; they are 'not divisible into one(s)' (see Irigaray, 2004 [1984]).

In Saariaho's flute music overall, the non-hierarchical presence of all kinds of embodied sounds of the flautist (and the flute) forms a starting point – rather than the outcome – of its sonic aesthetics. Sound production is based on an openness towards subtle variations of diverse sounds and their combinations. The elaborate degree of control required by these combinations demands a sensitive awareness of the relationship between lips and flute.

Laconisme de l'aile and *NoaNoa*

The fluid aperture of the flautist's lips is used very prominently in *Laconisme de l'aile*: the piece starts with the recitation of an excerpt from the poem *Oiseaux* (1962), by Saint-John Perse.[4] Gradually speech turns to whispering, which leads

---

[3]   Irigaray's thoughts have aroused a lot of discussion on the subject of essentialism (see, for example, Fruss 1989; also Whitford, 1991; Chanter, 1995; Stone, 2006).

[4]   'Ignorant, ignorant de leur ombre, et ne sachant de mort, de mort, que ce qui s'en consume d'immortel au bruit lointain des grandes eaux. Ils passent nous laissant et nous sommes plus les memes, ils sont l'espace.' ['Ignorant of their shadows, knowing of death

to the combining of consonant repetition and flute resonance (the flute is then in the playing position). This recitation passage also includes two composed breaths (inhalations) (line 1, bar 3 and line 3, bar 4), which could – depending on how they are realized – interrupt the line of speech or reinforce its subjectivity.

In this opening passage, the loose contact with the mouthpiece of the flute, combined with the abundant use of composed breaths, jeopardizes the assumed close – almost inbuilt – relationship between flautist and instrument. The flute can no longer be understood as a naturalized and musicalized extension of the flautist's body (a prosthesis), and is more like a particular cultural object with diverse socio-material connotations. In fact, in the flautist's hands, far away from the lips, it could refer to any kind of sound (there are no particular anticipations of a sound-type yet), or to performativity, sound theatre, happenings and so on. Its detached existence directs attention to the flautist's mouth, which now lacks the protection of the flute. The naked, breathing mouth oozes the moist abysses of the lungs, larynx, mucous membrane, windpipe, palate and lips, thereby deconstructing the assumed functional, solely sound-productive relationship between flute and flautist at the very beginning of the piece.

Breathing is a central texture in *Laconisme de l'aile*, even after its opening section. At line 20, bar 2, breathy sounds flow first through the flute, and then the flautist fully covers the blowing hole whilst inhaling and exhaling, interrupting the melodic lines of the piece. After some fragmented phrases with different messy sounds (hissing and key clicks, for example), the flute playing transforms into speaking, now via flutter-tongue technique and a gradual change to the repetition of the consonant 't' (at line 25). That repetition leads to the words 'traversé, traversé, d'une seule pensée' ['traversed by a single thought']. This line continues the excerpt from the poem quoted at the beginning, and the performer is advised to move the flute away from the lips when reciting it. Inherent in all the phrases throughout the piece is an undercurrent of unstable contact between the lips and the flute.

Speaking and breathing in *NoaNoa* always requires contact with the flute, but various speech-play-breathy-sound techniques are used. The whispering of actual words during the sound production is the most common speech-play texture, and it is significant that these textures are always combined with electronic sound manipulation.[5] The flautist synchronizes this electronic material (both its live

---

only that immortal part which is consumed in the distant clamour of great waters, they pass and leave us, and we are no longer the same. They are space.'] English translation by Robert Fitzgerald, 1971.

[5]   The text of the piece is a collage of excerpts from Paul Gauguin's diarial book, *Noa Noa* (1919). During the whole piece, the flautist whispers the following text: 'L'arbre sentait la rose la rose très odorant sentait rose rose sentait rose strt ststststtttttttt sentait la rose. Mes yeux voiles par mon coeur-r sentait la rose la fleur-r la fleur. Tttttt très odorant melange melange melange d'odeur l'arbre sentait la rose fleur. Tr tr tr. Fleur fanée fleur fleur lflfr melange d'odeur parfums parfums de santal très odorant s f tr f s z t f. L'arbre sentait fleur

Example 4.1   *NoaNoa* – **example of whisper-play phrase**

reverberations and pre-recorded textures) by use of a foot pedal. The whole piece contains some 63 pedal hits that make the pedal itself a kind of extra limb for the flautist, who both touches the electronic material and is touched by it at the same time. The spatio-sensory reaching forwards and backwards becomes one of the most central aspects of the flute playing here.

NoaNoa starts by introducing and accumulating various techniques (different vibratos with reverberation, changes in vibratos and pitch glissandi, trills with harmonic sounds). There are long whisper-play phrases at bars 23–8 (see Example 4.1), 48–55, and 71–5. These sections are always layered with electronic material: reverberation (in bars 23–8); pre-recorded male whispers, manipulated flute sounds, reverberation (48–55); reverberation and pre-recorded breathy flute sounds (71–5). Pre-recorded whispers are also present at bars 88–92 and 135–40. The end of *NoaNoa* bears a certain resemblance to the end of *Laconisme de l'aile* in that both include ascending scales with microtonal altering. The presence of

---

dorée. Je reviendrai. Mes yeux la fleur fleur fleur fanée. Trtrttttttttt je fl s trttttttttststtkstsksts trro jeje t je je t ta kata ka rot e re fl sa ka tr s z k z t k fl tr z t k ro fl tr ka z t fl tr ro z t k fl tr z t k st s t s. La fleur f r st s s t s. La fleur.' ['The trees smell rose, the rose, fragrant, the fragrance of the rose. My eyes catch my heart, the fragrance of the rose, the flower. Very fragrant, the mixture the mixture, the fragrance of the rose tree. The wilted flower, the mixture of fragrances, perfumes of the sandalwood. The fragrance of the tree, the golden flower. I return. My eyes, eyes, the flower flower flower, wilted. … I … the flower … the flower.'] English translation by TR.

silences is also part of the texture at the end of *NoaNoa*; there are several pauses that get longer and longer towards the close of the piece.

How a piece ends is significant – an ending can absorb, process and now carry the spatial and temporal sonic histories of a work – but the opening of a work can be equally important. The relationship between the player and the instrument is usually established at the opening of an instrumental piece, the presence or absence of the voice of the performer emerges, and the distance/proximity axis relative to the linguistic-semantic material is revealed on some level.

The Opening of *Laconisme de l'aile:* Secularization of the Flautist

As mentioned earlier, the solo work *Laconisme de l'aile* starts with the flautist's recitation of a passage from a poem written by Saint-John Perse (see Example 4.2 overleaf). The score advises the flautist to recite the text 'slowly and calmly, but with a clearly audible voice (if possible by heart, eyes towards the audience)'. The flute is in the hands of the flautist and is supposed to be 'very slowly lifted towards the lips' in order to reach them at the point indicated. During this opening section the flautist makes two radical disengagements in her or his identity as a performer: disengagement from the flute with the lips, and disengagement from eye contact with the score. Speaking and whispering (the recitation changes to a whisper at line 3, bar 4) without the flute in the playing position produce an embodied performer subjectivity, but the two composed breaths (at line 1, bar 4 and line 3, bar 4) define the flautist as being distant from a transparent sonic object. Depending on how these breaths are generated, the flautist can adjust the distance or closeness between body and flute-playing actions. This process of adjustment will give different meanings to the breaths.

Having interviewed several flautists who have played Saariaho's flute music, it is startling how diverse a range of approaches were adopted for the recitation section of *Laconisme de l'aile*. For example, Petri Alanko referred to the opening as 'more a kind of atmosphere-creating element', the aim of which is to 'prepare the piece'.[6] In other words, he defined the recitation as an introductory 'element', not as 'music': the work begins proper when the flute enters. On the other hand, Eva Tigerstedt said, 'These [the recitation and composed breathings] do not bother me ..., well, perhaps the recitation bothers me a bit because I don't have the training for reciting poems.' It seems that Tigerstedt is separating recitation performativity – speaking – from flute-playing performativity, positing herself as a flautist far away from a speaking subject. Anne Eirola, who premiered *Laconisme de l'aile*, further remarks that the flautist 'actually has to enter another ... performing genre' during the beginning of *Laconisme*. What

---

[6]   These and subsequent quotations are taken from my interviews with Petri Alanko (24 January 2001), Eva Tigerstedt (24 January 2001), Anne Eirola (14 March 2001) and Mikael Helasvuo (24 January 2001).

Example 4.2   *Laconisme de l'aile* – opening section

is significant in Eirola's statement is that she does not totally separate speaking from the authority of flute playing, although its otherness (compared to playing) is present in her remark.

Finally, Mikael Helasvuo approaches both speaking and breathing from a completely different standpoint; for example he states that 'It's great when you can start with this kind of poem and then the [flute] sound grows little by little … It has always been an essential part of this [flute] instrument, the breathing and the speech; it [the playing] starts from the mouth'. Helasvuo seems to emphasize a particularly embodied interrelation between the flute and the flautist, whereas Alanko, Eirola and Tigerstedt talk about playing the beginning of *Laconisme* from the perspective of a music–language relationship and the performance aspect within this. Helasvuo considers both speech and audible breathings as potentially expressive techniques that are always inherent in flute sound production. Therefore, speaking and breathing actually constitute flute playing, in contradiction to Alanko's statement which hierarchically separates these actions, at least in the context of *Laconisme de l'aile.*

The above statements show that the rupturing of the close flautist–flute relationship is not an insignificant issue for flautists and their experience as performers. It could be argued that the opening section of *Laconisme de l'aile* secularizes the flautist; it does not allow him or her to be first and foremost the disembodied *sonic* object. In most cases, by speaking, the flautist's gender is immediately revealed: the secularization is sexualization as well. The female or male flautist who speaks, breathes audibly and whispers, with eyes turned towards the audience, is a fully embodied person who produces and engenders a very different reaction from a flautist focusing solely on playing. At the start of the piece, several open relationships are established: between flautist and flute, between speech and flute sound (the two different 'voices' of the flautist), between composed breaths and unscripted inhalations, and between the flautist-as-sound-maker and listener-as-spectator. The listener (who does not know the piece) cannot fully anticipate the developmental processes of these relationships or how closely they are intertwined.

Listening and Breathing

I now turn to two flautists and their performances of the opening section of *Laconisme de l'aile.* Camilla Hoitenga's[7] and Manuela Wiesler's[8] very different breathing, speaking, whispering and playing illustrate how flautists can adjust the relationship between themselves, the flute and the sound within the playing body. Since both these performers are women, this investigation will focus on the particular significance of female sound production.

Camilla Hoitenga delivers the whole spoken section (line 1, bar 1 to line 3, bar 3) in an everyday voice, with speech-like intonation changes. The voice is close-miked, giving rise to the impression of listening to an ordinary story rather than a recitation, or performance, of a poem. The first composed inhalation (0'07"–0'08") is located in the cheeks, and it sounds like a breath that someone takes while telling a story: the openness of Hoitenga's mouth is audible. The second is much more intense and heated, and is located more in the windpipe, abdomen and the upper-side muscles than in the cheeks. Hoitenga's mouth is still quite open,

---

[7]   On the CD *Aile du songe*, Montaigne-Naïve MO 782154, track 1.

[8]   On the CD *L'Oiseaux tendres*, BIS CD 689, track 3.

but not as much as the first time. When the whispering section starts, she does not change her voice to a complete whisper, but produces some kind of speech-whisper combination,[9] incorporating both the pitch of speech and the noisy quality of a whisper. The resonance of the flute is audible for the first time in connection with the word '*l'espace*' ('space') (0'36"), and is easily audible when Hoitenga directs the 's' phonemes towards the lip-plate of the flute. She proceeds from speaking to playing quite quickly, given that the duration of the whole passage (line 1, bar 1 to line 5, bar 1) is only 47 seconds. The differences between breathing, speaking and playing are therefore clearly distinguishable.

Manuela Wiesler has a very different approach to the recitation section. She starts with a distant voice, a slow tempo and dramatic intonation changes. Her speaking resembles singing, and she strongly emphasizes the notated rhythms of the text. It is startling to notice that there are no breaks between the words. The first inhalation (0'12") is very long, taking three seconds. She executes it with a lip posture that *sounds* like a flute embouchure; the lips are puckered up, and the air stream moves from a very small hole inside the mouth. This hissing inhalation is located in the lips and the teeth, with the air streaming out quite audibly from the very front of the mouth. The second inhalation (0'47"–0'49") is faster, but it contains the same hissing quality, again giving the impression of a flute embouchure. From this, Wiesler proceeds directly to whispering which is even slower than speaking. The resonance of the flute is audible for the first time – just as in Hoitenga's version – in connection with the word '*l'espace*', but the 's' phoneme is broadened sideways, stressing the resonance of the front teeth as much as the resonance of the flute. The whole section, played by Wiesler, takes 1 minute and 42 seconds.

The long inhalations that Wiesler produces with the embouchure-like lip posture anticipate the controlled embodiment of actual flute playing. The breathing does not rupture her assumed flautist subjectivity, which is maintained as standardized through all the sonic expressions. Furthermore, in adopting a particular lip position she reconstructs her lips into a new instrument that acts as a substitute for her missing contact with the flute. Therefore, her mouth is primarily inaudible as an embodied, gendered sound-producer, because her lips are instrumentalized for the purposes of the controlled flute embouchure. This instrumentalization of the lips refers both to the absence of the standard lips–flute contact, and to the disembodied flautist-performer. In a way, Wiesler estranges the gendered materiality of her mouth by musicalizing her speaking and mimicking the flute-playing embouchure during inhalation. Subsequently, it could be said that

---

[9] In our many discussions on breathing, speaking and whispering on the stage, the actor and lecturer in speech technique Tiina Syrjä (Department of Drama, University of Tampere, Finland) has remarked that the difference between whispering and speaking is not clear at all for acting students. Syrjä says that often students assume their silent speaking to be whispering.

this estrangement also implicitly refers to the control of the feminine sexuality (see Irigaray, 2004 [1984]).

In Hoitenga's case, on the other hand, speaking, inhalation and playing are all produced with diverse embodied meanings. The everyday speech quality creates a feminine subject who is not associated with flute playing at all. In other words, the speaker at the beginning of *Laconisme de l'aile* is not necessarily the same subject (performer) as the player some bars later: there is a separation of roles here. The first inhalation places the authority of the speaking subject primarily in Hoitenga's mouth, where the apparatus of both breathing and speaking is located. The mouth as female is therefore a central construction in her performance. Hoitenga's mouth performs as a fluid aperture with blurred borderlines between various kinds of sonic material and narrative content. This potential for creating both sonic and semantic stories – mixed realities – from a particular female mouth emphasizes the constructive character of both flautist subjectivity and its related gender.

'Unduly Intimate' and 'the Facile' Linkage with the Flute

The intimate encounter between flautist and flute raises complex questions of distance and proximity between the two. During the recitation section of *Laconisme de l'aile*, the instrument in the flautist's hands is a liminal object: it could be understood as a musical instrument or a ritual artefact. Within this liminality there is constant reference to the lips of the flautist, but *which* lips? The opening recitation creates an immediate awareness of the existence of the vocal chords (as resonating, audible but invisible 'lips' in the throat). In the case of a female flautist – holding the flute far away from the lips of her mouth – the implicit consciousness of her third lips (the labia) is indisputable. Therefore, the flute in her hands is never just a flute in her hands. Without the predetermined mouth–lip contact it becomes a controversial object, loaded with diverse socio-sexual connotations.

To illustrate the particular liminality of the flute relationship in the context of Western performer identities, an extract from the interview with flautist Eva Tigerstedt reveals the crucial nature of intimate bodily contact during performance:

> ET: A Swedish composer sent me a piece ... There were things like ... 'make eye contact with someone in the audience' and [laughs] 'here you have to embrace your flute'. ... I thought I won't perform that ...
>
> TR: So, that was your limit? ...
>
> ET: Well, I think it is ... unduly intimate somehow. Of course, you could have an instrumental theatre, but I don't want to ... [mimics the stroking of the flute]. I think that's too much [laughs].

TR: But it's very intimate to speak into the flute [in *Laconisme de l'aile*] as well, isn't it ... and ...

ET: [interrupts] It is! Yes ... but it's not like ... that kind of ... I think that it's ... facile ... It doesn't bother me.

TR: Is it quite near ... playing [the flute]?

ET: It is quite near playing and it's near singing ... But these kinds of things like 'make eye contact' ... I mean, what does it have to do with the music ... with the sonic [material] any more? I think it's more like some kind of flirting.

Tigerstedt names two different actions that she does not want to do (at least as a flautist in a performance): making eye contact with a particular person in the audience and embracing her flute. It is intriguing that Tigerstedt seems not to problematize eye contact with the audience at the beginning of *Laconisme de l'aile*. Of course, there is a difference between looking at one person and having an unfocused view over the whole audience, but it seems not to be the object of the look that is at the heart of Tigerstedt's feeling of discomfort. The question is perhaps more: what makes the female flautist's gaze flirting in one context and facile in another? And, how do these gazes relate to the distance and proximity between the lips and the flute?

In *Laconisme de l'aile*, the flautist's speech is accurately notated in the score. In other words, speaking is performatized (as well as musicalized) and the flautist can adopt the role of the soon-to-be-playing performer if she or he so desires. This notated speech also helps to explain the distance between mouth-lips and flute. If the flautist follows the directions in the score and slowly starts to move the flute towards her mouth, the distance between flute and lips is an ambiguous and unmusical relationship for a moment within the whole recitation passage. Relative to this dynamic and functional movement towards flute playing, eye contact with the audience (as a whole) is part of a sheltered and legitimized performance practice: the flautist is not flirting with the audience, because she is reciting notated text during her gaze. She is on the threshold of sound-producing performance. On the other hand, in the Swedish work Tigerstedt mentions, eye contact is supposed to be a surprise, devoid of any musicalized behaviour that could mitigate the unwanted nuances of the gaze. The chosen member of the audience cannot know whether the flautist is really flirting with him or her as a performer, or on a more personal level. This kind of ambiguous situation could confuse the culturally restricted roles of both sound production (performer) and sound reception (audience). For example, in his reflections on 'contemplation', Richard Leppert has remarked that the etiquette of contemplated listening (in Western art music culture) forces the listener into a physical passivity that curtails bodily reactions as highly controlled, private, inaudible and invisible (see Leppert, 1993: 25; Small, 1998: 27; Goehr, 1992: 236).

There may be intimacy in the context of performing Western art music, but it typically occurs between the performer and his/her instrument through a particular music being played – but not between the performer and the audience. The predetermined ways of interacting with the instrument preserve the remoteness of the performer in relation to the audience. Embracing the flute excludes any culturally relevant reference to actual flute *playing*. As a gesture from a concert stage it may seem too intimate because it very quickly turns the flute into a fetish object, devoid of ('purely') musical content. The relationship between the performer and the instrument is then understood primarily as erotic. In fact, Pedro Rebelo, examining the performer–instrument relationship as 'a multi-modal participatory space', suggests (following Georges Bataille's work) that through the concept of 'difference', an erotic aspect in the relationship between the performer and the instrument always exists (Rebelo, 2006: 27–35).

> There seems to be a particular performative state that has the intangibility commonly associated with an erotic object of desire. The intangibility of this state only contributes to its status as object of desire. It is a state that manifests engagement, participation, and above all enunciates the instrument as entity. The instrument becomes distinct from other instruments and from the performer until what is left is difference. This object of desire, or rather desired state, questions the very ontology of instrument and performer. This desire is not directed at a particular object, but rather it emerges out of the difference that is manifest between the performer and the instrument (ibid.: 31).

It seems that Rebelo's definition of the presence of the erotic in the performer–instrument relationship is based on conceptualizing both the ephemeral sound and its heavily embodied production as the locations of difference *as* desire. The 'intangibility' of the erotic, then, is not only the abstracted difference as desired state, but it extends to the inestimable embodied intimacy between the player and the instrument: the accumulated touching-sensing as the relation between the two. As Rebelo suggests, the ontological difference arises from the ambiguity between instrument and performer in this constant mutual productivity. For example, does someone who is simply hearing/sensing a flute sound wish to know where the soft edge of the lips of the flautist ends and where the round edge of the blowing hole of the flute begins? At the moment of sound production these two are nuzzled against each other. They are reaching out to each other, passionately – and after decades of repetition, also unconsciously. While blowing into the tube, the flute is never a separate entity from the player, because the generated flute sound is always a body sound of the performer as well. Furthermore, this body-instrument sound inhabits a multi-levelled location, since breathing exits from the player's body while never having left it completely.

However, the process of amalgamation between the player and the instrument is highly restricted, as subtle control mechanisms form a hidden basis for the cultural negotiations concerning the embodied nature of the musician–sound relationship. Therefore, it could be suggested that any sense of eroticism between performer and instrument is linked to the (illusory) loss of a very detailed control process: the rupturing of possession of the predetermined sound-producing mechanisms, as the mastering of both the playing body and the instrument as an entity. This kind of eroticism is based on 'the elimination of temporality' as a total abandonment to the moment, 'a reaction against time itself' (see Weiss, 2002: 10). It is an attraction based on a kind of illusion of erasing the embodied history between performer and instrument, a yearning for an atemporal disembodiment. Moreover, Tigerstedt's unwillingness to embrace her flute in the performance situation may reflect an unwillingness to expose the loss of the temporal and spatial history of her flute–lips relationship. Given that any public interaction with the instrument is assumed to refer solely to sound-making in art music practices, gestures indicating erotic intimacy between any subjects and entities are taboo. Suggestive interaction with the instrument destroys its function as an objectified mediator of musical ideas and makes it a potential tool for individual, intimate, sexual pleasure. Therefore, it could be argued that the liminality of an instrument–player encounter is always both the liminality within the axis of embodied pleasure/disembodied aesthetic, and of sound felt as a multi-sensory experience. For the opening of *Laconisme de l'aile*, these interacting forms of liminality materialize both in complex adjustments of distance/proximity between the flautist's lips and instrument, and in the interrelation between gaze and speech.

Sensual Whisperings in *NoaNoa*

After focusing on the inter-relationship between female flautist and flute, we turn now to the relationship between male flautist and sound production in the context of bodily presence within Saariaho's flute music. This investigation concerns the exploration of whispering in *NoaNoa*. The materiality of whispering is particularly sensual in that it always implies extreme intimacy between the whisperer and the listener (see van Leeuwen, 1999: 27). In the context of Western art music, listening to a whispering flautist has particularly loaded connotations, given the relationship between instrument, lips, whispering, language, flute-sound and listener. Also, it is by no means inconsequential to consider how or what the flautist whispers, or how that whispered material relates to flute-sound production.

There are several whisper-play sections in *NoaNoa*, for which Jean-Baptiste Barrière, Saariaho's husband, has produced pre-recorded whisperings. Although these are often quite androgynous sounds – their gendered qualities may be difficult to trace – Barrière's whispers are recognizable as male: they are low-pitched and pronounced close to the microphone. The intriguing thing is that they seem to include two highly controversial qualities: on the one hand the words sound fragmented and messy, making the speaking subject ambiguous and vulnerable; on the other hand, despite moving from right to left through the loudspeakers, these whispers seem to dominate the sonic space. In a very subtle way they appear at the same time both emasculated and empowered.

The following extract from an interview with the flautist Mikael Helasvuo discusses listening to the pre-recorded, male whispers when they become immersed in the context of his own whispering and playing:

> TR: What do you think about these [in *NoaNoa* ...] when there are these male whispers and then you whisper and play at the very same time ... What approach do you have as a flautist when you play this?
>
> MH: Oh, you mean ... erotically, when ... here ... a woman and a man ...
>
> TR: Yes, or I mean as a flautist ...
>
> MH: Yes, it hasn't occurred to me that if the [live] performer is a woman, then it's going to be more erotic.
>
> TR: Yes, there are those [pre-recorded] male whispers in any case.
>
> MH: But there could be a deep eroticism between two men as well ... You could see it like that.

I was slightly confused when Helasvuo immediately contextualized both the pre-recorded and live whispers of *NoaNoa* as being erotic. Although I anticipated a subtle denial of the sensual aspects of the playing situation, the straightforward placing of heterosexual eroticism at the centre of the act of performing seemed surprising. Moreover, although it seemed at first that Helasvuo was maintaining some kind of hetero-normativity in his statement, his emphasis could actually be interpreted as being more concerned with the role of *listening* to erotic tension in the mixing of these whispers, than on the hetero/gay difference in terms of counterpart dualism.[10]

The embodied location of the voice assumes pertinence in the amalgamation of pre-recorded male whispers with live whispers (whether male or female). In his book, *A Voice and Nothing More*, Mladen Dolar argues that in the case of the human voice there is no such thing as disacousmatization,[11] because the actual source of the voice (the vocal cords) can never be seen. Thus:

> It [the voice as object] is not the haunting voice impossible to pin down to source; rather, it appears in the void from with it is supposed to stem but which

---

[10]   In her article 'No Bodies There: Absence and Presence in Acousmatic Performance', Linda Dusman remarks that new music (and acousmatic music) 'subverts the reproduction of the historical as natural, as queer sexuality subverts reproductive sexuality as natural' (Dusman, 2000: 342).

[11]   See Michel Chion's terms 'acousmatic' and 'de-acousmatization' (1994).

it does not fit, an effect without a proper cause. In a curious bodily topology, it is like a bodily missile which separates itself from the body and spreads around, but on the other hand it points to a bodily interior, an intimate partition of the body which cannot be disclosed – as if the voice were the very principle division into interior and exterior (Dolar, 2006: 70).

In the performance situation of *NoaNoa*, the listener can sense the very concrete division between the interiors and exteriors of two bodies: the sonic encounter between the openness of the lips of both the live flautist and the pre-recorded whisperer. The oozing quality of whispers seems to represent the resonance of touching between these two lips – and now I am speaking particularly about the *touch as heard*. Just as the touch of someone could leave a sense of imprint on the skin, the resonating pressure of a sound (vibrating back) could touch our bodies very comprehensively.[12] Touch is located in the sound, which is generated in two interior–exterior continua. In the case of *NoaNoa*, the touching as sound is a co-production of two distant bodies.

Helasvuo seems to conceptualize his aural experience of pre-recorded male whispers as *sensing*, as being able to touch and be touched by two simultaneous voices: his own voice and the voice of the pre-recorded whisperer. His description of an eroticism that emerges from the presence of several whispering mouths seems to highlight both the intimate nature of whispering (particularly as an amplified sound) and the sensuality of the indefinite touch of the voice (see Irigaray, 2004 [1984]). Therefore, his emphasis seems to lie more in the subtle variations of what sound as touch could *do*, rather than what it *is*. Such an emphasis is crucial for the performer, but interestingly its immediate outcome could be experienced by the listener as well. While listening to multi-embodied whispers, the listener is placed within the interior flow of creating sonic sensations, and not necessarily in the external stability of perceiving pre-determined ideas.

Stories from the Mouth

In the context of Western art music practices, the performer–instrument relationship as a bodily presence is a seriously under-theorized area of investigation. However, in terms of sound-producing actions, it has a quintessentially structural role. It is highly significant as to how the instrument is touched and what kind of distances and proximities emerge through interaction. Moreover, the different degrees of inter-relationship with the instrument may be located in particular bodily areas, depending upon the sonic textures and the cultural negotiations of the sound–body–meaning continuum.

---

[12]   I am indebted to fixed media composer Antti Sakari Saario for our many inspiring discussions on touching, listening and sensing different sounds.

In performances of Saariaho's flute music, the encounter between flautist and instrument is based on the mutually open flexibility between the flute and the lips of the flautist. Sound-production mechanisms are not standardized around a single type of sound, but they are situated between breathing, whispering, speaking and different kinds of flute sounds in a constantly evolving process. The flautist is thus confirmed as a multi-voiced storyteller; his/her stories from the mouth are told with constant fluidity. The subtle adjustments of breath, lip and air are intertwined with the socio-cultural changes in the authorial position of the flautist-as-sensation-maker. Similarly, the mouth-lips of the flautist are not just stringently controlled producers of a certain kind of dense flute sound, but more a complex junction between semantic, symbolic, embodied and socio-material meanings. The lips allow the outward emanation of the changing shapes of airstreams and breathing, as well as the resonant depth of imprints left by whispered or spoken words; they delineate the flautist's organic connection to the flute through the proximities and distances between the lip-plate of the flute and the lips. These actions place the lips at the core of the flautist's bodily presence, suggesting a range of different connotations in relation to musicalized/bodily/linguistic sounds.

The sociologist Henri Lefebvre asks in his book, *The Production of Space*, 'if the body, as capable for action, could create space?' (Lefebvre, 1991 [1974]: 170). His own answer to this question is yes, with an important emphasis on the mutually productive relationship between body and space: they are always in a constant interaction. In the case of performing and listening to *Laconisme de l'aile* and *NoaNoa*, the spaces these works create include definite bodily presences, the interior realms of fluid and sensual sounds. The intimacy of these spaces is produced by their being invisible, or aurally unrecognizable, consisting of sensitive interaction between several bodies in diverse time–space continua (of a live flautist, of pre-recorded speakers and flautists, of listeners and sound engineers and so on). Within this interaction, *the resonances of touch as sound* are the significant producers of the sonic meaning-making. Following Lefebvre's idea of an acting body being a creator of space (and vice versa), it could be said that in Kaija Saariaho's music the spatial production exists at a rather micro-tactile level. For example, a slight change in the angle of the airstream, the delicate adjustment of the blowing hole of the lips and the invisible but tactile controlled movements of the abdomen muscles – when combining speaking and flute playing – can create sonic spaces that permit certain social and historical meanings.

The opening section of *Laconisme de l'aile* could be understood as generating the flautist's performativity principally through speaking. Reciting the poem forms a simultaneous deconstruction and reconstruction of the voiced flautist, and the intimate relationship between the flautist's mouth, the instrument and its sound. Thus, the primary voice of the flautist is his or her own speaking voice, and not the sound of the flute. The relationship between the flautist and the flute is unstable during the whole piece, which makes the flautist an embodied subject rather than a disembodied sonic object. This embodiment contains a perspective on gender, since the voice (with all its other features) is always acknowledged as gendered.

The spatio-temporal flux of different reverberations, the sonic presence of diverse, controlled movements and the constant amalgamation of various multi-embodied and multi-gendered whispers, create the particular sensual realm of *NoaNoa*. Through the constant organic foot–pedal contact, the flautist both touches the electronic material and is touched by it at the same time. It actually offers the performer the possibility to be in contact with sonic material that is produced beyond the divided borderlines of different bodies. This dual touching also blurs a series of assumptions between the different authorial voices of *NoaNoa*; it is difficult to tell who is the maker and who and what is being made, as well as how and when such diverse sounds are/were created. The distributed authorities of the sounds seem to be constructed in the interstitial spaces between diverse acts, realized by several bodies in various temporal and spatial contexts. Such dualistic parameters as active/passive, complete/incomplete, self/other, male/female, language/music and original/reproduced are ruptured in these complex, multi-embodied, authorial spaces.

The flautist who performs music by Kaija Saariaho cannot stay mute or singular. She or he has to strive towards semantic and symbolic modes of expression, towards fluid processes of sound production, and towards plural embodiments of encountering the flute. The mouth of the flautist is a continually transforming umbilicus of the multi-voiced emanation of breathing, hissing, speaking, whispering, articulating, blowing and micro-controlling: a constantly adjusting diversity of sound-sensation-meaning production. In the fleshly stories from the mouth, the flautist can encounter the amalgamation and interconnection processes with persistently stratifying layers of various embodied histories and stories, spaces and instrument-relationships of sound making.

Chapter 5

Capturing Time and Giving it Form: *Nymphéa*

Michael Rofe

Music is purely an art of time, and the musician – with or without a composer –
builds and regulates the experience of the speed of time passing. Time becomes
matter in music; therefore composing is exploring time as matter in all its forms:
regular, irregular. Composing is capturing time and giving it a form. (Kaija
Saariaho, 2000)[1]

Music is a temporal art form. In the absence of a definitive spatial reality – scores,
recordings are mere representations of 'the music' – the temporal coordinates of
start-point and end-point act as the primary delimiting attributes of a work. And
as time is generally conceived to pass uni-directionally – the so-called 'arrow
of time' – music can construct relationships between the temporal domains of
past, present and future: memories of past musical experiences (from earlier in
the piece, or from earlier in one's life) shape present perceptions, giving rise to
expectations of future possibilities. In this model, musical narratives can develop
in a way similar to a literary plot:

Following a story ... is understanding the successive actions, thoughts, and
feelings in question insofar as they present a certain directedness ... We
are pushed ahead by this development and ... we reply to its impetus with
expectations concerning the outcome and the completion of the entire process ...
The primary direction of care is toward the future. Through care, we are always
already 'ahead of' ourselves (Ricoeur, 1980: 174 and 181).

Jonathan Kramer has suggested that the musical corollary – teleological listening
– is common in Western cultures largely due to the prevalence of tonal music,
wherein the listener constructs a sense of directed motion towards moments of
tonal stability. As he states, 'rates of motion [may vary], but not the fact of motion'
(Kramer, 1981: 550 and 555).

This last point highlights a fundamental difference between 'clock time' and
'musical time', a distinction that Thomas Clifton terms 'the time a piece *takes*'
as opposed to 'the time a piece *presents* or *evokes*' (Clifton, 1983: 81).[2] As such,

---

[1]   From Saariaho, 2000: 111; see Moisala, 2009: 54, for further discussion.

[2]   As Kramer points out, this distinction is most apparent in film, which rarely presents
a real-time unfolding of events (Kramer, 1988: 403).

not only can music be said to exist 'in' time, but time also exists 'in' music. By implication, music has 'the power to create, alter, disrupt or even destroy time itself' (Kramer, 1988: 5). Or, in Saariaho's own words, music 'builds and regulates the experience of the speed of time passing'. While this is true of most musics, the diminished role of tonal directionality in twentieth-century repertoire renders directed, teleological listening less of an inevitability, and, by implication, offers a wider range of compositional possibilities in which timescale can be explored.

Finding ways to control and structure the way time is felt to pass is a central concern for Kaija Saariaho; she has explored a range of possibilities throughout her career. In several formative works, the linear unfolding of time is vital,[3] acting almost as compensation for the lack of clear tonal directionality. *Vers le blanc* (1982, for tape) and *Verblendungen* (1982–84, for orchestra and tape), for instance, both involve a single transition – from one pitch cluster to another in the former; from loud to quiet in the latter – and in each, the gradual metamorphosis of materials between two states becomes the primary formal process. Yet in other (later) examples, Saariaho allows greater indeterminacy in the way form is constructed. Indeed, she has asked quite explicitly whether 'it [is] really necessary to create dynamic forms' (Saariaho, 1987: 132). This sentiment gives rise to rather different works. For instance, in *Mirrors* (1997, for flute and cello, originally a CD-ROM game), performers are given a series of musical fragments to be assembled as desired; the only instruction is that 'there should be always a mirror in one or several of the following musical dimensions: rhythm, pitch, instrumental gesture or timbre' (Saariaho, 1997: 2). Therefore, the essence of *Mirrors* does not reside in large-scale temporal directionality, but in small-scale time structures and their capacity for pattern generation. While this does not prohibit the construction – by performer or listener – of higher-level temporal narratives, it does break down the *need* for goal-directed order.

But these works have fairly straightforward temporal structures: Saariaho uses a single, governing principle in each. More often, her approach to timescale is both more subtle and more sophisticated: she has developed a variety of means to manipulate (and, at times, bypass) teleological listening. This in turn has a significant impact upon the construction of musical narratives. In order to abstract some of these processes and their effects, it is useful to focus upon a single example: *Nymphéa* ('Water Lily', 1987), for string quartet with live electronics. This piece is particularly interesting as it sits at the intersection of two series of works. Firstly, it constitutes Part III in Saariaho's *Jardin secret* trilogy. Secondly, it is the first of three 'Nymphéas': Saariaho reworked the material of the original in *Petals* (1988, for solo cello with optional electronics), and *Nymphéa Reflection*

---

[3] 'Linearity' is used here and throughout the chapter to mean a patterned succession of events, whereby 'earlier events imply later ones, and later ones are consequences of earlier ones' (Kramer, 1988: 21). Linearity is used in particular to define patterns wherein each successive step moves further away from the point of onset (as opposed to, say, cyclic organization, in which there is an underlying periodicity).

(2001, for string orchestra – and no electronics). Brief comparison of these works will be valuable as the discussion unfolds, but first it is necessary to consider a number of details of Saariaho's musical language, for which examination of the opening bars of the original *Nymphéa* will prove instructive.

Spectral Expansion: Harmony and Timbre; Harmony-Timbre

The opening of *Nymphéa* presents a rapid expansion of pitch space; 'expansion' implies the passing of time, as there is a definitively different 'before' and 'after'. Over the course of the first seven bars, we move from silence, to a unison A, to a chord that spans 3½ octaves (see Example 5.1 overleaf). This opening out of musical space is partly structured through intervallic symmetries: the A moves in whole-tone steps (up to B in the second violin, down to G in the viola), and in leaps (up a major sixth to F in the first violin, and [via a D] down a compound major sixth to C♯ in the cello); D♯s enter in inner parts, forming symmetrical tritones above and below the initial A. Voices continue their rising and falling trajectories, introducing additional pitches as they fragment into multiple parts.

Such patterns pervade much of *Nymphéa*, revealing a level of control that reflects Saariaho's careful approach to pitch organization.[4] Yet these rarely feature in the foreground as isolated phenomena: more often, pitch patterns develop alongside other aspects of the music in order to create broader perceptual effects and relationships. At the opening, individual notes are transformed through a host of timbral and pitch-based manipulations: techniques such as playing *sul tasto*, *sul ponticello*, with vibrato, or using glissandi, introduce a range of additional artefacts and harmonics. Most significantly, performers are asked periodically to apply additional bow pressure (see solid hair-pins above the staves in Example 5.1), resulting in gradual transitions into and out of noise. Finally, each voice of the quartet is modified independently through live electronic manipulation, which, at this point in the score, includes artificial phasing, harmonization and reverberation.[5]

Discussion of pitch organization in isolation is therefore problematic, given all the performance variations that in reality shape the sound; the listener is more likely to perceive a broader gestural shape: sonic expansion. This expansion occurs simultaneously across harmonic and timbral aspects of the music: not only do we move from unison to chord, but also from silence to *mf*, from timbral purity to

---

[4]   Damien Pousset has described some of these patterns, suggesting that *Nymphéa* shares its harmonic material with *Lichtbogen*, a work completed shortly before (Pousset, 2000: 93).

[5]   Phasing is a technique whereby a signal is passed through an oscillator in order to create additional peaks and troughs in the frequency spectrum; harmonization alters the frequency of a signal (in *Nymphéa*, harmonization values are less than a semitone); reverberation is akin to an artificial echo.

Example 5.1 *Nymphéa* – opening material

timbral diversity, from simplicity to complexity. This type of parametric conflation reveals the strong influence of Saariaho's spectral research. In physical terms, harmony and timbre are closely related phenomena. A 'single note' is, in fact, a composite of a fundamental frequency – the pitch we hear most prominently – and a series of quieter frequency resonances, or overtones. The timbral signature of the overall note – whether it is heard as a trumpet or a flute – results from the relative strengths of those overtones, and the way those strengths vary over time. As such, harmony and timbre can be manipulated as mutually contingent dimensions.[6] In *Nymphéa*, not only does the opening gesture expand and diversify in harmonic and timbral content, but there is a broader, synergetic expansion here of harmony-timbre: the initial pitch class, A, has widened by bar 7 to a chord that includes the pitch classes G¼♭, G♯, A¼♯ and B.[7] The effect is a sullying of the initial unison purity, a timbral distortion. Whether or not we perceive the specifics of this change is not the point (and one might even posit that we are not *supposed* to hear the specifics). Rather, it is the process that is important: changes in harmony can be conceived of as changes in timbre. And given the extended performance techniques noted above, changes in timbre give rise to changes in harmony.

The notion of expansion, of opening up a musical space, can be linked to certain visual images that inspired Saariaho during her work on *Nymphéa*: 'the plant's roots in the mud, the stem that brings the leaf to the surface of the water, and the flower that reaches toward the sky' (in Moisala, 2009: 56). Whether or not one constructs such visual narratives during the listening process, there is a directionality implied by states in expansion, and this, in turn, implies two points between which that change takes place. The starting point in *Nymphéa* is clear: silence, from which the purity of a unison sound tentatively grows. More specifically, this gesture allows the string quartet initially to approximate the sound of a sine wave, the purest possible timbre.

This principle of sonic purity (and impurity) formed an important creative impetus for Saariaho in the 1980s, most notably in her *Jardin secret* trilogy; as noted above, *Nymphéa* is the final part of that series. In each of these works, Saariaho explores what she has called her sound/noise axis: a continuum of sounds spanning pure sine tones at one extreme, and white noise at the other (see Anderson and Saariaho, 1992: 617). One can easily see how such a conception resonated with her spectral interests in parametric conflation. A sine wave is an oscillation of a single frequency; a musical 'note' is a composite of several specific frequencies (a fundamental and its overtones); white noise results from frequency saturation. Thus whilst the purity and impurity of sine tones and white noise respectively might be considered *timbral* extremes, they are, in a physical sense, extreme *harmonies*.

---

[6]   The opening of Tristan Murail's *Gondwana* is a famous example: he uses an orchestra to mimic the sound of a bell through careful selection of pitch, instrumentation and dynamics.

[7]   This is interlocked by a second cluster of C♯, D and D♯.

Saariaho has explained that,

> I began to use the sound/noise axis to develop both musical phrases and larger
> forms, and thus to create inner tensions in the music. In an abstract and atonal
> sense the sound/noise axis may be substituted for the [tonal] notion of consonance/
> dissonance. A rough, noisy texture would thus be parallel to dissonance, whilst
> a smooth, clear texture would correspond to consonance (Saariaho, 1987: 94).

If, in *Nymphéa*, we start from a position of purity and consonance, then there
is another dimension of expansion in the opening gesture: 'outwards' along the
sound/noise axis, as brought about by a change in sound density. But the end-point
of the initial expansion is not noise, dissonance, density saturation; we do not move
immediately to the other extreme of the axis. Rather, noise is used at a more local
level: performers are asked periodically to expand their sound into noise, then to
move back to a defined pitch. Again, the potential for visual narratives abound – a
flower straining to open, small steps upwards and outwards. Importantly, though,
noise is set up as a local tension within the overall sound-world, and not as a goal
of a uniform expansion process.

Growth, Life and Decay

The initial gesture of *Nymphéa* serves to populate an empty sound-space. That
population process ceases in bar 8 (see Example 5.1), from which point materials
are closely related to those already introduced: the pitch-class content of the next
ten bars is largely a composite of pitches added over the initial seven bars (with
the addition of a prominent melodic E, and, later, C); extended performance
techniques continue to dominate the perceptual surface; noise gestures continue
to phase in and out of (and between) individual voices. Each of these features thus
serves to prolong the sound-world of bar 7: harmonies and timbres slowly evolve,
but with no new goal.

But, as this second phase unfolds, pitch elements gradually start to coalesce
into melodic cells. Initially, these appear to have no consequence, and contribute to
the non-directional prolongation of the sound-world. However, from bar 17, these
cells combine to form a longer melodic line, and, by bar 21, this line dominates
the texture. Moreover, other voices drop out from bar 21, isolating this melody; it
quickly wilts by glissando on to a single D♯ (as earlier, symmetrical tritone to the
initial A). The opening expansion has thus been counterbalanced by a subsequent
contraction, and, again, that contraction covers several musical parameters: from
chord to single pitch; from timbral density to timbral purity.

Three distinct phases can therefore be heard over the initial 24 bars of *Nymphéa*,
defined loosely as growth (expansion), life (prolongation) and decay (contraction):
see Example 5.2. This notional shape offers an important mirror to the life cycles
of the natural world: the theme of nature hinted at in the title '*Nymphéa*' is thus

Example 5.2 *Nymphéa* – **growth-life-decay cycle**

given musical expression. Moreover, the symmetries of the opening voice leading are composed out through various axes of formal symmetry: spatially, a middle-register unison expands its pitch content upwards and downwards, populating that space through changing timbral density; temporally, that space later contracts to another middle-register unison. Of course, these symmetries are not exact: the unisons are different; the prolongation phase is not itself symmetrical about its centre point; clock time durations are not mirrored exactly. Yet there remains a conceptual symmetry here, the significance of which will be discussed later.

For now, this process begins to highlight the fundamental concern of this chapter – the organization of time. 'The speed of time passing' (*pace* Saariaho) does not follow simply from degrees of rhythmic activity. For instance, there is no real sense of rhythm over the opening seven bars, yet we still experience a sense of change, and, by implication, we are aware of time passing. It is change, then, that is crucial. Both expansion and contraction – growth and decay – involve materials in flux, motion *between* two points of definable difference. Prolongation, on the other hand, involves exploration *within* an existent sound-world, a sense of free-floating, non-focused discovery. Time – that is to say, linear, progressive time – inheres in expansion/contraction gestures more prominently than in prolongation gestures due to the extent of ordered directionality.

Saariaho's approach to composition at the time of writing *Nymphéa* bears out the significance of these observations: 'in exploring the development of form, I … found my attention naturally drawn to the significance of dynamism and stasis' (Saariaho, 1987: 94). By setting up processes that involve transitions between two states, Saariaho invites a sense of dynamic motion (even if the specific goal cannot be intuited, as might be the case in tonal music). Conversely, prolongational states set up a greater sense of stasis,[8] for although gestures come and go, they do not

---

[8] Stasis is defined here following Lewis Rowell: '[Static] music is consistent, continuous, and relatively unarticulated; it fails to imply a sense of progression, goal direction, increasing or decreasing tension, movement hierarchy, structural functions, contrasting rates of motion, culmination, phrases or other internal units that might suggest a temporal scale of periodicities. It is, in a word, a "pool" of sound, a sustained aesthetic

combine into larger directional patterns.[9] Perceptions of temporality follow on: time can be felt to pass 'more quickly' in dynamic music than in static music – just as it would in tonal repertoire – offering a means of building patterns of *musical time within clock time*.

Anamorphic Impressions and the Construction of Form

If *Nymphéa* makes general reference to the theme of nature, then its title also fosters a more specific association with the most famous series of artworks concerning water lilies: the Monet *Nymphéas*. Over a period of roughly 40 years, Monet produced some 250 canvasses of the lily pond in his garden at Giverny. But, as art critic Andrew Forge has noted,

> Increasingly as [Monet's] understanding of the specific nature of his vision matured, he came to see that his real subject matter was not so much the scene in front of him in terms of its ingredients – trees, figures, boats, whatever – as the 'effect', that is, the particular condition of light-filled atmosphere that enfolded them all under the circumstances of the hour, making them all one (Forge, 1975: 8).

If, in the Monet *Nymphéas*, details of form and line, composition and representation, are subsumed under broader patterns of 'light', then one can see a clear parallel with the spectral synthesis of musical parameters within a universal currency of 'sound'. It is hardly surprising, then, that several prominent spectral composers – Gérard Grisey and Tristan Murail, for instance – have drawn quite explicitly from the work of Impressionist artists in their music.[10] As such, Saariaho belongs to a wider tradition of interdisciplinary pollination; she spent some time studying the Monet *Nymphéas* prior to her own experiments (Moisala, 2009: 58), reinforcing the significance of (this) visual image in her music.

In an interview with Thiébault-Sisson, Monet described in more detail the way in which he approached his subject:

surface in which the beauty lines in one's response to the surface itself, not in the syntactical relationships among its components ... The general illusion is one of a state rather than a process, a music more of being than becoming, a continuous Now' (Rowell, 1987: 184).

[9]   Kramer has another useful analogy here: when on an aeroplane, one is largely unaware of 'moving'; the journey feels essentially static (Kramer, 1988: 13). But during phases of take-off and landing – transition between two definably different states (land and cruising altitude) – there is a more perceptible sense of motion through time and space; a greater dynamism.

[10]   See Malherbe, 2000, for more discussion of these parallels, and analysis of several spectral works that draw upon Impressionist concerns.

I have painted these water lilies a great deal, modifying my viewpoint each time, transforming the motif according to the season and according to the different light effects that each season brings. Besides, the effect varies constantly, not only from one season to the next, but from one minute to the next, since the water flowers are far from being the whole scene; really, they are just the accompaniment. The essence of the motif is the mirror of water whose appearance alters at every moment, thanks to the patches of sky which are reflected in it, and which give its light and its movement. The passing clouds the freshening breeze, the storm which threatens and breaks, the wind which blows hard and then suddenly abates, the light growing dim and then bright again – so many factors, undetectable to the uninitiated eye, which transform the colouring and disturb the planes of the water (Monet, in House, 1983: 162).

This description is remarkably similar to several images that inspired Saariaho's *Nymphéa*, as she outlined in the programme note for its premiere:

The image of the symmetrical structure of the water lily, yielding as it floats on the water, transforming. Different interpretations of the same image in different dimensions; a uni-dimensional surface with its colours, shapes and, on the other hand, different materials that can be sensed, forms, dimensions; a white water lily feeding on the underwater mud (Saariaho, in Moisala, 2009: 58).

In the Monet *Nymphéas*, lilies do not themselves form the primary foci; in the Saariaho, there is no single lily 'theme' or sound-world. Rather, in each, lilies are distorted by their surrounding conditions, and these conditions themselves come to capture the attention of the observer/listener. Fineberg argues that this type of anamorphosis is an important spectral technique, as it allows composers to present fairly simple subjects (or processes) from different perspectives, distorting them anywhere up to the point of non-recognition (Fineberg, 2000b: 109). While variation technique is deeply rooted in Western music in general, the idea of *ana*morphosis (change *in*), as opposed to *meta*morphosis (change *between*), has a specific resonance here, given its parallel with the stasis/dynamism polarity explored earlier.

Example 5.3 overleaf shows an anamorphosis of the opening sound-world of *Nymphéa*, taken from later in the work (compare with Example 5.1). As can be seen, both passages begin with a unison A, and both include exactly the same pitch content in their rapid expansion of harmony-timbre. However, in the later extract, we move further along the sound/noise axis: the goal of the expansion is as close as a string quartet can come to producing unadulterated noise; the sound-space is now populated to its maximum possible density. So where noise previously played a non-integral role within the expansion process – fluctuations were less ordered – it now functions as an end-point in a uniform growth phase. Saariaho thus inflates the sound-mass *further*, yet does so over a comparatively brief duration; in fact, a duration roughly the same as at the opening of the work. That we move further

Example 5.3 ***Nymphéa* – anamorphosis of opening materials**

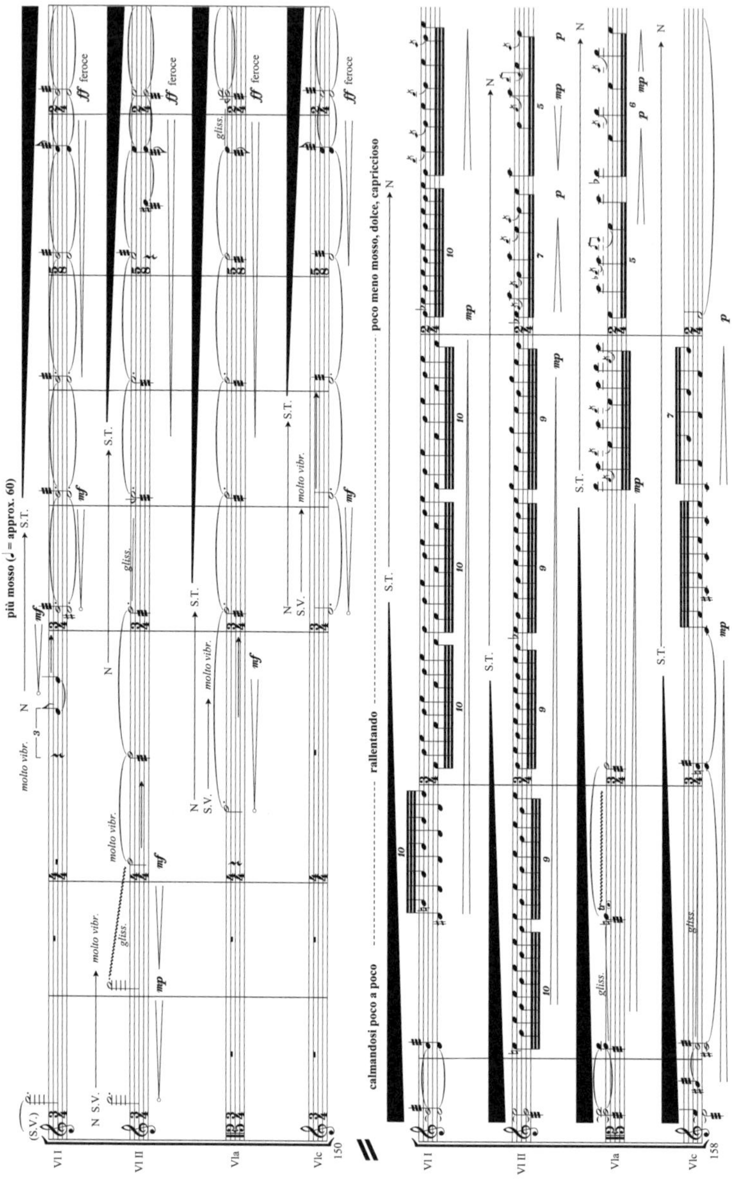

over a similar duration invites a sense in which time is moving more quickly: there is greater dynamism due to the greater distance – or dissimilarity – between start- and end-point. And there is no doubt that this stage of the work is more dissonant and dynamic than the opening: the metaphorical lily has been distorted by more aggressive conditions.

The extract in Example 5.3 also differs from the opening in the way the music proceeds after its initial expansion. Whereas, at the opening, the expanded sound-world is prolonged, we now experience an immediate and partial deflation from the noise of bars 157–8 to the interim state of bar 161, and it is this sound-world – somewhere between sine wave (unison) and noise – that is prolonged. Over the following bars, Saariaho presents a series of subsequent expansions to noise, and partial contractions back to variants of that interim state, before events finally contract fully on to a single pitch – C_2 – in bar 208. So not only is the opening material distorted, but so too is the path that material takes: its growth-life-decay cycle is distorted. The basic shape of Example 5.2 is thus transformed into the more complex pattern of Example 5.4, in which the density of sound – that is to say the music's position on the sound/noise axis – is now shown through shading.[11] By implication, we are invited to experience different configurations of dynamism and stasis from those of the opening, and thus perceive new patterns in the passing of time. Overall, there is a greater sense of dynamism here due to the higher number of uniform density changes: this phase of the work projects the strongest sense of motion and directionality; the most vivid experience of time passing.

Example 5.4   *Nymphéa* – **anamorphosis of growth-life-decay cycle**

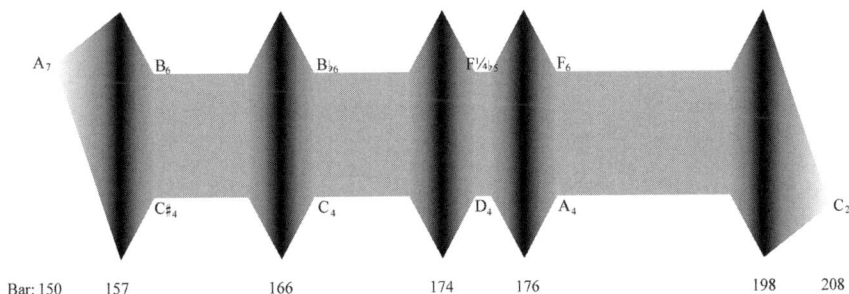

That this phase of the music is a variant of the opening implies its structural discreteness, and, by implication, the possibility for divisibility in general. As such, variations – or the various conditions to which the lily is subjected – are articulated through the closed/cyclic nature of the shape: a state of rest expands into a particular set of (musical) conditions, then retreats to the initial state. Time is thus 'captured' (*pace* Saariaho) into discrete units. The parsing of time in this way

---

[11]   The pitch-space extremes at the onsets of intervening sound-worlds are shown, as are the initial and final unisons.

Example 5.5   *Nymphéa* – **captured sound-worlds; overall form**

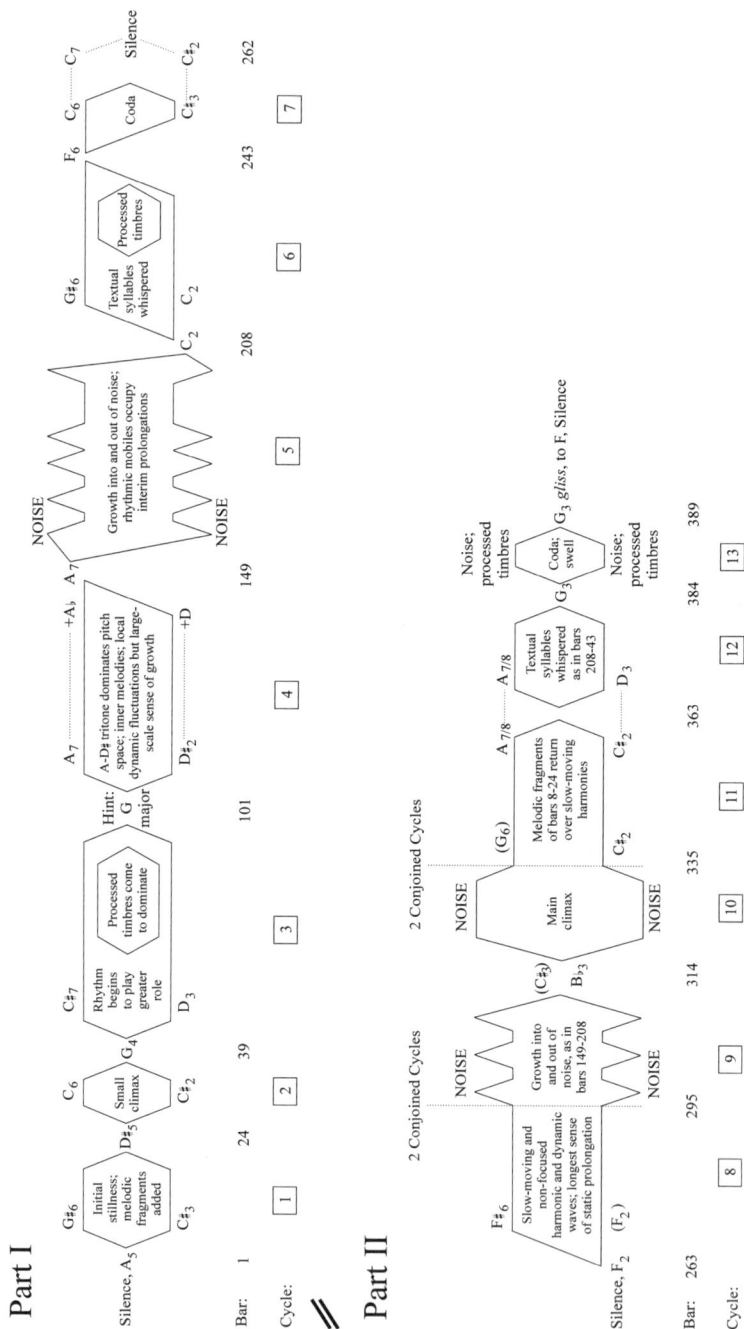

gives rise to a particular conception of the work's overall form: a series of varied growth-life-decay cycles, as shown in Example 5.5. Immediately apparent is the diversity of shapes into which the original cycle is cast. Some retain the temporal and spatial symmetries of the original, while others deform this shape. At times these are fused, at other times there are cycles within cycles.

Importantly, there is a close link between each shape and its content. As described, cycle 5 (Example 5.4) contains some of the most dissonant timbres and goes through a series of dynamic growth and decay phases. On the other hand, cycle 8 contains slow-moving, relatively consonant harmonies, giving rise to one of the longest prolongation phases – and, consequently, one of the most static periods – in the work. The variation process thus encompasses both form and content, reflective of Saariaho's conception of form in the 1980s: 'When I say "form" I mean precisely the idea that Vassily Kandinsky defined as the following: "Form is the external manifestation of inner meaning"' (Saariaho, 1987: 93). As each of Monet's *Nymphéas* presents a snapshot (an impression) of a particular moment in time – a particular set of visual conditions encompassing both composition and texture/tone – so each cycle in the Saariaho captures a particular set of musical conditions. The stasis or dynamism of each part – its temporal form – is inherently linked to the consonance or dissonance of its harmony-timbre – its content.

Symmetry as Temporal/Spatial Construct

> I am very interested in the structures found in nature – especially the symmetry of leaves and flowers … When composing, I often draw sketches of form about the musical events moving in time. Formal structures often aim at either creating symmetry and/or breaking it down. In both cases, the awareness of symmetry is present in my works … [to a greater degree] than is generally the case (Saariaho, in Moisala, 2009: 56 and 91).

Symmetrical structures have already been observed in various domains of *Nymphéa*: the foreground swells into and out of noise; the opening voice leading; the spatial and temporal symmetry of the original growth-life-decay cycle, and the deliberate asymmetry of certain later variants. Moreover, as noted earlier, Saariaho identified in her programme note the symmetrical structure of the lily as a specific source of inspiration for the work.[12]

It is notable, then, that *Nymphéa* projects a two-part structure at the highest level of formal organization (see Example 5.5). This is articulated primarily through the use of silence at bar 262, the only complete decay and complete (re)growth aside from the extremes of the work; its double bar-line is the only structural indication in the score. Further, there are several correspondences between cycles from each

---

[12] Saariaho has also written of the significance of symmetry in the first part of the *Jardin secret* trilogy; see Saariaho, 1987: 124ff.

part, giving rise to a notional symmetry (or, at least, equivalence) between the two large-scale formal stages. The use of extreme noise in cycle 5 (complete with the dynamism of its frequent growths and decays), for instance, is reproduced in cycles 9 and 10, while the melodic fragments of the first cycle (and the static prolongation to which their presentation gives rise) recur in the eleventh. The most notable parallel, though, is between the sixth and twelfth cycles, both of which require performers to whisper extracts from a poem by Arseniy Tarkovsky:

Now summer is gone
And might never have been.
In the sunshine it's warm,
But there has to be more.

It all came to pass,
All fell into my hands
Like a five-petalled leaf,
But there has to be more.

Nothing evil was lost,
Nothing good was in vain,
All ablaze with clear light
But there has to be more.

Life gathered me up
Safe under its wing,
My luck always held,
But there has to be more.

Not a leaf was burned up
Not a twig ever snapped
Clean as glass is the day,
But there has to be more.[13]

Given the work's title, and the growth-life-decay cycles of its form, it is significant that Saariaho's choice of text contains such prominent natural imagery – summer; sunshine; leaf; light; life; twig. Moreover, for the present purpose, there are implicit references to time: 'summer is *gone*'; 'might never have been' (negates the passage of time); 'it all came to pass'; 'there has to be more' (anticipation of the future). Importantly, these are references to *clock* time: to the past and to the future. Up to this point, the focus of this chapter has been primarily upon aspects of *musical* time in *Nymphéa*, which is to say (following Clifton) the time the work evokes: dynamism, stasis; change, prolongation.

---

[13]   Translation by Kitty Hunter-Blair, taken from the score of *Nymphéa Reflection*.

But clock time relationships also play a vital role here. That material originally presented in cycle 6 *returns* in cycle 12 connotes the passage of time: repetition is a temporal process. Likewise, the return of cycles 1 and 5 respectively in 11 and 9/10 projects an explicit sense of time having passed, as, in a more general sense, does the very notion of anamorphosis.

Musical memory thus plays a role in creating higher-level formal narratives. It is in this way that the two-part background form of *Nymphéa* can take shape. As stated above, both parts are framed by silences at their extremes (see Example 5.5), but both parts also contain their most dissonant/dynamic cycles (5 and 9/10) at their centres. In each part, this central 'swell' is followed by the texted sections, setting up an additional equivalence. The growth-life-decay cycle is thus notionally projected to the background of the work, as shown in Example 5.6. This formal shape has a certain symmetry, with two large-scale cycles that have a degree of equivalence (note that the 'symmetry' here is not a palindromic symmetry, but one borne out of repetition, similarity). But there is also a certain asymmetry: Part I is itself asymmetrical, taking longer to grow than to decay; Part II is a compressed version of Part I, as it lacks an analogue to cycles 3 and 4 (see Example 5.5). Saariaho's aforementioned affection for symmetrical structures – and the distortion of those symmetries – carries significant structural function here through the (a)symmetrical packaging (capturing) of time. Moreover, the notion of anamorphosis is fundamental even at this highest level of structural organization, further reinforcing the form–content link so vital in much of the composer's work.

Example 5.6 *Nymphéa* – **background shape**

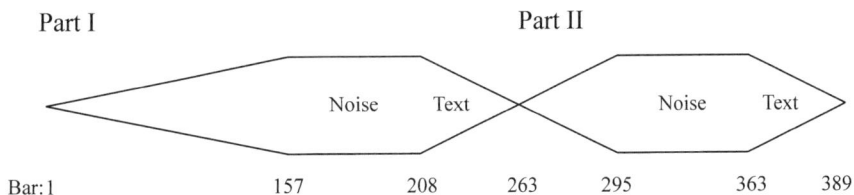

Part I   Part II

| | | Noise | Text | | Noise | Text | |

Bar: 1   157   208   263   295   363   389

A six-stage architecture thus begins to emerge: two parts, each containing the three-stage growth-life-decay pattern. As such, it is notable that Saariaho introduced a six-movement plan when she came to rework the piece as *Nymphéa Reflection* in 2001 (see Example 5.7 overleaf). These movement divisions explicitly articulate the six-stage grouping outlined in Example 5.6, and their titles point to the expressive characters that prevail therein. Material in *Nymphéa Reflection* follows closely that of the original, aside from a few expanded codettas at the ends of certain movements. However, there are two substantial differences, both of which have an effect upon background symmetry. Firstly, Saariaho completely cuts cycles 3 and 4 from the original *Nymphéa* in the later version. As described above, it is the presence of these sections in Part I of the original that gives rise

Example 5.7 *Nymphéa* and *Nymphéa Reflection* – **formal comparison**

Nymphéa	*Nymphéa Reflection*
PART I	
Cycles 1 and 2 (bars 1–38)	I. '*Sostenuto*' (expanded codetta)
Cycles 3 and 4 (bars 39–148)	[CUT]
Cycle 5 (bars 149–207)	II. '*Feroce*' (expanded codetta)
Cycles 6 and 7 (bars 208–62)	III. '*Dolcissimo*' (no voices; extra materials)
PART II	
Cycle 8 (bars 263–94)	IV. '*Lento*'
Cycles 9, 10 and 11 (bars 295–362)	V. '*Furioso*' (expanded codetta)
Cycles 12 and 13 (bars 363–89)	VI. '*Misterioso*' (expanded codetta; ends on C root)

to the overall asymmetry of Example 5.6; by removing this material in *Nymphéa Reflection*, a more precise background symmetry now emerges.[14] Secondly, cycles 6 and 7 from the original are recast in the later version without the use of the Tarkovsky text; what used to function as 'accompanimental' material to the voices is now expanded to form the sole focus for this section. So while the cut of cycles 3 and 4 serves to tighten background symmetries, this second change disrupts that balance, creating a greater sense of end weighting as voices are now used only in the final bars of the work.

The six-movement architecture of *Nymphéa Reflection* functions as a spatial framework within which to situate the perceptual present; the expressive quality of each movement is captured in its 'subtitle', inviting expectation. Moreover, the expanded codettas of this later work bring about a greater sense of finality at the end of each movement, making it easier to perceive these subdivisions. It is therefore fair to assume the possibility of large-scale directional listening: the background symmetry can take shape during the listening experience through evolving expectations. But in the original *Nymphéa* there are no such structural clues, rendering the possibility for large-scale expectation less likely. For instance, the implication from Example 5.6 is that bar 157 is somehow a large-scale goal of bar 1. But is this really the case, or is it simply the peak in one of many local cycles? In other words, does Example 5.6 grow over time – is that growth perceptible during the listening process – or is it simply a spatial, conceptual plan, only to be understood post-listening?

---

[14] Saariaho cuts the equivalent of bars 39–145 of the original. An expanded version of bars 146–8 is retained in order that the first large-scale section can end on an A (rather than G). The expanded codettas mentioned above are sufficient to counteract the 'loss' of material from the cut. In fact, the later work is slightly longer.

Cyclic and Linear Time

That *Nymphéa* consists of a series of individual scenes or impressions implies a kind of formal patchwork; a succession of variants. In this model, each variant moves from a state of rest (unison) into activity (a particular 'scene'), then back to rest; the process repeats. I have been referring continually to each pattern of growth-life-decay as a *cycle*. Yet I have presented these cycles *linearly* in diagrams. This highlights a fundamental paradox in this piece (and, indeed, one that recurs throughout Saariaho's work): it is possible to hear *Nymphéa* as a series of independent cycles – as in Example 5.5 – but it is also possible to construct higher-level narratives by connecting up these phases. Two modes of temporal organization emerge: cyclic time and linear time.

In the cyclic mode, each phase of activity projects a different musical scene; a different set of conditions in which the lily is viewed (heard). But the cyclical basis of that varied repetition is further reinforced by successive stages sharing their interim points of rest: the G of bar 39, for instance, is the end-point of cycle 2, and also the start-point for cycle 3. Cyclic renewal is important here. But how important is its being a G? On one hand, the pattern A-to-G occupies multiple structural levels: it is one of the first foreground changes we hear in the piece; it occupies the middleground between the opening and bar 39; it is the primary background change from the opening to the end of the work as a whole. Certainly, then, this relationship is *conceptually* significant, providing a compositional logic and a supplement to tonal pitch relationships. But how *perceptually* significant is it? This will no doubt vary between listeners; what is important is that if one does not make that connection, the G of bar 39 can be interpreted in its simplest form: a unison. And if this is the case, then all interim points of rest are connected, for all are unisons, or, at least, points of quasi-unison, consonance and purity. As such, the form of *Nymphéa* (Example 5.5) might better be rationalized not as a linear succession of cycles, but as a cycle of cycles (see Example 5.8 overleaf).

In this model, the central core represents a single state of rest, from which the music expands into, and contracts out of, successive states of activity. As Saariaho has noted, 'a chord which is familiar [in this case, not a chord, but a unison] somehow assumes the function of consonance' (Saariaho, 1987: 122). The sound/ noise axis is thus given a more subtle expression: the further each cycle moves out radially from that central consonance, the further along the sound/noise axis it has travelled. Interestingly, there is something quite flower-like in the overall shape of Example 5.8, another (albeit elaborate) expression of natural imagery in the work, perhaps. Each stage is anchored to the common core, recalling Saariaho's inspiration, quoted earlier: 'the plant's roots in the mud … yielding as it floats on the water, transforming'. Or, if the centre point is conceived to have some type of magnetic 'pull', then the arcs of activity about that core are notionally comparable to magnetic field lines, or solar flares. Given Saariaho's apparent interest in these themes – *Lichtbogen*, *Solar*, *Notes on Light* – such an interpretation may not be as frivolous as it first appears.

Example 5.8   *Nymphéa* – form as a cycle of cycles

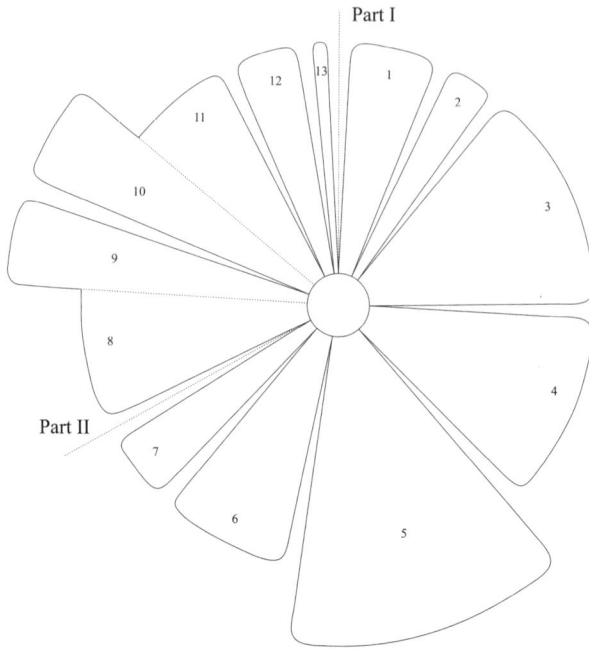

Importantly, regarding issues of time, the process of continually returning to similar states of rest results in a curious effect: this music never really 'goes' anywhere; returning sound-worlds reinforce this impression. There is no overall linear journey on which the listener is taken: changing conditions cause motion but not *loco*motion. It is as if the *listener* is rooted in the mud, observing, and stirred by, a series of diverse conditions that pass him or her by, rather than being actively transported between musical states. This sensation is remarkably common, at least for this listener, in Saariaho's work.

The cyclic understanding of Example 5.8 reinforces the notion of *Nymphéa* as a series of discrete musical scenes. However, we have already seen several ways in which cycles work together: correspondences between the sound-worlds of certain cycles, and the consequent background shape of Example 5.6; the cycles-within-cycles layout of phases 3 and 6 (see Example 5.5); the multi-level A-to-G connections.[15] And, as observed earlier, individual cycles are fused together through their shared points of rest, leaving the move to silence at bar 262 (with its attendant double bar-line) the only unambiguous structural *division* in the entire work.

---

[15]   Interestingly, in *Nymphéa Reflection*, the final chord of the work is not rooted on G, but on C, negating any multi-level A-to-G significance. Instead, this C reinforces the importance of the C♯-C sound-world used at various strategic points in both works. Likewise in *Petals* – Saariaho's 1988 version of the work – C functions as the primary pitch focus.

Example 5.9 *Nymphéa* – **second cycle**

In this respect, it is useful to reconsider the opening stages of the work. The initial cycle has been described in detail: the unison A expands then contracts to the D♯ of bar 24. However, when we consider the second cycle, bars 25–39, the D♯ of bar 24 is now given a new context: it is the brief end-point of a glissando; it falls to D♮, which itself expands quickly to the sound-world of bar 25 (see Example 5.9, which follows on directly from Example 5.1). This sound-mass then opens out into the C♯-C 'climax' of bar 31, before contracting more purposefully on to the G of bar 39. In other words, the G between cycles 2 and 3 is a more stable point of rest than the D♯-to-D between cycles 1 and 2. There is therefore a higher level of growth-decay that encompasses two lower-level cycles: the relative instability of the D♯ means that the C♯-C peak can be felt (retrospectively) as the climactic goal of not only the second cycle, but also the first-and-second cycles. Middleground patterns, themselves based on the growth-life-decay shape, thus begin to emerge.

Over the next few cycles, an increasingly forceful projection of rhythm sets up an additional linear narrative. At the opening, there is no real sense of rhythm and metre: even the melodic fragments from bar 8 initially seem like free-time flourishes. But, as these fragments converge, a greater sense of rhythm is established. From cycle 3, the listener encounters the first feeling of pulse (see bar 39 in Example 5.9 above). And by cycle 5 this 'pulse' has been taken to its extreme through the use of tremolandi marked *feroce* (see Example 5.3). There is therefore a large-scale process of growth in the rhythmic domain towards cycle 5.

This pattern of linear growth is also brought about in the harmony-timbre domain. As shown in Example 5.10, the increasing rhythmic activity across Part I of *Nymphéa* is mirrored by three successive climaxes. Each supersedes its predecessor in volume – *mp, ff, ff tutta la forza* – and each moves successively further along the sound/noise axis – the C♯-C extremes of pitch space in climax one are followed by semitonal clashes (D♯/D, A/A♭) at the extremes of climax two, and then full-scale noise in climax three. So just as the C♯-C climax acts as a point of focus over cycles 1 and 2, climax two plays a similar role over the first four cycles: it is felt retrospectively to be the most significant moment *up to that point*. Likewise, climax three supersedes both its predecessors, giving rise to the background shape of Part I, shown in Example 5.6. A fractal-like growth process thus emerges: the growth-life-decay shape is echoed over successively higher structural levels. This process of reduplication means that the growth of material gradually determines large-scale form; as in nature, the plant grows *into* its shape through cumulative steps. The Kandinskian conception of form as 'the external manifestation of inner meaning' can again be seen as vital in the way *Nymphéa* takes shape.

Importantly, such fractal-like growth-by-reduplication is inherently linear in its temporal organization: one is constantly re-evaluating *past* musical events in the light of *present* perceptions. Therefore, the background shape of Example 5.6 is more than a (retrospective) conceptual construct. It can be felt to grow linearly over time, with successive stages in the fractal acting almost as middleground connections between the local cycles and the developing background form. So, despite the strong patterns of cyclic time seen in Example 5.8, there remains an

Example 5.10 *Nymphéa* (Part I) – fractal-like growth

important linear element in this music, albeit one that is more subtle and less all-encompassing than might be the case in other musics.

Time and Narrative

Nymphéa demonstrates several means by which Saariaho manipulates the passing and parsing of time: dynamism and stasis as a way of controlling how quickly *musical* time is felt to elapse; reminiscence and variation as a way of highlighting the passing of *clock* time; interactions between the temporal domains of memory, perception and expectation; symmetry and asymmetry as a means of perceiving (dis)order; cyclic and linear modes of temporal evolution, and their effect upon the extent of directionality; teleological listening as one of several possibilities. Saariaho finds ways of integrating processes that seem, on paper, quite incompatible.

Of the wide-ranging influences that underpin Saariaho's work – musical and non-musical – it is useful to highlight two in which time plays a notable role.[16] First, Tim Howell has described the particular relevance of timescale in Nordic life:

> ... extremes of light and dark, and the very slow rate of evolution that takes an entire year to achieve, undoubtedly affects human perceptions of how time passes. Furthermore, this cyclic quality is offset by abrupt seasonal changes: winter-to-spring happens in a couple of weeks – you can observe on a daily basis how a tree moves from brown to green; the change back at the onset of winter is no less dramatic (Howell, 2006: 276).

Howell goes on to argue that a range of Finnish composers – from Sibelius to Saariaho – have turned to such variations in timescale for compositional inspiration (Howell, 2006: 276ff). Given Saariaho's Finnish roots – and the frequency with which she looks to nature for inspiration (as she does in *Nymphéa*) – it is interesting that the manipulation of time plays such a crucial role in her music; her view that music 'builds and regulates the experience of the speed of time passing' resonates with Howell's interpretation.

Secondly, Saariaho's move to mainland Europe in the early 1980s gave rise to a host of new influences. Foremost amongst these was contact with Grisey and Murail, and the spectral research of IRCAM. As Grisey has written, time plays an integral role in spectral music:

> Strengthened by an ecology of sounds, spectral music no longer integrates time as an external element imposed upon a sonic material considered as being 'outside-time', but instead treats it as a constituent element of sound itself ...

---

[16]   See Howell, 2006: 203–5, for greater exposition of these influences.

whereby pleasure … is the result of a perfectly parallel relation between the perceiving body and the conceiving spirit (Grisey, 2000: 2).

Since the work of John Cage, time (particularly measured/measurable time) has frequently come to act as a (if not, *the*) primary ordering principle in music. But in spectral works this takes on a particular significance: the initial motivation of spectralists 'to control the finest possible degrees of change' (Murail, 2000: 7) has, as Joshua Fineberg states, led this group of composers to 'a central belief that music is ultimately sound evolving in time' (Fineberg, 2000a: 2).

These two influences clearly resonate with one another, and seem to find expression in many of the processes described in this chapter. Exploration of temporal organization – and how time might be 'captured' within a musical form – can be found throughout Saariaho's work, from early pieces such as *Verblendungen* and *Stilleben*,[17] up to more recent works such as *Notes on Light*. Importantly, the way in which time is structured in each of these cases necessarily impacts upon the construction of narrative: in the absence of consistent teleological processes, the type of directed narrative proposed at the opening of this chapter becomes less straightforward (in both senses of the word(s)).

In *Nymphéa*, the presence of two contrasting modes of temporal organization – cyclic and linear – gives rise to the possibility for constructing *multiple* narratives, depending upon the extent to which the listener connects successive cycles. This is a question for the individual, and will vary depending upon a host of factors, not least familiarity with the music: it is logical that subsequent listenings to a work will give rise to additional linear connections, as memory will play a sharper role in creating a spatial (a-temporal) model for comparison. But this balance between cyclic and linear order does not reside fully in the listener, as Saariaho subtly controls the relative dominance of these modes at different points: the re-use of text in cycle 12, for instance, invites a sense of return by referencing memorable events from the past. Yet this phase is also an independent cycle; one of many free-standing growth-life-decay shapes. So while Examples 5.8 and 5.10 undoubtedly stand in some type of theoretical opposition, they also work together. A useful analogy is the idea of wave motion. In this model, there is both cyclic repetition (as each wave constitutes a single period) and linear progression (insofar as there is an overall passage through time). That Saariaho's music somehow passes by in waves of activity resonates closely with earlier observations, and offers a possible interpretation of how the composer manages to offset and balance aspects of cyclic and linear order.

Example 5.8 (the cyclic model), Example 5.10 (the linear model), and the wave-like synthesis of the two, offer different narrative paths through the work

---

[17]   Saariaho has described *Stilleben*, which literally means 'still-life', as a work that is 'suspended in time' (in Kankaanpää, 1996: 91). The implications for time (and timelessness) in *Stilleben*, along with its references to the time-structures of *Lichtbogen*, are discussed in Kankaanpää, 1996: 87–92.

based on different aspects of its temporal organization. And there are a host of other possible narratives that have not been considered in detail: 'ecological' (the way in which the work mimics sounds from nature), based upon the title; textual (those relating to the Tarkovsky poem); genre-based (the extent to which Saariaho plays with the genre of the string quartet); real/artificial (the changing balance of acoustic and electronic timbres); and many others. There is no single route through this music; Saariaho invites listeners to choose from a range of possible narratives, each supported by its own musical logic.

Given this multiplicity of meaning, it is interesting that Saariaho, like Monet, has returned to the subject of 'water lilies' at various points in her career. In the Monets, 'whole groups of canvases are identical in formal structure, but the individual paintings are differentiated by endless variations in lighting and colour' (House, 1983: 162). The same can be said of Saariaho's *Nymphéas*: their differing forces give rise to differing musical shapes, which, in turn, emphasize different narrative routes. In *Nymphéa Reflection*, for instance, the presence of a full string orchestra increases Saariaho's options: effects that were generated electronically can now be produced solely by acoustic instruments. In 'reflection', the six-movement architecture offers a more extensive, spatial sense of form relative to the original: clear subdivisions function as reference points between which the listener can construct more wide-ranging linear narratives.[18] But in *Petals*, the reduced timbral palette (solo cello with optional electronics) leads to a work of compressed dimensions. The same basic materials are used, and these remain packaged in phases, but everything is simplified.[19] Saariaho has described *Petals* as a 'petal of the water lily' (in Moisala, 2009: 34); its narrative scope is thus concentrated relative to the original *Nymphéa*.

Nymphéa, *Petals* and *Nymphéa Reflection* each offer a different perspective on the same underlying subject, a creative recycling process common to Saariaho's work. Yet differences in context (as with Monet) bring a host of new narrative possibilities to the fore. If a 'narrative' is understood to mean the intelligible whole that governs a succession of events, then narrative and time are reciprocal processes, as Ricoeur explains: 'I take temporality to be that structure of existence

---

[18] Interestingly, the use of separated movements is a rarity in Saariaho's early works; rather, the types of evolving temporal patterns seen in *Nymphéa* are more frequently found. Subdivisions are used more often in her later works, resulting in the predominance of more spatial forms like that of *Nymphéa Reflection*. Clearly the balance between form as a noun – a spatial construct – and form as a verb – a temporal process – is a carefully considered issue in Saariaho's music.

[19] Now, two types of sound-world alternate: static, sustained harmony-timbres, and phases of rhythmic activity. But, again, there is a sense of linear connectivity: the penultimate phase (bars 17–27) places a particular focus on a low, *pizzicato* C; this C acts as a kind of 'fundamental' in the two sustained phases that surround this material. Moreover, there is a sense of large-scale growth towards the end of the work, where noise features most prominently.

that reaches language in narrativity and narrativity to be the language structure that has temporality as its ultimate referent' (Ricoeur, 1980: 169). For narrative to develop, time must have passed, and wherever disparate events unfold over time, it is possible to construct narrative order. That Saariaho explores such intricate time structures, through which there is such a multiplicity of interpretative routes, thus makes a vital contribution to the communicative power of her music: 'Each [of my works] consists of sentences that somehow relate to each other and eventually tell a story. This story does not have a concrete meaning, but it is a kind of narrative with its own logic' (Saariaho, in Moisala, 2009: 60). This logic – its form – is deeply rooted in the capturing of time.

Chapter 6

Whispers from the Past: Musical Topics in Saariaho's Operas

Liisamaija Hautsalo

> The nightmare of modernism made some of us think that musical meaning, in any ordinary sense, was finished. But all that is past. (Raymond Monelle, 2006: 273)

Although Kaija Saariaho is now recognized as a leading composer of opera – her works are frequently performed throughout the world – it was far from clear earlier in her career that this would be the case. Saariaho emerged in the early 1980s writing small-scale vocal and chamber works, while in the 1990s, her style gradually started to change and she began writing more extensive orchestral and vocal works. But it was not until the 2000s that larger stage works started to appear. Her first opera, the five-act *L'Amour de loin* ('Love from Afar'), was premiered at the Salzburg Festival, Austria in 2000, and her second, the two-act *Adriana Mater* ('Adriana the Mother'), was unveiled at the National Opéra de Paris, France in 2006. And since these two full-length operas, Saariaho has continued writing works for the stage: *La Passion de Simone*, an oratorio for soprano, chorus, orchestra and electronics, was seen for the first time in Vienna also in 2006; her latest stage work, *Emilie*, is a monodrama for single soprano soloist and orchestra, and was premiered at the Lyon Opera in 2010.

This chapter is divided into two parts: the first charts Saariaho's development as an opera composer, whilst the second considers her two full-length operas, *L'Amour de loin* and *Adriana Mater*, in detail. In particular, the operas will be examined from the point of view of musical semantics in a semiotic-hermeneutic framework, applying Raymond Monelle's theory of musical topics (Monelle, 2000 and 2006). This will reveal that Saariaho's operas actually align in several respects with the wider operatic tradition, despite the prevailing modernism of her style. Importantly, this alignment goes beyond a shared genre: Saariaho frequently takes traditional musical devices – topics that have been common since operas of the early seventeenth century – and uses them as part of her contemporary language.

From Anti-Opera to Pro-Opera

In 1984, Saariaho stated in an interview that the symphony and, to an extent, the opera were 'outdated art forms' (Lehtonen, 1984: 49). However, behind this view lies a broader modernist aesthetic: one that dominated the generation of Finnish composers born in the 1950s. In particular, it betrays two important influences stemming from her time as a student in the 1970s. Firstly, Saariaho was taught by Paavo Heininen, who was a strict modernist and serialist, having himself studied with Zimmermann in Cologne, and later with Persichetti and Steuermann at the Juilliard School of Music in New York. Heininen actually taught the vast majority of Finnish composers born in the 1950s, influencing a whole generation, and acting as a link particularly with the European avant-garde. Secondly, Saariaho was a member of the radical *Korvat auki* ('Ears Open') society, founded as a mouthpiece for the Finnish avant-garde by the younger generation.[1] Following its European prototypes, the critical polemic aimed at the Finnish musical establishment by *Korvat auki* was directed above all towards opera, which was seen as an old-fashioned art form.[2] This even gave rise to the pejorative term *karvalakkiooppera* ('fur-hat opera'), which has since become used more neutrally to describe a Finnish national style of tonal opera.[3]

Despite Saariaho having argued for the outdated nature of opera, her attitude differed from the strictest views of the *Korvat auki* activists. In the same interview in 1984, she says that 'as far as I myself am concerned, opera could perhaps mean some kind of multimedia experience' (Lehtonen, 1984: 49). And although Saariaho chaired the anti-opera *Korvat auki* (1979–80), her personal relationship with the genre was a more favourable one. For instance, her interest in Wagner's *Tristan und Isolde* – particularly while she was writing *L'Amour de loin* – was confirmed in an interview in 2000:[4]

---

[1]   Other members included Eero Hämeenniemi (the first chairman), Magnus Lindberg, Tapani Länsiö, Jouni Kaipainen, Olli Kortekangas and Esa-Pekka Salonen. See Heiniö, 1995: 433; Korhonen, 2007: 174–5.

[2]   See Heiniö, 1995 and 1999. A critical view of opera was taken in particular by the European avant-garde. Boulez, for example, was famously provocative in his command to 'Blow up the opera houses!' (Heiniö, 1989: 67). Likewise, in 1971, Ligeti expressed his relationship with opera: 'I cannot, will not compose a traditional "opera"; for me the operatic genre is irrelevant today – it belongs to a historical period utterly different from present compositional situation' (in Griffiths, 1981: 248). Interestingly, Ligeti later wrote the stage work *Le Grand Macabre*, which is in fact a parody of traditional opera. At the same time, many composers did not completely abandon opera, but instead tried to look for new forms of stage work that avoided the headline 'opera' (see, for example, Heiniö, 1989: 67; Stoïanova 2006: 110).

[3]   The first operas to be called '*karvalakkiooppera*' were Sallinen's *Punainen viiva* (1978) and Kokkonen's *Viimeiset kiusaukset* (1975). See Heiniö, 1995: 434; Heinö, 1999: 32–7.

[4]   Also in this interview – the first she gave on *L'Amour de loin* – Saariaho highlighted thematic links between *Tristan* and *L'Amour de loin*. By 'thematic links' she was referring to their similar plots, but expressed doubts as to whether there were any musical similarities (Hautsalo, 2000a: 18). Just before the Helsinki premiere in 2004, the composer asked for no connections to be made with *Tristan* in the programme notes. However, I suggest elsewhere that there are in fact certain congruent musical elements in the works, such as their stream-like flow of endless musical textures (see Hautsalo, 2008b: 180–88).

I have always loved *Tristan* and I cannot really say how much it has contributed to my own music. I have had a page from *Tristan* hanging on the wall of my studio since 1978 and I have glanced at it over the years with different eyes. When I began writing Clémence's music, I looked again at the faded page hanging on the wall that was now twenty years old. On it, the lovers sing in German 'Isolde, Tristan Geliebte!' At just that moment I was trying to internalize the places of different vowels in my throat and I thought for a long time then about the high 'i' vowels Wagner had written (Hautsalo, 2000: 18; see also Saariaho, 2006: 131).

The fragment concerned is the beginning of Act II, scene 2 of *Tristan*, where an ecstatic love scene between the principal characters begins. Clearly *Tristan* has been an important influence on Saariaho since her student days.

Towards Opera: Multimedia

Although Saariaho was always interested in music and played a variety of instruments in her youth, she had also been fascinated by the visual arts since early childhood. She had synaesthetic abilities, seeing music as colours (Moisala, 2009: 2–4 and 55), as borne out in her earliest attempt at composing: a small sketch called *Keltaista ja hermostunutta* ('Something Yellow and Nervous'), since lost, for solo guitar.[5] The title of the piece thus shows how, already in her youth, the musical, the visual and the emotional were essentially bound together. Saariaho was educated at a Steiner school,[6] which encouraged individual creativity, and, before beginning to study composition at the Sibelius Academy in 1976, she also attended the University of Art and Design in Helsinki. Additionally, Saariaho was an avid reader of literature, and, with an absence of female composers as role models, she was influenced by women writers such as Virginia Woolf and Sylvia Plath (see Iitti, 2005; Moisala and Diamond, 2000). Thus three different forms of media – musical, visual and literary – interact from an early stage during Saariaho's development.

It is telling, then, that Saariaho mentions 'multimedia' as a possible way of approaching opera as an art form. Robert Morgan defines 'multimedia' as a form that mixes vocal and instrumental performances with other modes of artistic expression, such as acting, dance, mime, film and slides (Morgan, 1991: 448). Importantly, such a definition easily describes a variety of projects that Saariaho undertook in the 1980s and 1990s: projects that variously combine music, text, electronics, tape, video and dance. For instance, *Study for Life* (1981) for female voice and tape calls for various theatrical lighting effects (of particular interest given Saariaho's synaesthetic ability); she also planned for

---

[5]   Taken from an interview with Saariaho by the author, 29 November 2003.

[6]   It is apposite that 'the thing [Saariaho's former classmates] remember about Kaija is that she was always drawing' (taken from telephone conversation with Suurla, 31 December 2007).

scents to be discharged into the auditorium during the performance.[7] *Kollisionen* ('Collisions', 1984), on the other hand, presents a different kind of multimedia experience: a theatrical piece, written for percussion and live electronics (see, for example, Nieminen, 1994: 73). Consequently, it is worth noticing that, almost twenty years later, Saariaho planned multimedia elements for *L'Amour de loin*: her sketches reveal that, even at a fairly late stage in the composing process, Saariaho had planned to use video in the opera at the point of the sea voyage – the word 'film' appears in the margin of a sketch dated 28 December 1997.

Towards Opera: Diatonicism

For a student in the late 1970s, where modernism was the prevailing aesthetic ideology, and post-serialism the method used by the most predominant composers, writing opera must have seemed impossible. But attitudes and approaches gradually began to change, even among Saariaho's peer group. The move towards musical pluralism at the end of the 1980s and in the beginning of the 1990s was mirrored by similar moves in other countries, and with it came greater tolerance towards opera. In Finland, changes in attitudes were aided by Paavo Heininen, teacher and figurehead of the younger generation, who began composing opera himself in the mid-1980s. As Esa-Pekka Salonen concluded in 2006, the most important task of composers of his generation has been to find ways out of the backyard of modernism (Salonen, 2006: 137).

In his discussion of operatic art after World War II, Paul Griffiths states that 'Thematic, diatonic music is ready ground for the narrative metaphor, but there have been notable few successful atonal operas; those which exist have generally found some alternative to diatonic harmony as fuel for continuous forward motion, or have retained sufficient diatonicism to guarantee a certain dynamism' (Griffiths, 1981: 249). The new attitudes of the 'postmodern' age allowed the re-introduction of such principles, and for Saariaho, her research into timbre during the 1980s provided an additional and alternative source for such quasi-tonal 'dynamism' (see Saariaho, 1987).

Towards Opera: The Soprano Voice and Melody

From a musical perspective, the key individual stimulus for Saariaho has been the human voice; she prefers writing for female voice, because it is '[her] own

---

[7]   Taken from an interview with Saariaho by the author, 29 November 2003. Other multimedia projects include *Piipää* (1987), directed by Marikki Hakola, and composed in collaboration with Jean-Baptiste Barrière; the text for the work was written by Jouni Tommola. *Piipää* is actually described in Saariaho's list of works as a 'multimediashow' (see <www.fimic.fi/Saariaho>). Saariaho also recorded music for Joakim Groth's play *Skotten i Helsingfors* (1983), for *Kollisionen* (1984), and for the sound installation *La Dame à la licorne* (1993).

voice, a woman's voice' (Saariaho, in Hautsalo, 2000: 20). Most of her songs have been written for soprano,[8] and all four of her works for the stage composed in the twenty-first century cast a soprano in the lead role or in a key supporting role. In fact, her entire career as a composer began by writing vocal music for female voice. According to Pirkko Moisala, at the beginning of Saariaho's composition studies she 'could only compose songs and other vocal music inspired by literature and poems, but her teacher [Heininen] insisted that she began to write for instruments' (Moisala, 2009: 6). Nevertheless, her first publicly performed work was *Bruden* ('Bride', 1977), written for soprano and percussion to a text by the Finnish-Swedish modernist poet, Edith Södergran.

However, the most important trigger for future operas was the ballet *Maa*, commissioned by the Finnish National Opera in the late 1980s, and given its first performance in 1991. By writing for an opera house, it was possible for Saariaho to familiarize herself with such a venue as an instrument of expression (Hautsalo, 2000: 17). There was also a change in Saariaho's musical language in the vocal works of the mid-1990s, starting with *Château de l'âme* (1995) and *Lonh* (1996): melody was no longer a forbidden musical device. It is fair to say that by coming to understand the opera house, and by developing the melodic dimension of her musical discourse, Saariaho was now in a position to compose opera.

Past in Present: The Musical Topic

Before *L'Amour de loin* and *Adriana Mater* are examined in detail, it is useful to set out the semiotic-hermeneutic theory of musical topics used in the remainder of the chapter. Originally, the Greek word *topos* (plural: *topoi*) meant a place, a region, or something commonplace. Used in a musical context, according to Fritz Noske, 'a musical *topos* may have a descriptive or imitative configuration', but 'it generally communicates in a purely intellectual way, i.e. through persistent association with a certain idea, a situation or concept', and 'is transmitted from one generation to the next' (Noske, 1977: 172).[9] Musical topics thus make use of traditional and recognizable rhythmic, melodic or harmonic figures (see Noske, 1977: 172; also Ratner, 1980: 9), in order to orient the listener to particular semantic meanings. Raymond Monelle refers to the ubiquity of such topics by pointing out that,

---

[8] Of Saariaho's entire output of vocal music, only three songs have been written for male voice (baritone); these appear alongside two songs for soprano in her *Tempest Songbook* (1992–2004).

[9] During the Baroque period, a 'doctrine of figures' (German: *Figurenlehre*) had already been developed in the German-speaking world. This partly corresponds to the present-day Anglo-Saxon 'topic theory'. A notable contemporary commentator on the doctrine of figures is Dietrich Bartel (see Bartel, 1997); in this study, I shall refer to several of Bartel's 'figures', but for the sake of conformity I will refer to them as 'topics'.

> Some topics are to be found throughout our culture, from the sixteenth century through to the twenty-first. Although musical topics have acquired their specific theoretical articulation rather late, it has always been possible to recognize associative passages or patterns in music, which have been transferred from one work or from one style to another (Monelle, 2006: 4).

As Monelle concludes, 'Western music has signified through topical reference throughout its history' (Monelle, 2000: 40).

Originally, the theory of musical topics was intended for the semantic analysis of Viennese classical instrumental music, and was formulated in the early 1980s by Leonard G. Ratner (1980). From this, Monelle (2000 and 2006) has developed his own semiotic application, based firstly on C.S. Peirce's (1940) and secondly on Ferdinand Saussure's (1915) concept of the semiotic sign.[10] Monelle's starting point is the idea that a musical topic parallels the concept of the sign. Following Peirce, he demonstrates how a topic can therefore function either as an icon – whereby sounds directly imitate a signified object (such as the musical imitation of a cuckoo) – or as an index – whereby sounds imply associated meanings (as a cuckoo might imply the onset of spring) (Monelle, 2000: 14ff). And following Saussure, Monelle demonstrates that a topic consists of two dimensions – the signifier (content) and the signified (expression) (Monelle, 2006: 22). Each of these principles offers a different viewpoint from which to analyse a musical topic, and, as the remainder of the chapter unfolds, they will be used variously.[11]

As topic theory was originally conceived to analyse tonal music, it is not applied so frequently to post-tonal repertoire. Yet despite the lack of tonal harmony in Saariaho's musical language, her operas often make repeated reference to *recognizable* musical gestures, passages and patterns; the structure, form, direction, rhythm or instrumentation of these passages resonates closely with certain standard musical conventions – or topics. At times these reinforce textual content, but at other times they recur without any links with the text at all. Importantly, these topics often have their precise equivalents in a tonal frame of reference. Thus, the aim for the remainder of this chapter is to highlight the strong cultural-historical connections whereby *L'Amour de loin* and *Adriana Mater* continue the tradition of Western classical music and opera.

L'Amour de loin

Since the early songs, a central theme of Saariaho's work has been that of love. During the 1990s, her major vocal works – *Château de l'âme* (1995), *Lonh* (1996)

---

[10]   Musical significance from the viewpoint of semiotics has also been examined by Hatten (1994 and 2004) and Tarasti (1994), while topic theory has been applied by (amongst others) Allanbrook (1983), Agawu (1991), Kallberg (1996) and Välimäki (2005).

[11]   Gadamer (2004) exemplifies a similar approach. Monelle refers to his own musical analysis as 'topical hermeneutics' (Monelle, 2006: 8).

and *Oltra mar* (1999–2000) – all focus on this subject. *L'Amour de loin* ('Love from Afar') follows in this vein, and deals with the idealized, unobtainable love between a man and a woman, mirroring the cultural-historical context and plot of Wagner's *Tristan und Isolde*. For like *Tristan*, Saariaho also focuses on love in a medieval, feudal, social system; a love that ends unhappily with the male lead dying in the arms of his beloved.

Set in the twelfth century, *L'Amour de loin* is based on the life story of a troubadour – Jaufré Rudel, Prince of Blaye in Occitania, southern France. Weary of his pleasurable but empty life, Jaufré hears from a Pilgrim about a woman who lives across the sea – Clémence, Countess of Tripoli. On the basis of what the Pilgrim tells him, Jaufré falls in love with the woman and, pretending to be a Crusader, sets off to meet her. However, the troubadour falls ill on the voyage and dies in the arms of his beloved when he reaches harbour. Clémence decides to withdraw to a convent and devote the remainder of her life to God.

Commissioned jointly by the Salzburg Festival, the *Théâtre du Châtelet* in Paris and the Santa Fe Festival in the US, *L'Amour de loin* was written on a tight schedule between 1999 and 2000, although the work had been coming to maturity throughout the 1990s (Hautsalo, 2000: 17). Its three lead characters – lyric soprano, lyric baritone and mezzo-soprano – are supported by a female chorus, representing the women of Tripoli who accompany Clémence, and a male chorus, who represent Jaufré's friends. The instrumentation follows that of a traditional symphony orchestra, albeit with an expanded percussion section. However, this is supported by pre-recorded electronic materials, which consist of 80 passages, triggered by the pianist throughout the performance.[12] The opera is cast in five acts without an interval, and lasts for roughly two hours. It opens with an extensive overture, which introduces the main musical elements of the opera and sets up the musical dramaturgy in miniature. Subsequent events proceed largely in the form of musical prose, using recitative-like dialogues or monologues.

The Historical Jaufré Rudel and the Medieval Background of the Plot

There are no precise dates for the life and death of the historical Jaufré Rudel, but from various sources it has been possible to date his active days as a troubadour from 1125 to c. 1148. Six of his texts survive – three of which deal with the theme of 'love from afar';[13] a short and partly fictional account of Jaufré's life – *Vida* – also survives from the thirteenth century, written after his death.[14] Jaufré's story and the

---

[12] All characters have their own electronic 'chords'. As such, these chords function almost as leitmotifs (Hautsalo 2008b: 46). For more technical details about the pre-recorded material in the opera, see Battier and Nouno (2003).

[13] See, for example, Pickens (1978), van der Werf (1983) or Niiranen (1998). Some sources suggest that seven poems have in fact survived (see Gaunt and Kay, 1999: 286).

[14] The author of *Vida* is unknown; it can be found in four different collections of songs (see Pickens, 1978: 53).

Example 6.1   Jaufré Rudel's troubadour melody and its use in
**   *L'Amour de loin***

a) Version of Original Melody

Lanquan li jorn son,   lonc   en   may,   M'es belhs dous   chans, d'au-zelhs   de   lonh

b) *L'Amour de loin*, Act I, scene 1

101   Aparler   du___   bon-heur   j'ai app-ris,   à ê-tre   heu - reuxpoint n'ai app- ris.___

idea of an unattainable love have subsequently run through Western literary history, appearing both in novels and in dramas. Petrarch (1304–74) mentions Jaufré in his sonnets, while in 1575 Jehan de Notredame published the story in connection with biographies of the troubadours. Jaufré's story has been taken up and retold by several Romantic writers, including Algernon Charles Swinburne, Giosuè Carducci, Ludvig Uhland, Heinrich Heine and Stendahl.[15] The theme is also touched upon in Monteverdi's *Combattimento di Tancredi et Clorinda* (c. 1626). The libretto for *L'Amour de loin* is based on Jaufré's own poem, *Lanquan li jorn son lonc en may* ('When the days are long in May'), and also on the thirteenth-century *Vida*.[16]

Four melodies by the historical Jaufré survive, including that of *Lanquan li jorn*. Although Saariaho does not quote this melody directly, she does paraphrase it in some of Jaufré's material (Hautsalo, 2008b: 64–7 and 98). This lends a distinctly diatonic, modal flavour to the sonorous identity of Jaufré's material in *L'Amour de loin*, despite the overall modernist idiom (see Example 6.1).[17] Functioning like a Wagnerian leitmotif, this imparts to Jaufré's material a distinguishing sonorous identity with respect to other characters: the music of the Pilgrim frequently features a descending motif from piccolo to double bass; Clémence is frequently set against high-register instruments, such as bells, triangle, piccolo, harp and violins (Hautsalo, 2008b: 145–51 and 175ff).

L'Amour de loin opens with Jaufré composing a song and accompanying himself on the lute while his friends try to interest him in entertainments that no longer amuse him. In this situation, we hear a tarantella – originally a Neapolitan

---

    [15]   See, for example, Haapanen-Tallgren, 1925: 69–86, or Wolf and Rosenstein, 1983: 95 and 102–7.

    [16]   The Frenchman Jacques Roubaud was initially commissioned to write the libretto, but subsequently withdrew from the project to be replaced at the last moment by the half-French, half-Lebanese writer Amin Maalouf (see Hautsalo, 2008b: 32).

    [17]   Noske's concept of 'sonorous individuality' refers to the musical unity of an opera character (see Noske, 1977: 19).

Example 6.2   *L'Amour de loin* – **tarantella as topic**

folk dance in 6/8 or 3/8 time (see Example 6.2).[18] Because the tarantella imitates another musical style, it can be deemed an indexical topic (see Monelle, 2006: 29). The tarantella in *L'Amour de loin* can be interpreted in many ways. For instance, its sharp rhythm might be interpreted as a reinforcement of the text – at this point, Jaufré's friends are expressing their astonishment that he has changed, and has stopped taking part in their shared activities. But from the signifier/ signified viewpoint, it is not simply the rhythmic dimension that operates as the signifier, but also the presence of certain instruments. In particular, the use of tambourine, which reinforces the rhythm of the tarantella, also loosely suggests something 'medieval'; it gives the scene the feeling of a specific place and time.[19] The tambourine is the signifier of the tarantella topic together with the 6/8 rhythm.

The tarantella can also be examined from a wider perspective, whereby dance topics can be said to parallel different social classes. According to Andrea Batta, in *Don Giovanni*, Mozart brings out the social distinctions between people by using the minuet to mark out the upper class – it is danced by masked guests Anna, Elvira and Don Ottavio – while he uses the *ländler* for the servants' dance (Batta, 2001: 348). Likewise in *L'Amour de loin*, the tarantella – which originates in folk music –can be seen as making a distinction between Jaufré and his friends: Jaufré is the lord of the manor, but his friends, despite their friendship, have lower social status. This hierarchy is communicated above all through the music: the popular 'folksy' tarantella belongs to the subordinates, and stands in contrast to the music of Jaufré himself, which follows the conventions of troubadour music in its well-developed and refined nature.[20]

---

[18]   It is also said that the name refers to the poisonous spider *Lycosa tarentula*, whose bite is believed to inflict tarantism on the victim, an illness which causes the victim to move about violently in a way that resembles dancing (see Schwandt, 2008).

[19]   In the same way as the castanets used for the inn scene in *Carmen* suggest something 'Spanish'.

[20]   A similar contrast occurs in Act IV, scene 3, when Jaufré's friends make fun of him because they think he is afraid of the sea.

Example 6.3   *L'Amour de loin* – the noble horse as lord-of-the-manor
texture

Chivalry played a key role in maintaining the *status quo* within the feudal
system of southern France in the twelfth century, and Jaufré's status as lord of
the manor would have involved a range of chivalrous pursuits such as hunting.
Monelle draws particular attention to 'the Noble Horse' – a recurring musical
topic – wherein the signifier is rhythmic, directly indicating a galloping horse as
the signified (Monelle, 2000: 5). While the libretto for *L'Amour de loin* does not
mention horses, horsemanship or riding, Saariaho does allude to horses in the
music of the opera. Through the whole of the introduction to Act III, a regular
6/8 rhythm can be heard, written for marimba, vibraphone, harp and piano. This
sound-world is iconic of horses, and contributes to a 'lord-of-the-manor' texture in
the opera (see Example 6.3). Thus in *L'Amour de loin* we can hear a musical horse,
and we can imagine the fictitious Jaufré Rudel to be riding around his demesne,
engaged in chivalrous pursuits.

Despair and the Pianto

L'Amour de loin contains a good deal of dysphoric, negative emotion. Monelle
suggests that music has its own conventions for describing such states, the most
concrete and easily perceivable of which is the *pianto* topic – an interval of a
falling second, used as a sighing gesture to indicate tears, complaint, sorrow or
death (Monelle, 2000: 1, 17–18 and 66–79). The *pianto* (Italian, *piangere*: to cry)
can be traced as far back as the sixteenth century madrigal (ibid.: 66–73), but the

Example 6.4 *L'Amour de loin* – the *pianto* **topic**

topic also appears in contemporary music.[21] Since the *pianto* is an imitation of an actual phenomenon – a falling tear – it could be termed an iconic topic (ibid.: 17). From the point of view of the signifier/signified division, the falling second acts as a simple signifier in its reference to a falling tear; the signified is just as simple in its reference to a dysphoric mood.

The *pianto* contrasts with other topics Saariaho uses insofar as it occurs in its original form despite the atonal surroundings in which it appears. In *L'Amour de loin*, the *pianto* is written primarily for the chorus, whose role is to comment on the events taking place in the opera. For instance, it is heard in Act II, scene 2, sung by the chorus, to indicate Clémence's loss of her childhood for ever (Example 6.4). Although the *pianto* topic usually appears in the context of text dealing with complaint or sorrow, it can also be associated with hesitation and concern. For instance, it accompanies the doubts that come into Clémence's mind in Act II, scene 2, when she begins to think about her own unworthiness in relation to the troubadour.

Topics of Death

Jaufré Rudel dies with his love from afar still unrequited. A range of musical topics – iconic and indexical – that refer to his death are used in the latter stages of *L'Amour de loin*. Jaufré's death in Act V is the central event in the opera, but is referred to musically prior to this moment. The most evident topic of death in *L'Amour de loin* is *catabasis*, originally isolated by the German theorists of *Figurenlehre* (lately Dietrich Bartel, 1997). During the fourteenth and fifteenth centuries, *catabasis* referred, as Benestad (1978: 116) has argued, to death, the grave or hell. Thus, this descending figure is iconic in nature. In *L'Amour de loin*, *catabasis* appears several times, always as a descending scale, and always in

---

[21] For instance, Torvinen has demonstrated its use in Erik Bergman's work *Colori ed improvvisazioni* (Torvinen, 2007: 225–36). The *pianto* topic is particularly characteristic of opera: for example, it appears in *Don Giovanni* when Donna Anna finds her father dead; and in *La traviata* when Germont forces Violetta to relinquish her beloved (see Karbusicky, 1986: 66).

Example 6.5   *L'Amour de loin* – catabasis

connection with text dealing with Jaufré's death or dying.[22] It appears first when Jaufré and his friends face the storm in Act IV, scene 3, foreseeing the forthcoming death of the troubadour (Example 6.5).

In Act V, scene 2, the dying Jaufré is carried to the castle; his passing is presaged by a soft and slow 3/4 rocking rhythm, which is heard mainly on Jaufré's own instrument, the harp, softened by a faint string texture. The rocking cradle song gently lulls Jaufré to eternal rest; to death (see Example 6.6). The *berceuse*, or cradle song, is a recurrent topic in many musical cultures throughout the world, usually heard in real-life situations where a mother sings her child to sleep. But from the earliest examples, the cradle song has not only been associated new life and childhood, but also with death. In ancient mythology, for instance, sleep and death – Hypnos and Thanatos – are brothers (see Pentikäinen, 1990: 183). Transferred to classical music, too, the cradle song frequently refers to death as well as sleep, as occurs here in *L'Amour de loin*.[23]

As Jaufré's death comes ever closer, the score is marked 'cease playing, one after another' (bar 448) and *morendo* (gradually dying away) (bar 458). Thus the music for the death scene represents the gradual ebbing away of life from

[22]   There are two kinds of *catabasis* topics in *L'Amour de loin*: they either foresee or frame the death (Hautsalo 2008a: 129–32).

[23]   Particularly in Finnish opera, the cradle song often refers to death. For example, this is the case in Armas Launis's *Kullervo* (written in 1930 and based on the *Kalevala* epic), Aulis Sallinen's *Horseman* (1975), and Olli Kortekangas' *Daddy's Girl* (2007) (see Hautsalo, 2010).

Example 6.6 *L'Amour de loin* – cradle song

the human body. As Jaufré exchanges his last few frail words with Clémence, there is a steady repeating microtonal motif written for the first violins, which remains within the region of B♮ then likewise dies away (bars 438–62). A further prominent icon of death is the rhythm-based 'heart motif', which is heard on the timpani to suggest a beating heart: it ceases at the moment of Jaufré's death (bar 461). The flute, too, is used iconically at this moment: a small gesture made by blowing into the instrument imitates the snuffing out of a candle (bar 462).

Immediately after Jaufré's death, the full chorus sings a chorale (bars 474–519); its chant-like, Lutheran style acts as an indexical topic of death (Example 6.7 overleaf). The chorale proceeds in common time, or *alla breve*, with brief 3/4 interjections: there is a strong tradition of the *alla breve* chorale especially in church music, often indexically signifying lofty, solemn or ponderous subjects. Clémence's material further supports a chorale interpretation, as she refers explicitly to the context of Christian prayer: 'You are goodness and mercy, you are grace'. The chorus repeats the text, swapping it between registers. Saariaho's

Example 6.7   *L'Amour de loin* – chorale

reserved method of writing for four voices refers to the devout Lutheran chorale: this music is pious, and it is sorrowful.

Adriana Mater

After the poetic *L'Amour de loin*, Saariaho wanted to write a work that would be firmly planted in the stark reality of our own age (Saariaho, in Hautsalo, 2008b: 12). In her second opera, Saariaho thus distanced herself from the romantic-nostalgic idiom of its predecessor: *Adriana Mater* ('Adriana the Mother') tells a brutal story of the ravages of war on the fate of individuals and, in particular, focuses on women as victims of war. Act I follows the young Adriana (mezzo-soprano), who lives with her sister Refka (soprano) in a village within a war zone. The home defence forces are on standby, with Tsargo (bass-baritone), a former schoolmate of Adriana, as one of its soldiers. Adriana fends off advances by a drunken Tsargo, but he later comes back and rapes her as revenge. Nine months pass and a son, Yonas, is born as a result of the rape. Act II takes place 17 years later, by which time Yonas (tenor) has grown up. Tsargo returns home from the war, blind and crippled. Yonas is told who his father is, and the circumstances surrounding his conception; at first he wants to kill Tsargo, but then thinks again – after all, the man is his father. The libretto – which was written by Amin Maalouf, Saariaho's librettist from *L'Amour de loin* – is not based on an existing story, and sets the opera in the present day ('an unprepossessing quarter before the war').[24] Like its predecessor, love remains a central in *Adriana Mater*, but now it is an all-embracing maternal love: the love between a mother and her child in exceptional circumstances.

Ivanka Stoïjanova points out that, in contrast to *L'Amour de loin*, *Adriana Mater* is a musical drama with a strong moral dimension (Stoïjanova, 2006: 28). In dealing with war as something grotesque, something that distorts people, *Adriana Mater* is an anti-war opera with a clear political undertone. And in examining one woman's experiences of war, the work also takes a stand on behalf of women and children: the opera is focalized from a woman's viewpoint, and includes themes that are rarely seen in opera, such as the intimate relationship between mother and child, and the painful and taboo subject of rape. Saariaho has always tried to avoid being labelled as a 'woman composer' or a 'feminist composer', preferring to be known simply as a 'composer' (Moisala, 2008: 28–9), but by addressing themes particularly associated with the female gender, this opera could be said to take a feminist stance.

Written in 2004 and 2005, *Adriana Mater* lasts roughly two hours, and is dedicated to the memory of Saariaho's own mother.[25] Its two acts further subdivide

---

[24]   Maalouf has said in various contexts that the location for the opera could well be the Balkans; the former Yugoslavia. See, for example, Hautsalo, 2008b: 12.

[25]   It is also dedicated to Peter Sellars, who directed the premieres of Saariaho's two operas.

into seven 'tableaux';[26] it can therefore be conceived of as a *Stationendrama* ('Station drama') given its independent, episodic passages, which follow one another in a loosely linked manner (Stoïanova, 2006: 27). Instead of the diatonic-modal flavour of its predecessor, the musical idiom of *Adriana Mater* is extremely dark and depressed. The four lead characters are supported by a mixed chorus and an orchestra with an expanded percussion section. And like *L'Amour de loin*, the sound-world of *Adriana* again includes electronic elements, but, on this occasion, there is no pre-recorded material: sounds are edited electronically in live performance.[27]

Topics of Lament and Cry

The overture of *Adriana Mater* differs from typical opera overtures: it includes the chorus, which foresees the terrible events of the opera using the *pianto* topic, as described in *L'Amour de loin*. The *pianto* is heard prominently throughout this overture: the chorus sings the phoneme 'A', reinforcing the sigh-content of the topic.[28] Similar to the opening scene of *L'Amour de loin*, where Jaufré Rudel is singing and playing, Act I begins with Adriana singing a song: *'une sorte de vieux rondeau'* (an 'old rondo'). Her melancholic song refers to sensual pleasure, which gives some indication of Adriana's state of mind: Adriana is a girl on the threshold of adulthood and hungry for life; she sinks into an erotic dream, failing to understand the drunken Tzargo's aggression. There is a static string texture in the background to this song that creates a threatening atmosphere; the violas stand out from this by repeating the *pianto* topic.

In fact, there are many instances throughout the opera of the *pianto* topic appearing particularly on viola: this instrument is associated with the character of Adriana. But wherever it is used, it is always associated with something negative – sorrow, threat or death. For example, at the point of the rape, the lamenting *pianto* topic is sounded by the chorus. As the extreme form of this topic, Saariaho uses pure sigh – written in the score as 'inhale and exhale' – without any pitch (see Example 6.8).

Topics of War

War is a psycho-material state in *Adriana Mater* that shapes the events, characters and musical soundscape of the work. Historically, there is a genre of 'war operas': Handel's *Rinaldo*, with its Crusade theme; Berlioz's *Les Troyens*; Prokofiev's

---

[26]   The opera is defined in a subheading as '*Opéra en sept tableaux*'.

[27]   This technique is used particularly in the opera's four dream scenes, where chorus material is added to alter the spatial effect and to add a feeling of surrealism. Saariaho's subsequent monodrama, *Emilie*, also makes use of live electronics.

[28]   A texture built up using a similar *pianto* topic is repeated later in Act I, at the beginning of the dream sequence, where it leads into an oppressive nightmare.

Example 6.8 *Adriana Mater* – use of the *pianto* topic in its extreme form

War and Peace; and B.A. Zimmermann's *Die Soldaten*. Monelle offers extensive analysis of the military topic in eighteenth-century music (Monelle, 2006: 113–81). Although *Adriana Mater* is set on the edge of a battlefield, the war does not have its own music or specific theme. Nevertheless, Saariaho describes the war through an enormous sonority created by heavy orchestration, dark tone colours, and dynamic extremes of *tutti fff* passages.

Example 6.9 *Adriana Mater* – execution topic

At the same time, war and violence are also given a more concrete expression in *Adriana Mater*. One important example from the viewpoint of topic theory is the use of a rhythmic theme for side drum, used in both acts, but in different contexts. In Act I, scene 2, this tremolo-and-triplet figure has powerful and oppressive associations, referring to military marches and even to the drum-roll often used to portray executions in film. Thus, the theme could be called an execution topic; it is indexical as it is associated with the wider genre of military topics (see Monelle, 2006: 113–60).[29] In the first act of the opera, the execution topic is used to refer to Tzargo and to his military rank: during the war he is the 'Protector', with the right to decide who should live and who should die (Example 6.9).

---

[29] The execution topic can be found in other operas: for example, in Puccini's *Tosca*, it is heard in the third act when Cavaradossi is to be executed. It also appears throughout the whole of the last tableau of Poulenc's *Dialogues of the Carmelites*, when the nuns are executed.

Example 6.10   *Adriana Mater* – musical icon of the rape

Icons of Rape

One of the defining features of *Adriana Mater* is its inclusion of a rape scene. Although opera as an artform has historically been used to confront human weakness, sickness, violence and death, rape has largely remained a taboo subject.[30] But in *Adriana Mater*, the rape is central: it is the point of departure from which all subsequent events ensue. Although the libretto does not mention rape directly, it is given its own musical expression in the work. First, the chorus senses the approaching tragedy: the women's chorus communicates despair with a *pianto* topic written for the phoneme 'O' (bars 195–203). Then, in the rape scene itself, an extremely loud mass of sound with a pulsating rhythm increases in density several times to presage the act of sexual violence. The scene culminates in a musical description of the rape itself: a series of blows marked *sffz*. We thus have a musical imitation of the sexual act; a musical icon of rape (Example 6.10). As Tzargo rapes Adriana, her singing voice metamorphoses into an uncontrolled shout of '*Non!*', for which no pitch is written in the score; the chorus articulates a shout of horror culminating again in the phoneme 'O' (bars 392–6). The last '*Non!*' by Adriana and chorus is framed by the snare drum rhythm (bars 387–406) – the execution topic – emphasizing the horrific nature of this moment.

---

[30]   Benjamin Britten's *The Rape of Lucretia* (1946) is one notable exception, yet, even here, Britten distances himself from the act of raw violence by placing it in the Ancient Etruscan era.

Topics of Hope: Nightingale, Cradle Song and the Heart Motif

Despite the dreadful events in *Adriana Mater*, the work also contains elements of hope. This is reflected in the subtitle of the third scene in Act I: 'Two Hearts'. Several months have elapsed since the rape, and there is a conversation between Adriana and Refka about what has happened since: the young Adriana has been left pregnant, but has decided to keep the child. Although one might think this is a dark, depressing scene, it is in fact filled with hope, as suggested by a musical gesture referring to spring and awakening nature. This takes the form of a trill on the piccolo, iconic of birdsong (see Example 6.11); it can be considered as an example of Monelle's bird song topic, itself associated with the great pastoral genre (Monelle, 2006: 235–6).[31] The same scene also contains a musical reference to the unborn child: the conversation between Refka and Adriana is framed by fragments of the indexical cradle song topic (as seen earlier in *L'Amour de loin*). It is used here without any connotations of death; rather, it symbolizes the lulling to sleep of a child. Adriana has accepted the idea that she is soon to give birth.

Example 6.11   *Adriana Mater* – nightingale as topic of hope

A further topic that connects the two operas is the 'heart motif': it is used in *L'Amour de loin* as a musical icon referring to death, but acts as a topic of hope in *Adriana* (see Hautsalo, 2008a: 119–22). In fact, this motif is used frequently in Saariaho's operas, and was used for the first time in her orchestral work *Du cristal* (Moisala, 2009: 102). The heart motif is a dotted rhythmic theme for percussion – usually timpani – that imitates the beating of a heart; it therefore functions as an iconic topic (see Example 6.12 overleaf). Saariaho has explained that the idea for the heart motif emerged when she herself was pregnant with her first child, and was thinking about the idea of two hearts beating inside a woman's body: the third scene's subtitle, 'Two Hearts', comes from this idea (Hautsalo 2008b: 15). This motif appears in several scenes, first when Adriana is expecting the baby, and later when mother and son are together. Its first appearance occurs in scene 1, where it leads up to Adriana's song (bars 56–8); it returns in the 'Two Hearts' scene, played by the bass drum when Adriana is

---

[31]   Saariaho has used bird themes in the titles of several works, and frequently imitates bird song in her music. Examples include the flute concerto, *Aile du songe* (2000–01), the solo flute work, *Laconisme de l'aile* (1982), and *... sah den Vögeln* (1981), for soprano and ensemble. In both operas, the piccolo refers iconically to the nightingale and indexically to the awakening spring.

Example 6.12   *Adriana Mater* – the heart motif

defending her right to keep the baby (bars 116–21) and when she describes how she has heard the heartbeat of her baby (bars 127–43).

If the heart motif is heard as silent, cautious and hardly noticeable in Act I, in Act II it occurs in a totally different manner. In scene 4, when Yonas accuses his mother of not telling him the truth about his father, the heart motif is played loudly and dissonantly by marimba, bringing the relationship between the two into focus (bars 45–8). The motif now appears in fast quavers: Adriana is horrified when the secret has been revealed.

The Dual: A Synthesis of Topics

Act II, scene 6 – 'Dual' – describes the 17-year-old Yonas's first encounter with his father, Tzargo, and brings together a range of topics heard earlier in the opera. First, the side drum execution topic is used as Yonas addresses his father: Tzargo's answer refers to the past, at which point the topic is heard as a macabre echo (bars 21–34). It is also heard later in the scene, when Yonas threatens Tzargo, demanding to know if circumstances led to the rape of his mother. Hence, the topic of execution performs two functions in *Adriana Mater*: it refers to Tzargo as a murderer and as a rapist.

As in *L'Amour de loin*, death is written into the musical textures of *Adriana Mater*: the most striking topic of death is again *catabasis*. Throughout *Adriana*, Saariaho connects *catabasis* particularly to Tzargo, even though he does not actually die in the opera. The most alarming statement is in Act II, scene 6 (bars 115–16), when Tzargo is talking about his own death (Example 6.13). This is followed by a statement of the *pianto* topic (bar 124), as Yonas accuses Tzargo: *'Que tu sois résigné à payer pour tes crimes ne fais pas de toi un innocent'* ('Just because you are willing to pay for your crimes does not make you innocent'). In the end, Adriana is not the only victim: they are all victims, even Tzargo. Finally, the heart motif is re-stated following the discussion between father and son, now scored for the darker timpani and bass drum (bars 193–206).

Aspects of Love

Saariaho's stage works consistently deal with themes characteristic of traditional opera: love, God, hate, violence and death. As noted earlier, different aspects of love form the central theme in *L'Amour de loin*: at the heart of the opera is the love and longing between a man and a woman, a love that approaches the transcendental. It is clear that *Adriana Mater*, too, is about a deep love, but now

Example 6.13 *Adriana Mater* – catabasis

this love is confused and contradictory. Adriana refuses the abortion since she already loves her unborn son, even though the child is conceived as a result of sexual violence. The sisters, Adriana and Refka, love each other, even though Refka accuses Adriana for the rape. And Yonas loves his mother and also his aunt, even though they did not tell him the truth about his father.

Most interesting of all is the relationship between Yonas and his father. Why does the former stop from killing Tzargo, even though he now knows the truth? Is that love? The French philosopher Emmanuel Levinas, who has dealt with questions of Otherness and love, says when discussing fatherhood that, 'Paternity is the relationship with a stranger who, entirely while being Other, is myself' (Levinas, 2000: 91). This may be of relevance to Yonas's state of mind: Tzargo, a rapist and a murderer – and his father – is the Other, but also himself. By killing Tzargo, Yonas would metaphorically kill himself. So in Act II, scene 7, when Yonas finally confesses he could not kill his father, Tzargo, Adriana ultimately feels relieved. The heart motif, played now on timpani, appears for the last time (bars 596–600): it connects the mother and the son more tightly than ever before. Consequently, this theme expands to become the all-encompassing core motif of the entire work.

Whispers from the Past

At the start of a new decade, Kaija Saariaho is one of the most sought-after composers in the world. She is regularly commissioned to write orchestral and chamber music as well as works for the stage. Her success as an opera composer is quite extraordinary, evidenced by numerous international performances and by the positive reviews – almost amounting to eulogies in some cases – which she has received. *Adriana Mater*, for example, has been seen in both Europe and the US, and the premiere of *L'Amour de loin* led to some eight completely new productions. In 2000, critics at both the *New York Times* and the *BBC Music Magazine* voted

L'Amour de loin the best opera of the year (see Hautsalo, 2008a: 2). How Saariaho has come to reach such a successful position is worth reflecting upon, helping us to draw some conclusions. As mentioned earlier, her compositional development gradually shifted towards creating large-scale stage works, despite a long-standing commitment to modernist and post-serialist concerns dating back to the 1980s. On the other hand, even during that early phase in her career, Saariaho engaged with multimedia, interdisciplinary approaches: painting, light, mime, text and electronically modified material. Developing and fully integrating a narrative element into her music made it possible for her to create larger, unified entities for the stage.

These preoccupations with narrative concerns have changed Saariaho's musical idiom and expression. As this chapter demonstrates, the libretto is not the only means by which these operatic works achieve a sense of narrative: musical topics and icons also support and underline this process – sometimes even telling a story of their own. Certain conventions in Western opera, such as love scenes, *travesti* roles, or *deus ex machina* mechanisms, alongside semantic icons – *pianto* for sorrow and crying, *catabasis* for death and the grave, for instance – have always been in use. The musical topics within Saariaho's works, often modified into the musical language of our time, could be described as whispers from the past: a link between tradition and the composer's individual expression.

A musical-semantic analysis of Saariaho's two operas reveals a solid adherence to some of the historical conventions that have been in existence since opera first emerged in the seventeenth century. Conveyed through the thematic and musical structures she deploys, the purpose of this approach is not to identify the composer's intentions, but to interpret her works within a specific frame of reference, in a search for musical signification and meaning. What is at issue, therefore, is a particular perspective, constructed by and through this research: an interpretation rather than any absolute truth. Topic theory offers the opportunity to untie some of these musical knots. This opening up and increased understanding of different historical layers is especially important within a genre where the musical language remains relatively challenging for the listener.

Based on the modernist aesthetic of uniqueness, the musical language of today is not necessarily well suited to operatic composition. Elements of periodic structure, repetition and a predominance of melodic writing, alongside the requisite emotional and dramatic dimensions of this music, are still the basic materials of opera; yet in many ways these traits are at variance with post-war, modernist ideals. Saariaho may be seen as a pioneer in this regard, preserving the essentials of operatic conventions but without compromising the originality of her personal aesthetic. Her musical language offers a blend of expressiveness and dramatic tension; this forms a motivating, driving force in the operas.

'The nightmare of modernism', as Raymond Monelle has called it, no longer monopolizes the aesthetics of contemporary music (Monelle, 2006: 273). Kaija Saariaho seems to have brought us out from this nightmare, so that composers do not need to see opera as being directly at odds with their musical language, as did the generation of post-war modernists and their heirs. Rather, opera today can be a highly effective platform for contemporary composers, allowing them to create and experiment in a more pluralistic manner. Overall, it appears as if these whispers from the past are now contributing to the operatic narratives of the future, and they are doing so with a level of success that is appreciated by a significantly wide range of audiences.

Dialogues

Chapter 7
Dualities and Dialogues: Saariaho's Concertos

Tim Howell

Concertare: (i) 'to contend, dispute, debate';
(ii) 'to work together with someone'.

The concerto is one of the most long-standing and enduring of all musical genres. Despite the enormous changes of style and language that characterize its evolution, an apparently infinite adaptability has ensured a continued relevance for contemporary music. Whereas the 'symphony' is often shunned as being outdated by those engaged with modernist concerns, the 'concerto' does not carry the same historical baggage and many composers today still find new ways of approaching concerto-like preoccupations. The attraction of the solo concerto – which pits the individual against the mass, exploring issues of dramatic conflict, dialogue and resolution – seems undiminished in its appeal; this is a genre that quite directly 'speaks' to its audience, often by evoking extra-musical associations. For Kaija Saariaho, it has always occupied a special place in her thinking and thus provides a useful focus for discussions of aesthetic conception, compositional process and listener perceptions. In an article entitled 'Some Thoughts on my Concertos', she speaks of the value of collaborating with particular performers – 'the style of a concerto is always born of a particular interest not only in the instrument but also in a specific soloist' – subscribing to a tradition that seems as relevant now as was ever the case (Saariaho, 2005).[1] The contradictory definitions of 'concerto' given above are creatively synthesized in this process. Musical conflicts so central to the genre are paradoxically the result of a concerted effort: combining forces with the soloist to discover new possibilities. Duality in the actual composition arises from dialogue in the act of composition.

Saariaho goes on to explain something of her aesthetic stance regarding concerto writing:

> Even though each work has extra-musical associations attached to it, this does not mean that I strive to describe these things in my music. It has sometimes been claimed in print that I need an extra-musical impulse as the seed for my music. I would prefer to say that, in my consciousness, music is strongly connected with other senses and that I am only partly aware of these connections. Human

[1]   I am grateful to Andrew Bentley for translating Kaija Saariaho's article, 'Some Thoughts on my Concertos', which appeared in Sivuoja-Gunaratnam, 2005.

breathing, bird flight, continuous changes in light, the rhythms and smells of the sea have all produced materials for my concertos, but when I process them at my work desk they become 'just' the sounding materials, rhythms and pitches, with which I operate (Saariaho, 2005).

This is especially significant for a composer who values titles so highly: 'When I feel I have the right title, I can focus my material. The title is very important for feeding my imagination' (in Beyer, 2000b: 6). Saariaho's first concerto, *Amers* for cello, ensemble and electronics (1992), is a good example; the title here means 'sea-marks' (more typically, 'landmarks'), echoing the 'rhythms and smells of the sea' as mentioned above. 'It is a metaphor. I often make drawings when I start composing and I was imagining the cello being a kind of boat moving in different directions in this sea of sound of electronics and ensemble' (Saariaho, 2001).[2] More directly, though, *Amers* is the French word for 'navigation beacons', strategically placed along the coast for sailors, so the idea that the soloist negotiates some kind of journey is significant here. Indeed, that metaphor recurs in Saariaho's recent cello concerto, *Notes on Light* (2006–07). Other connections include the poet Saint-John Perse (1887–1975) whose book of verse dedicated to the sea has the title '*Amers*'; his work inspired the extra-musical dimension in the later flute concerto *Aile du songe* (2001).

As the first example of this genre, *Amers* deserves some further comment. Like any concerto, the role of the soloist is crucial and here a microphone wired to the cello allows each string to be amplified separately. Despite such super-soloist potential, though, any traditional principles of duality are deliberately eschewed in favour of a three-way discourse: soloist, ensemble and (computer-generated) electronics. *Amers* clearly belongs to an earlier stylistic phase for the composer, and it is interesting that as Saariaho moves towards more lyrical and vocal explorations, an interest in concerto writing develops. This piece is a crucial landmark in her stylistic development. Although its spatial qualities have a three-dimensional aspect (given its three competing forces), the overall structural layout is in two parts: '*Libero, dolce, misterioso*' and '*Sempre molto energico, ma espressivo*'. This concept – the second stage being an intensification of the first – informs later examples; *Graal théâtre* and *Aile du songe* both adopt a similar binary scheme, as discussed below. While the narrative shaping of events corresponds to that of a journey, somehow the soloist remains hampered by his surroundings.[3] This is a work of unpredictable disruptions and interruptions. However, there is a sustained energy and intensity which, coupled with references to fundamental pitch-centres (most notably E♭), give both momentum and focus to this otherwise

---

[2]   The CD-liner note for the 2001 recording of *Amers* (Sony-SK60817) includes an interview of the composer by Martin Anderson, from which these quotations are taken.

[3]   The male personal pronoun refers to the soloist for whom the work was written, Anssi Karttunen.

fragmentary discourse. To challenge listener perceptions of musical continuity in such a direct way is a recurrent preoccupation of Saariaho's work.

The crucial role of titles can be seen throughout Saariaho's concertos, feeding her imagination and giving structural focus. Inspired by the writings of Jacques Roubaud, *Graal théâtre* for violin and orchestra (1994/97) is no exception, the composer being drawn to an unexpected combination of words. '*Graal*' refers to what is innermost, sacred – the Holy Grail; '*théâtre*' to something extrovert, dramatic – a concerto soloist – here portrayed as if a character in an abstract musical drama. Such binary oppositions become embedded within the genre and are reflected in a two-movement form: '*Delicato*' (which portrays lyricism and restraint through linear continuity) and '*Impetuoso*' (where drama and conflict are projected in block-like contrasts). These dualities – the pairing of opposites – operate on a variety of levels in this piece, offering a number of listening strategies: conflict, complementation, dialogue and resolution. *Aile du songe* ('Wing of Dreams') for flute and orchestra pursues those ideas; the literary influences that lie behind its portrayal of bird flight are conveyed through a precisely imagined structure. This concerto is also in two parts: '*Aérienne*' ('Ethereal') and '*Terrestre*' ('Terrestrial') – air and land – titles taken from the Saint-John Perse collection of poems that inspired it.[4]

Notes on Light invites us to (re-)consider the importance of visual stimuli. The significance of light for Finnish composers in general, and to Saariaho in particular, cannot be overstated. Extremes of light and dark (and the very slow rate of evolution between them) condition perceptions of how time passes, for both composers and listeners. Also, that cyclic quality is offset by abrupt seasonal changes: winter to spring, brown to green, takes just a couple of weeks. The differing qualities of light envisioned at each stage of this five-movement work – 'Translucent', 'On Fire', 'Awakening', 'Eclipse' and 'Heart of Light' – act as a powerful metaphor. Collectively they offer a vivid perspective on timescale. Gradual evolution of light conveys a horizontal, temporal process, resulting in an expressive continuity; sudden contrasts of colour exert a vertical, spatial impulse, creating formal articulations. Mapped onto the concerto genre, an inherent dialogue and duality is conveyed through these reflections on time and space. Elsewhere, *Mirage* for soprano, cello and orchestra (2007) offers a new outlook on the 'double concerto' idiom: 'two interpretations setting out from the same point of departure', as Saariaho explains in her programme note. Rather than being in conflict, these two soloists complement each other in a truly concerted effort. The cello elaborates upon its vocal partner as both follow parallel courses towards a final synthesis. This discourse between text and texture, word and sound, highlights their relationship as a combination of forces which, in turn, is set against contrasting orchestral sonorities.

Beyond this overview of Saariaho's concertos, where each example makes a distinctive contribution to the genre, lies the composer's preoccupation with

---

[4]   See Howell, 2006: 216ff, for more details.

treating a particular instrument as a focal point. Consider the flute in *Lichtbogen* (1986), for instance: here it adopts the role of a protagonist, whose presence frames the formal arch of the work, adopts three personas (alto, flute in C, piccolo) and undergoes various transformations – ranging from the human and down-to-earth to the surreal and distant.[5] At the closing stages, the flautist recites phonemes taken from one line of Henry Vaughan's poem, *The World*: 'I saw eternity the other night', again indicating the importance of the solo 'voice' within an instrumental context. The diptych *Du cristal ...à la fumée* (1989–90), two separate yet conjoined orchestral works, deploys soloists (amplified alto flute and cello) in its second stage only; they offer individual perspectives on the orchestral material, something complementary rather than opposed. In this context of 'pairings' operating on a number of levels, the elevation of two instruments is merely another facet within an ongoing discourse and not intended as evidence of true (double) concerto thinking. It is, however, part of a compositional mindset that clearly values the personal 'voice' as a significant strand in communicating with the listener.

The Search for the Holy Grail: *Graal théâtre* (1994/97)

A special relationship between opera and concerto has long been recognized in the history of music, especially as it informs the emergence of the concerto genre itself. For instance, as Charles Rosen asserts, 'Mozart's most signal triumphs took place where Haydn had failed: in the dramatic forms of opera and concerto, which pit the individual voice against the sonority of the mass' (Rosen, 1971: 185). Saariaho's output suggests that such long-standing connections are still relevant. *Graal théâtre*, even by its title, is a dramatic work embodying strong music-theatre elements. Moreover, the composer sees her first opera, *L'Amour de loin* ('Love from Afar'), premiered in 2000, as the culmination of many aspects of her work: 'Actually everything I've written since 1983 is directly connected to my opera, which uses borrowed material' (in Beyer, 2000b: 6). Indeed, the highly developed lyrical dimension of *L'Amour de loin* is directly foreshadowed by a new preoccupation with melody that makes *Graal théâtre* distinct from previous works. An individual voice striving to be heard is the common thread here. It is also interesting that Saariaho returns to the genre of concerto immediately after the opera: *Aile du songe* was her next major composition.

Graal théâtre, by being scored for violin and orchestra, offers a more personal view of concerto conflicts. Saariaho was herself a violinist and something of a compositional struggle is portrayed through the soloist's role here: 'I had a kind of vertigo, a fear of high places, when I started this concerto. I played the violin as a child and I loved many violin concertos passionately – and I was afraid to step into this domain' (Saariaho, 2001). Against a background of frustrated ambitions, wistful hankering – and the sheer love of the genre – Saariaho has tried to move

---

[5]   See Howell, 2006: 210–16, for details.

away from traditional virtuosity to delve into the soul of the instrument. In order to help conquer her fear, she consciously engaged with the weight of tradition by researching the repertoire and developing an interest in the violin concerto genre *per se* (see Saariaho, 2005). While the final work is uniquely her own, some veiled references to iconic examples may spring to mind: there are some intimations of the Beethoven, for instance, not least because of a pitch-centre on D♮. And, of course, the violin concerto has a very special place in the history of Finnish music, given Sibelius's renowned contribution to the genre.

In this broader context, and with an emerging melodic lyricism that becomes so overt in *L'Amour de loin*, it is fair to say that *Graal théâtre* occupies an important place in Saariaho's overall output; it also marks a turning point within her concerto writing. Commissioned for the BBC Symphony Orchestra (1994) and premiered at the Proms in 1995, the piece was composed especially for Gidon Kremer as soloist. It was arranged for chamber orchestra in 1997 and this slight re-profiling brings the soloist rather closer to the other instruments, though the violin part remains unchanged. Comparing the two, it is striking that an essential *concertante* dimension is fully preserved despite reduced forces. (This chapter refers to the second version, as it is the more often performed and recorded.) *Graal théâtre* typifies much of Saariaho's aesthetic given her preoccupation with time and space, expressed through the blurring of traditionally distinct parameters (such as timbre, harmony, texture and dynamic) and an overriding sense of economy. Significant characteristics include the slow transformation of evolving materials, the sculpting of sound into fluid formal shapes, a highly individual emphasis on texture and timbre and an underlying sense of narrative continuity.

Example 7.1   *Graal théâtre* (*'Delicato'*) – **opening material**

Amounting to some 30 minutes in duration and 716 bars in length, its whole conception is expansive. Indeed, a sense of spaciousness is immediately striking: this is music that unfolds on a grand scale. Example 7.1 shows the opening materials as these are the generator of subsequent events. Initial cadenza-like iterations run to some 60 bars before any real orchestral engagement, and this quasi-dominant feel

Example 7.2   *Graal théâtre* ('*Delicato*') – episodic overview

Formal Episodes	I	II	III	IV	V	VI	VII	VIII	IX	X
Bars	1–59	60–88	89–164	165–86	187–218	219–65	266–309	310–344	345–405	406–444
Character/ Expression Marks Bold = Ensemble Non-bold = Solo	**Rubato; delicato; dolce; poco nervoso;** *più agitato; poco furioso; calando, dolce; espressivo* **accel....**	**Più mosso; più energico**	**Meno mosso, dolce; più mosso, energico;** *poco furioso;* **furioso; subito dolce; meno mosso, più espressivo; dolce**	**Meno mosso; agitato; dolce; agitato; dolce; agitato;** *poco disperato;* **grandioso; poco più mosso;**	**Meno mosso; espressivo; dolce;** *espressivo; poco furioso;* **dolce,** *grazioso;* **subito dolcissimo**	**Più mosso; più energico; meno mosso, dolente; energico; poco nervoso; misterioso; poco rubato; più calmo,** *molto espressivo*	**Più mosso; subito dolcissimo;** *più agitato; con forza; energico;* **più mosso; leggiero;** [**accel. poco a poco**]	**Più energico; più mosso; agitato;** *con fuoco; con ultima forza;* **rit. molto; calando**	**Sempre espressivo; sostenuto; sempre calmo, ma intenso;** *più energico;* **poco passionato; intenso, poco largando; grazioso; dolce, misterioso**	**A tempo; più energico;** *con fuoco;* **calando;** *con fuoco;* **meno mosso: calmo, espressivo; libero; dolcissimo.**
Duality	Expressive	Energetic	Expressive	Energetic	Expressive	Energetic	Expressive	Energetic	Expressive	Energetic/ Expressive
Dialogue and Narrative	Cadenza-like violin iterations; establishes wide-ranging soloist potential; anticipatory tension prevails	Solo melody acts as link; orchestra is far more decisive, creating a sense of conflict; significant stage in concerto contrasts	Regained lyricism is short lived; contrasting energy is subdued through combined efforts of soloist and orchestra	Dramatic contrast allows soloist to set a chain of events in motion; sustained climax is primarily orchestral: Climax I	Orchestra initiates events but the soloist projects an 'expressive' character overall; sense of stasis marks the 'end' of this episode	Feeling of being more developmental with greater variety and increased fragmentation of events; soloist prepares for next phase	Prevailing *dolcissimo* orchestral music is undermined by solo outbursts; as a result, orchestra sets the tone with *leggiero* material	Rapid exchanges of material between the two forces; build up of tempo, dynamic and energy to establish Climax II	Stasis; sense of time being suspended; lyricism dominates; yet soloist initiates material, as orchestra holds regular pulse	Strongest sense of dialogue between the two forces as the on-going potential for synthesis of materials is achieved; final sense of lyricism
Formal Continuity										
Pitch-Class Focus										

is an early indication of how the soloistic writing may manipulate perceptions of timescale. Anticipatory tension is paramount. Despite that expansiveness there is also economy, as only a limited amount of material is deployed – and this is carefully focused. A broad, expressive palette is the product of a deliberately restricted range of elements and the tension of large-scale effects emerging from small-scale gestures conditions much of the progress of this concerto. A fundamental trait of counterbalanced oppositions is established at the outset, where the soloist dominates but seems rather trapped. We question what is fixed rather than freely improvised, discovering that the nature of improvisation may lack real direction, despite surface activity and apparent motion. It seems as if the orchestra helps to free the soloist from a slightly claustrophobic space, yet much of the writing for ensemble involves repetition patterns (pedal points, ostinati, rhythmic cells) that are themselves rather obsessive and potentially static. Such oppositional strategies are quite paradoxical – offering a compositional potential that Saariaho is keen to exploit.

Oppositions and Tensions: 'Delicato'

Tensions within this first stage of the piece arise from setting up a number of oppositions, establishing their individual characteristics and playing them off against one another.[6] Any structural framework is informed by these processes, resulting in a loosely woven tapestry of diverse episodes. Despite such formal freedoms there are underlying levels of control as well. While a foreground sense of dramatic contrasts is predominant (consider tempi, expression marks, timbre/orchestration), middleground narrative (arising from solo/orchestra interaction and their struggle for supremacy) and background continuity (emerging from larger patterns of tension and release and pitch-class centricity) are also discernible. Typical of Saariaho's approach is an antithesis between two formal impulses: organic – music that unfolds and finds shape over time, and architectural – a sequence of events sculpted in space. Any relationship between them arises from a careful manipulation of timescale.

Example 7.2 groups the complex web of surface contrasts into ten episodes. With frequent use of transitional material, any suggestion of separate 'blocks' is carefully removed: these episodes are phases of activity within a continuum. Indeed, this synopsis shows considerable diversity, indicated by the number of expression marks involved; larger groupings are correspondingly fluid – alternative segmentations are equally valid – but at least some idea of how the listener may perceive a formal shape emerges. Consequently, these ten episodes contract to a sequence of five contrasting pairs; these alternate between predominantly 'expressive' (*dolce, espressivo*) and 'energetic' (*energico, agitato*) music(s). To simplify further, the more lyrical and expressive music is associated with a slower (*meno mosso*) tempo, while its rhythmically more active, dynamic counterpart uses a faster (*più mosso*) rate of change: it is more energetic. Things are not quite

---

6   Saariaho has said in the past that 'of course the construction of musical form has always used the principle of oppositions' (in Saariaho, 1987: 97).

so simple, however. Within this spatial, architectural framework of duality is a temporal, organic impulse: a dialogue. A glance at any particular episode reveals the extent to which orchestra and soloist work in conflict with the prevailing mood; though elsewhere, they combine and complement each other.

This ongoing narrative creates formal continuity. Listeners might engage with the piece on a number of timescales, be it varieties of surface contrasts or their grouping into a middleground discourse, but ultimately these events subscribe to a background level. A sense of large-scale momentum generates a balanced formal shape articulated by two climactic peaks (the culmination of episodes I–IV and V–VIII), with the last two episodes (IX and X) offering a sense of closure (albeit a temporary one, given the *Impetuoso* movement to follow). These waves of evolutionary motion, where local activity subscribes to an ongoing sweep of events, nevertheless make reference to principles of opposition. Both prolonged climactic passages are offset in the ensuing episode (see V and IX) by their expressive counterpart: static calmness (*dolce*). With such a dramatic interleaving of diverse materials and two emotionally protracted climaxes, it is possible to lose sight of the '*Delicato*' title of this movement. However, as an exploration of oppositional processes, these expressive extremes are being held in a delicate balance. Additionally, the weighting between 'expressive' versus 'energetic' music – at least when measured durationally – is clearly in favour of the former; a restrained lyricism seems to prevail in this ('*Delicato*') movement.

Much of the piece may be understood by the listener without reference to pitch organization. By this stage in her output, Saariaho is so in control of patterns of tension and release which hinge around a particular pitch-centre that her music does not place huge demands on the listener. There is an instinctive coherence at work. As stated in her programme note, 'When compared to my other music, *Graal théâtre* is the exception in a long row of pieces where I combine acoustic instruments with some kind of electronic extensions. Unlike these earlier works, my starting point here was the delicate violin sound and its interaction with an orchestra'. Such a deliberately restricted timbral palette allows a particular focus on the violin itself and the choice of D♮ as the pitch-centre here, being one of the soloist's open strings, seems part of the mindset of a spectral composer: D is quite 'fundamental' on a number of levels. The larger-scale formal continuities to emerge are positioned in relation to the harmonic gravity surrounding this focal point. A final sense of closure is underlined by the closing sonority of a D-major triad, scored for the soloist and orchestral double-basses. It is something about the inevitability of that outcome, how and when this centre lodges in the mind of the listener, that is so carefully handled.

Example 7.2 offers a brief summary of this process by charting the main pitch-class referents as the piece unfolds, aligning these with the various levels of formal process (episodic, oppositional and continuous) as part of an overall sculpting of events. Initial materials centre upon the open strings of the violin and the first orchestral entry to project a pitch-centre moves in descending steps from A to E (bars 32–42) – which is then prolonged (over bars 42–54). With fifths being highlighted in this way, the orchestra extends upon this feature: the next phase is based on a B♮

pedal. The principle of some kind of counterbalance – of fifths or thirds – either side of a D centre allows for an ongoing momentum and equilibrium. Allowing this centre to remain implicit for such a long time adds to the prevailing tension, especially when at the moment of clear establishment (bar 173) it is immediately undermined. The first climax being centred on a D pedal that gives way to C♯ (bars 173–86) is a significant departure from earlier patterns and creates dramatic disruption. Thereafter, the condensed and intensified build-up to Climax II involves more wide-ranging reference points, more distantly related to D♮ centricity. A main element of final resolution is the prolonged return to that centre in the last two episodes, while the contained (but very striking) use of chromaticism (and also microtones) over bars 381–8, offers a degree of synthesis at this stage. Large-scale pitch referents provide focus and direction in support of overall formal continuity.

Example 7.3   *Graal théâtre ('Impetuoso')* – **opening material**

Drama and Conflict: 'Impetuoso'

The second 'movement' is both shorter and more dramatically eventful than its counterpart; Example 7.3 shows its opening events. Temporal compression allied to expressive expansion is highly effective and from the outset, where the soloist repeats virtuosic material from earlier in the work, the listener is invited to measure events here in relation to the first movement. Formal outlines correspondingly amplify that model; an episodic scheme is retained but based on far more abrupt and disruptive contrasts: soloist and orchestra explore new levels of conflict.

Example 7.4 *Graal théâtre* ('*Impetuoso*') – descending figures

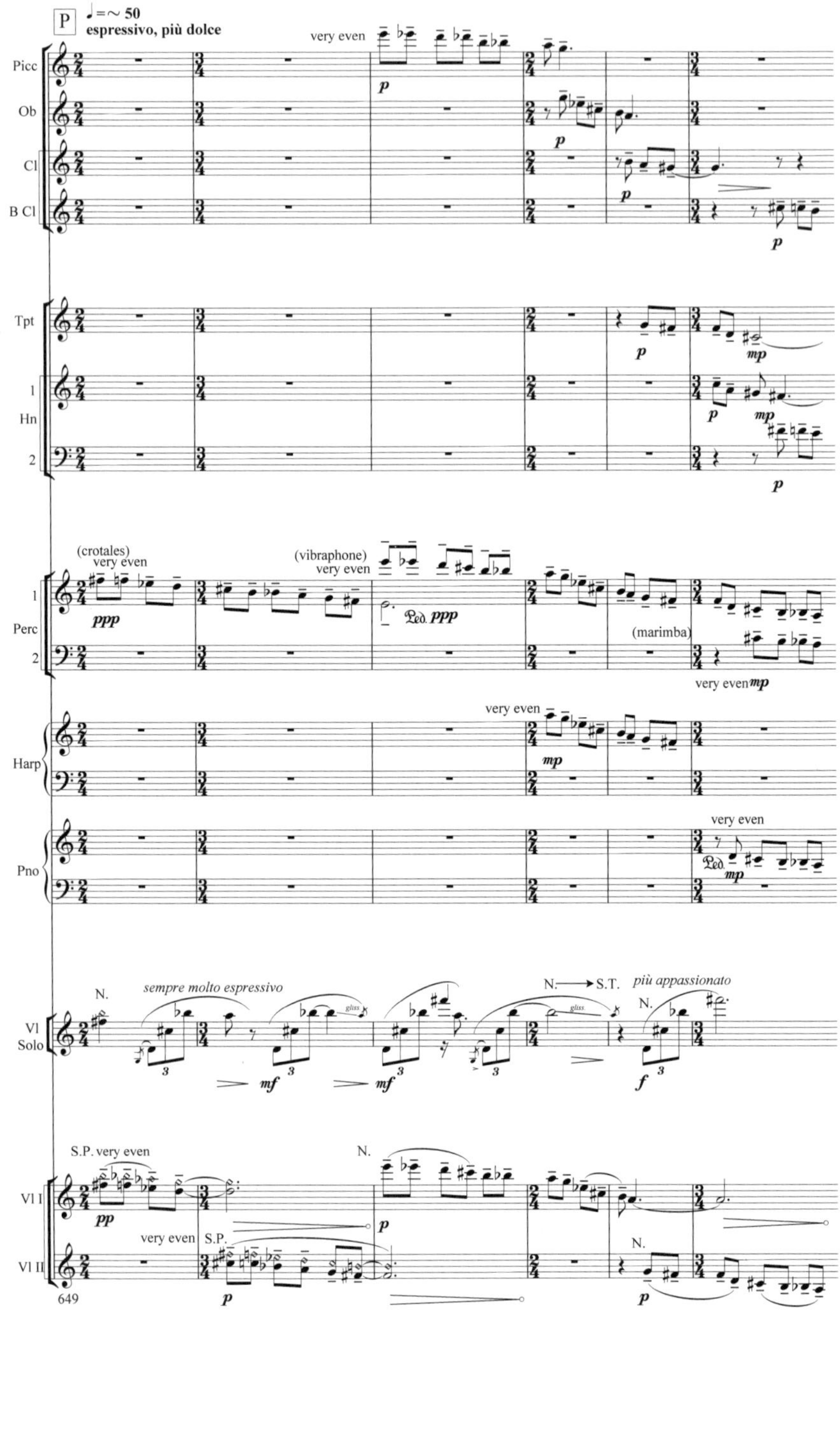

Heightened drama brings greater distance between the two forces, with violin virtuosity taken to an extreme. Soloist cadenzas are strategically placed – at the opening (bars 445–59), following the main climax (bars 617–31) and at the end (bars 698–716). For the listener, these passages play a significant part in any recall of formal shape.

Moving from the *furioso* outburst of the first cadenza, through to the *espressivo* lyricism of the last, these structural signposts mark notable stages in an organic process: conflict gradually gives way to resolution. The 'central' statement needs further comment as it plays a crucial role in mediating between extremes. After a climactic passage for both violin and orchestra, where at its peak the soloist plays *con ultima forza, disperato* (see bar 600), the ensuing cadenza combines materials of contrasting moods: *energico/più dolce*; *agitato, ma dolce*. It finally projects an atmosphere of *calmo, espressivo* music. The next episode, dominated by the orchestra, resumes the prevailing 'Impetuous' mood but culminates in very striking material – marked *espressivo, più dolce* – that is, exclusively associated with the full ensemble: see the descending figures of bar 649ff, shown in Example 7.4. As duality gives way to dialogue, this proves to be a decisive turning point, paving the way for the final violin cadenza that replaces virtuosic assertiveness with contemplative lyricism.

The pairing of opposites that has conditioned every level of *Graal théâtre* – title, genre, large- and small-scale form, atmosphere, expression, texture, pitch organization – is again manifest in our perception of this movement in relation to the first. Such a process of comparison invites new considerations of how to define techniques of variation and repetition. Indeed, events appear to have come full circle as the closing moments so clearly recall those of the opening. It is less a change of atmosphere – there are plenty of 'delicate' moments within this 'impetuous' music (and vice versa) – and more a repositioning of similar materials at a different time that is so effective. Saariaho's interest in variation processes that are essentially temporal are significantly advanced in the structuring of this concerto.

A Visual Narrative: *Notes on Light* (2006–07)

> ...I could not
> Speak, and my eyes failed, I was neither
> Living nor dead, and I knew nothing,
> Looking into the heart of light, the silence.
> (T.S. Eliot, *The Waste Land*, 1922)

As its soloist and dedicatee, Anssi Karttunen, concludes: '*Notes on Light* is a rich voyage that leads us to the very heart of light', and Saariaho's quotation of T.S. Eliot (on the last page of the score) makes that intention explicit (Karttunen, 2007).[7] The metaphor of a voyage helps to convey the narrative qualities of the piece and also gives some insight into its shape; a destination that reaches the source of light – silence – suggests a cyclic quality overall. The multi-movement phases of this work, a scheme of apparent diversity yet implicit continuity, collectively explore various qualities of light. Saariaho has explained the original idea of the piece in terms of 'light filtering in various ways through transparent sound material' (in Moisala, 2009: 106). Ranging from absolute brightness to total darkness, characteristics of transparency, reflection, diffraction, translucence, opaqueness – and even the soloist being eclipsed – are all envisioned here. Along the way, soloist and orchestra explore the relationships between light and speed that convey horizontal continuities, and their specific qualities – colour and tempo – which articulate vertical contrasts. Above all, this is an eventful journey that places the solo cello in a range of different situations relative to the orchestra, allowing both parties to assume many versatile roles. As Karttunen summarizes: 'The soloist is not just the hero of *Notes on Light*, he/she has to stand up for his rights, fight, lead, collaborate with and sometimes submit to the orchestra'.

At first glance, the five-movement layout bears little relation to that of a conventional concerto. However, the principle of duality can be seen to operate on the highest level, with the grouping of contrasting pairs of outer movements – each with its balance of oppositions – acting as a counterweight to each other. An overall tripartite design emerges, supported by a durational symmetry between its first two parts and a more extensive final stage (which the *attacca* indication between IV and V helps to confer): see Example 7.5. Such fundamental concerto principles also operate within individual movements and help the listener to shape formal perceptions. Charles Rosen's view of the classical concerto, that 'the most important fact about concerto form is that the audience waits for the soloist to enter and when he [*sic*] stops playing, they wait for him to begin again' (Rosen, 1971: 196), holds good even in this contemporary context. The initially mysterious ('secret') world of translucence – where light may be transmitted but nothing is transparent – gains clarity through the relationship between soloist and orchestra. From the outset, the cello establishes its soloistic credentials, but in a ruminating, almost hesitant, quasi-improvisatory manner. Successions of these recitatives are subject to varied repetition, where subsequent utterances are always intensified; there is a rhetorical quality to this gentle articulation of time passing: an essentially horizontal process. The orchestra, on the other hand, gradually moves from early refractions of the cello line to a position of conflict: sustained, vertical, block-like punctuations threaten to suspend time, interrupting the flow. Nevertheless, these disruptive pauses create a sense of anticipation – itself an inherently forward-moving impulse – as well as separating events in musical space.

---

[7]   This comment, along with others below, are taken from a programme note by Anssi Karttunen (January 2001), published by Chester Music.

Example 7.5   *Notes on Light* – **movement layout**

Movement	Title	Duration	Quality of Light	Character
I	'Translucent, Secret'	4:57	Translucent	*Misterioso, espressivo*
II	'On Fire'	3:12	Blazing	*Sempre energico*
III	'Awakening'	7:52	Colourful	*Dolce, languido*
IV	'Eclipse'	4:22 [*attacca*]	Darkness	*Molto calmo*
V	'Heart of Light'	7:06	Brightness	*Dolce, espressivo*

Embedded in this duality of solo and orchestra contrasts is an implicit potential for dialogue that helps to articulate later events: the piece constantly re-evaluates soloist/orchestra tensions and partnerships. Extreme conflicts characterize movements II and IV; the fiery exchanges in the former prevent both parties from speaking at the same time, while the soloist is eclipsed by the orchestra in the fourth movement, (though it finally manages to break through the darkness by initiating – *attacca* – the closing voyage towards light). In the intervening central movement, 'Awakening', combined forces make a concerted effort to build broad and colourful gestures, and these will be recalled in the final synthesis of the work: 'looking into the *heart of light*, the silence'. Extra-musical associations that have influenced the aesthetic conception of the piece also inform the concerto idiom and its attendant formal shaping: both architecturally – in space – and in terms of narrative continuity – of time.

Spatial Duality

The relationship between spatial duality and temporal dialogue is fundamental to Saariaho's engagement with the concerto genre and *Notes on Light* illustrates this well. In order to chart this process, Example 7.6 overleaf summarizes the formal scheme of its opening movement. These early stages of the work are important. An initial sculpting of events into a larger design is both reflected in the layout of the piece as a whole and refracted through each of its five phases. A carefully worked balance between potentially opposing elements – instrumental forces, textures and timbre, section lengths, dynamics, metres – lies at the root of this concerto. At its most simple, an alternation of solo/tutti contrasts provides a basic framework, with the closely related recurrences of orchestral material almost assuming the guise of ritornelli. (There is something of a reversal of traditional practice here, as the work begins with what is essentially an episode.) While horizontal/vertical contrasts mark the most obvious delineation between the two forces, different metres underpin a separation between dynamism (the cello passages are distinctively fluid) and stasis (the tutti statements are consistently in 4/4 time). Even that balance is brought into question, though. The soloist's 'dynamism' is the product of a subtle sense of translucence; it has a thoughtful, meditative presence that, when threatened by

Example 7.6   *Notes on Light* ('Translucent, secret') – formal architecture

Sections	A + A1	B	A2	B1	A3	B2	A4	B3	A5 + Coda
Concerto Contrasts	Cello bb. 1–14	Orchestra bb. 15–17	Cello bb. 18–28	Orchestra bb. 29–32	Cello bb. 33–42	Orchestra bb. 43–44	Cello bb. 45–52	Orchestra bb. 53–58	Cello bb. 59–66; 67–76
Formal Balance	2 x 7-bar phrases	3-bar ritornello	11-bar episode	4-bar ritornello	10-bar episode	2-bar ritornello	8-bar episode	6-bar ritornello	8-bar episode
Totals	14 bars		14 bars		14 bars		10 bars		14 bars; 10-bar coda
Character/ Expression Marks	*Misterioso; Sempre molto espressivo*	*Misterioso*	*Sempre dolce, espressivo*	*Ben sonante; rit. molto: Con tristezza*	*A tempo: Dolce*	*Subito maestoso; rit. Morendo*	*A tempo: Misterioso*	*Subito doloroso; rit. molto: Lamentoso*	*A tempo: Delicato*
Summary of Main Events	Balancing cello recitatives; 2nd statement intensifies 1st: last 3 bars orch. prepares for......	Vertical contrast. Trills grow out of refractions of the earlier cello line, offering some continuity.	Cello resumes 2nd statement with more assertiveness; 3-bar orchestra prepares for......	TUTTI *mp* statement; more sustained and disruptive gesture.	*Più dolce, espressivo* version of last recitative.	TUTTI *mf* statement; more dissonant and assertive.	Reverts to initial *misterioso* world. Suggests a kind of retreat, relative to the orchestra.	TUTTI *mff* Most extensive, tense orchestral outburst, crisis point: chromatic descent.....	Almost cadenza-like cello response; Coda of 4 bars, then 2 x 2-bars *intenso,agitato/ calmo, misterioso.*
Soloist Pitch-Class Centres	*[musical notation]*								
Orchestral Pedal Points	*[musical notation]*								

orchestral outbursts of increasing intensity, retreats further into a contemplative, more secretive world. Conversely, the 'static' tutti statements, limited in both activity and duration, nevertheless gain a gradual dynamic and timbral impulse; the sheer forcefulness of a full orchestral sonority becomes ever-more assertive as concerto conflicts reach a crisis point (see B3: bars 53–8). The cello response is measured and contained, though with deliberate references to cadenza-like gestures; the soloist articulates a change of mood from intense and agitated to calm and mysterious.

Despite such a clear separation between potentially competing forces, there are subtle overlaps as well. Orchestral accompaniments, especially at the end of soloist episodes, frequently prefigure the blocks that follow: they are almost transitional. Conversely, the cellist often has sustained single- (or two-) note gestures during these passages, maintaining a presence but in a supportive role. Beyond these glimpses of formal continuity are shared pitch-related materials that explore competing demands: conflict and complementation. The supremacy of an F♯ centre (so particular to the cello soloist) is undermined by an orchestral focus on C♮, giving each element its own pitch-space – a focal point; see Example 7.7 overleaf. However, when viewed together, these are merely equal and opposite. Their tritone 'polarity' offers some equilibrium: there is stability in a symmetrical division of the octave. The most striking surface feature, yet one that also informs underlying, middleground motion, involves semitone neighbour-notes either side of these centres: F♯/F; C/D♭. A significant element here is the falling cello motive, countered by a rising orchestral figure, with the cello chromaticism seemingly more decorative, relative to an ascending motion that may assume a more functional ('leading-note') role. This contrast between what may be ornamental or fundamental – and its potential for constant re-definition – is reflective of the changing roles of tutti/solo contrasts in the overall form. It is highly characteristic of Saariaho's method that surface details encapsulate larger structural issues in this way.

Chromatic gestures operate on different timescales. The four orchestral statements (see Sections B–B3 inclusive in Example 7.6) outline a large-scale semitone ascent: G–A♭–A–B♭; and its peak, which marks the crisis point of the movement, is characterized by a chromatic *descent* (from B♭ to D). Indeed, the orchestral closing stages pursue that stepwise motion, falling in semitones to a C♮ 'outcome'. Focal points within the cello ruminations revolve around a central F♯: exclusive territory for the soloist. It is during the orchestral ritornelli (see B1 and B3, for instance) that the cello assumes the pitch-space of its counterpart, though personalizing and influencing that gesture: now an *ascending* C♯–D (that will eventually move via G♮ to a final C). Indeed, the cadenza-like Coda is a conciliatory passage with the cellist's closing note offering compromise: it capitulates in favour of a C♮ outcome. Controlled chromaticism within both soloist and orchestral domains is fundamental to patterns of tension and release shared between them, and underpins the formal architecture of concerto conflicts. With chromaticism representing the more opaque side of 'Translucence', the presence of focal points and pitch-class centres offers transparency: a glimpse of things to come in this journey to the heart of light.

Example 7.7 *Notes on Light* **('Translucent, secret') – opening material**

Fiery exchanges between soloist and orchestra define the next phase of duality; 'On Fire' is characterized by a deftness of pacing that sets it apart from anything else. A reservoir of ideas that are strikingly simple in themselves is subject to a process of complex manipulation; a uniformity of content is set within a variety of contexts. The overall shape is informed by an initial discourse between cello and orchestra that gives way to altercation, a subsequent exchange of materials, and a final – though rather elusive – hint of resolution. Fundamental contrasts of mood dominate, and the two forces never actually play at the same time. An overwhelming sense of atemporal impulse (*energico, tempestoso, furioso*) that relentlessly drives the music onwards is stopped in its tracks by a *subito dolce* contemplation from the orchestral strings (bars 63–7), itself the result of an earlier *dolce* episode (bars 54–6, for harp and celesta). Time is suspended – it becomes space – and events seem to float in a motionless vacuum as a new ethereal quality emerges. Though only temporary, given that the soloist soon resumes his/her energetic outbursts, something of the unique register/ timbre associated with this momentary calm is subsequently absorbed by the cellist. There is a paradox here. A relatively large degree of (registral) space occupies a very small amount of (metrical) time and this challenges listener perceptions, especially as this brief episode has long-term consequences. Despite a constantly articulated temporal flow, there is little sense of progress; energy is divorced from motion, activity from direction: events move onward but not necessarily forward. Even-more compressed sequences of repetition patterns, now frantically alternating between soloist and orchestra in ever-closer successions, add to the prevailing fieriness of the (*energico/furioso*) Coda. Nevertheless, that fleeting sense of a registral exchange between these competing partners offers a hint of resolution as deeper, more mysterious forces intimate some degree of compromise.

Separation of materials within the concerto format is raised quite acutely again, in the fourth movement – 'Eclipse'. Quite literally the darkest point of these notes on light, this correspondingly short – but far less fleeting – phase explores the same conceptual discourse of transforming time into space. Everything is paired down to absolute basics in a 38-bar reverie; the cello only proffers three statements: five notes in total, using only two pitch-classes. It returns to an earlier semitone, rising motive – C♯-D – which marks the two complementary stages (bars 1–10 and 11–21) of one larger formal block. Thereafter, from the *misterioso* of bar 22, the orchestra eclipses the soloist whose final gesture (bars 36–8) is further reduced – to a single C♯ – which then acts as a pivot into the last movement. Though characterized by an appropriate stillness, the progress of this eclipse is subtly achieved. Initial string sonorities refract the soloist's timbral qualities in a slow dissolution of events defined by their falling gestures and sustained sonorities. There is, however, an underlying pulse, but this is deliberately a-rhythmic – merely marking time – as it has no energy or momentum. Any suggestion of 'rhythmic' interest is illusory, part of an aura of intensity as dynamic and timbre expand; there is some sense of change evoked by this process, but rather than disturbing the prevailing stasis it merely 'colours' it. While a degree of varied repetition defines an overall shape, forming a sequence of timbral variations, local events are locked, fixed and inert. The expressive impact considerably outweighs any evaluation of the events concerned: it amounts to far more than the sum of its parts. This is Saariaho at her most economical, using an absolute minimum to generate maximum effect.

Temporal Dialogue

The title 'Awakening' elicits a range of associations, suggesting that this central movement occupies a critical stage on a journey to the heart of light. Certainly the

Example 7.8   *Notes on Light* **('Awakening') – cyclic structure**

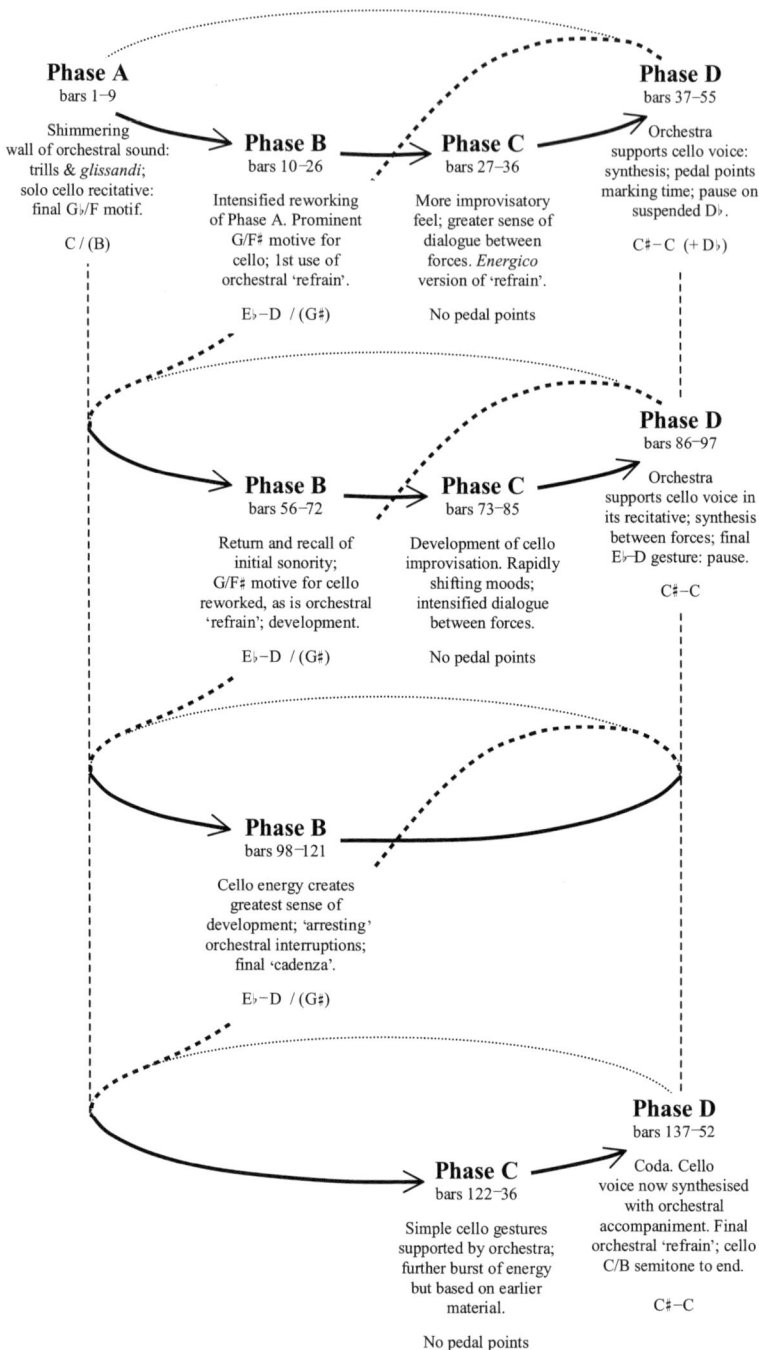

Phase A
bars 1–9

Shimmering
wall of orchestral sound:
trills & *glissandi*;
solo cello recitative:
final G♭/F motif.

C / (B)

Phase B
bars 10–26

Intensified reworking
of Phase A. Prominent
G/F♯ motive for
cello; 1st use of
orchestral 'refrain'.

E♭–D / (G♯)

Phase C
bars 27–36

More improvisatory
feel; greater sense of
dialogue between
forces. *Energico*
version of 'refrain'.

No pedal points

Phase D
bars 37–55

Orchestra
supports cello voice:
synthesis; pedal points
marking time; pause on
suspended D♭.

C♯–C (+ D♭)

Phase B
bars 56–72

Return and recall of
initial sonority;
G/F♯ motive for cello
reworked, as is orchestral
'refrain'; development.

E♭–D / (G♯)

Phase C
bars 73–85

Development of cello
improvisation. Rapidly
shifting moods;
intensified dialogue
between forces.

No pedal points

Phase D
bars 86–97

Orchestra
supports cello voice in
its recitative; synthesis
between forces; final
E♭–D gesture: pause.

C♯–C

Phase B
bars 98–121

Cello energy creates
greatest sense of
development; 'arresting'
orchestral interruptions;
final 'cadenza'.

E♭–D / (G♯)

Phase C
bars 122–36

Simple cello gestures
supported by orchestra;
further burst of energy
but based on earlier
material.

No pedal points

Phase D
bars 137–52

Coda. Cello
voice now synthesised
with orchestral
accompaniment. Final
orchestral 'refrain'; cello
C/B semitone to end.

C♯–C

overall sonority is very different here, a new timbral palette bringing increased anticipation. The orchestra opens with a wall of sound made up from shimmering trills and sustained, repeated notes; set against this sonorous fixity is an agile, repeated-note cello entry that acts as an upbeat to a truly vocal outburst (*molto espressivo*). A struggle of the individual voice pitted against a mass of sound, so central to the concerto aesthetic, is given new life. The transformation of initial oppositions into a concerted effort gradually evolves over time, and it is this linear unfolding of a formal impulse that distinguishes this 'movement' from its surroundings. Rather than blocks of material grouped into an architectural scheme, there are cycles of activity – some four in all – each a further reflection of its predecessor in an ongoing discourse. This cyclic quality is rather special in its concern for renewal rather than return, thereby generating a forward-moving 'awakening' of the inherent potential of its materials: it creatively re-cycles earlier events. A sense of dialogue is the key factor. It is the relationship, not the conflict, between solo and orchestral forces that conditions their progress through time.

Example 7.8 summarizes the layout of materials (though a spatial representation of a temporal process has inevitable limitations). Nevertheless, a basic pattern is immediately apparent: phases of materials are being rotated. However, the extent to which Saariaho's sheer invention disguises this framework should not be underestimated. Through constantly evolving surface activity, slow, transformational cycles using background pitch-centres are subtly projected here. The idea of wheels-within-wheels is also present; the first cycle (of four) itself comprises four phases (A–D) that form the basis of later developments. Issues of repetition, return, recall and renewal are all in a state of flux, imparting a sense of continuity; nevertheless, the use of pauses at the end of each cycle (literally at bars 97 and 121, and through a sustained D♭ over bars 52–5), has the effect of marking out passages of time. Durations are of interest, not least because of a disparity between observation and perception that arises. With Cycle III being a mere 24 bars, Cycle IV just 31 bars, a glance at Example 7.8 suggests a drastic compression of initial events; indeed, added together, these last two cycles exactly amount to the duration of the first: 55 bars.

On paper then, observing their combination may suggest a three-part formal scheme in total. Listener perceptions are very different, though. Cycle III is especially eventful with an increase in expressive intensity that is inversely proportional to its compressed timescale: extremes of character, tempo and gesture are tightly confined. Put simply, there is far more in this 24-bar passage than its length would suggest, as temporal restriction has an emotionally expansive effect. Moreover, the concerto-form conflict also reaches a peak: the soloist achieves greater energetic momentum (see *Più mosso, energico*, bar 105ff) while, conversely, the ensemble exerts more interruptive control. Balance and complementation remain important; the soloist's material builds on earlier gestures, while the orchestral punctuations are a reduction of its 'refrain' element. A compromise is reached as the cello is finally subdued into a (*Più calmo*) cadenza-like reverie. The last formal cycle of the movement (from bar 122) has a suitably strong emphasis on recall, if not return: its initial *Tempo primo* indication is significant. Of course, temporal continuity remains paramount and there is a renewed burst of activity during this phase, making the final sense of synthesis (bar 137ff) all the more satisfying.

The pedal points themselves – their presence or absence, pitch-class focus, length and recurrence – help to articulate the cyclic constructions deployed. Given the central image of 'Awakening', this is the point in the work most concerned with 'colour'; an emphasis on 'chromaticism' has extra meaning, as timbre and pitch-class complement each other. The semitone motion from C to D♭ that defines the outlines of Cycle I eventually is resolved as part of a chromatic descent, E♭–D–C♯–C, during Cycle II, and is distributed again (though in a rather fragmentary way) over the last two cycles. A pedal C♮ was the first pitch-class centre projected by the orchestra at the very start of the concerto and deployment of chromatic neighbour-notes has been a recurrent feature throughout, operating on all levels. Establishment of such a strong background degree of stability is offset by the use of Phase C: episodic materials that have no fixed pedal points. Correspondingly, these passages feel far freer, exploring the more improvisatory qualities associated with concerto writing, though within the carefully-defined limits of this schematic shape. An unpredictable balance between freedom and restraint, so fundamental to a linear (rather than vertical) formal process, is engendered by these phases of activity; they offer an essential sense of renewal within a cyclic unfolding of recall.

Example 7.9 *Notes on Light* **('Awakening') – soloist chromaticism**

A few observations of surface-level activity help to confirm more immediate perceptions of that rotational process: there are close connections between content and form. Chromaticism within the soloist's material remains consistent; the use of a G/F♯ figure (given the associations surrounding F♯ in the first movement) is particularly striking (see Example 7.9), though it is merely one of a number of such semitonal gestures. Set against these cello recitatives is music that remains distinctive to the orchestra (see Example 7.10) and is subject to recurrence: an orchestral refrain. Consistently marked *Grave* (though it may be *subito*, *più* or *poco*) and varied in directness, length and intensity, its developmental treatment mirrors that of the soloist's material. What remains exclusive is a strongly etched

Example 7.10 *Notes on Light* ('Awakening') – orchestral refrain descending outline of non-chromatic elements, while the inclusion of chromatic neighbour-notes offers a potential for synthesis between these two bodies of material. The very last appearance of this refrain (bars 147–50) is one of its most dramatic, though by now there is a strong sense of complement (rather than potential conflict) relative to the cellist's closing recitative. Overall, it is the use of dialogue between these two forces that both conditions the surface activity here and informs the cyclic nature of its formal scheme.

Structural Synthesis

As the piece reaches the final stage of its journey to the 'heart of light', issues of synthesis become paramount. Following on immediately from 'Eclipse', where the soloist is completely overshadowed by the orchestra, the re-alignment of initially opposing forces into a concerted effort is all the more telling: both sides of fundamental concerto definitions are brought into play. As the soloist asserts a central position, there is a return to a block-like formal scheme that alternates between the two forces; this directly recalls the opening movement, along with a number of references to associated material. Such clear recollections offer a degree of cyclic continuity that operates alongside block-like separations, as both formal impulses of the work (organic and architectural) are brought together. Balancing out these oppositions is the key element: contrast gives way to complementation, segregation becomes synthesis.

Example 7.11 shows a ternary-form outline and its attendant sense of balance operates on a number of different levels – formal subdivisions, solo/orchestra partnership, tritone-related pitch centres – that collectively provide a sense of resolution for this finale. A glance at this architectural summary reveals an underlying framework: a journey that is precisely articulated in 12 stages. The first section of this ternary form (bars 1–52) is itself in four parts and the first of these (bars 1–23) is further divisible into four stages, suggesting that the systematic way in which time is parcelled up into units of activity is a multi-levelled conception. Initially the soloist part dominates proceedings, and the way in which it alternates between two types of material encapsulates much of the oppositional momentum that the rest of this movement pursues. Events may be summarized as follows:

A   Bars 1–12: Recitative-like, vocal, melodically sustained cello writing – *Dolce, espressivo*
B   Bars 13–17: Cadenza-like, semiquaver flourishes in shorter outbursts – *Più energico*
A   Bars 18–21: Varied reworking and, in the light of 'B' material – *Con forza, agitato*
B   Bars 22–3: Reworking of semiquaver flourishes – *Più, espressivo*

While distinctive contrasts allow such subdivisions, an overriding process of *varied* repetition provides continuity; the re-working of this 'A' material takes

Example 7.11   *Notes on Light* ('Heart of Light') – formal scheme

Section	Bars	Tempo	Pitch-Centre
Statement	1–23	*Dolce, espressivo*; *Più energico*; *Meno mosso*; *Più espressivo*	Focal pitch-class of C, gradually emerges; Tritone: F♯-C thereafter; culminates on F♯ climax; soloist moves back to C (bar 52)
	24–30	*Più mosso, Dolce*	
	31–41	*Dolce, leggiero*	
	41–52	*Poco a poco più pesante*; *Con forza*; *Energico*; *Calando*	
Development	53–60	*Meno mosso, Libero*; *Espressivo*	C♮ as sustained, overall centre gives way to F♯; other semitonal motifs add uncertainty
	61–6	*Più mosso, Dolce, nervoso*; *rit. Libero*	
	67–77	*A tempo, Subito energico*; *Calando*; *Dolce*; *rit. Libero*	
	78–90	*A tempo, energico*; *Dolce*; *Lento*	
Synthesis	91–5	*A tempo, intenso*; *Più libero, Molto espressivo*	Return to C♮, supported by increased use of 5ths; eventual emergence of initial centre of the piece, F♯ as the goal of the work
	96–103	*A tempo, dolce*; *Lentissimo molto libero*	
	104–9	*A tempo, Misterioso calmo*; *Lentissimo molto libero*; *A tempo, subito più energico*; *Calando*; *rit. molto*;	
	110–17	*Senza tempo* (follow the soloist): *Lentissimo molto libero*; *Misterioso*	

on something of the character of 'B' (and vice versa). A fundamental principle of how apparent contrast and discontinuity may actually contribute to a sense of ongoing dialogue is set up during these opening stages. Thereafter, the orchestra refracts these materials and ultimately guides the soloist to the heart of light. Antithesis leads to meaningful exchanges and ultimately both forces come to engage in a concerted effort to find resolution: a temporal process.

Once again, perceptions of what may be ornamental or fundamental are creatively brought into question. Thus, in addition to such balance on formal, genre-based and gestural levels, issues of timescale – in terms of actual versus perceived duration – support this architectural infrastructure in an organic way. The length of each subsection is varied but with a tendency for compression as the form unfolds over time. Characteristically, this is offset by an increase in the range, amount and variety of activity within each of these blocks, adding to a sense of continuity and momentum. Example 7.11 illustrates this, as suggested by the basic tempo/character indications that Saariaho provides; perhaps the passage between bars 104 and 109 – a mere 6 bars – is the most obvious instance of a wide expressive range being contained in a short period of time. Paradoxically though, there is a single, prevailing mood despite that variety. This slow, still, calm, mysteriousness allows time to be more and more drawn out as the piece reaches a close: at the heart of light, time becomes space, music gives way to silence.

An architectural spatial design overlaid by an organic temporal process is the ultimate balance that this movement holds in check. In doing so, this structural synthesis encompasses many of the issues explored throughout the piece as a whole. With the explicit duality of one level being countered by the implicit dialogue on the other, a resolution is achieved. The basic ternary infrastructure retains a degree of equilibrium. Each of its sections (Statement, Development and Synthesis) is of remarkably similar duration if measured in clock time, with a marginally shorter (but more eventful) central portion flanked by two equal outer stages. Set against such arcane precision are varying degrees of formal articulation, which work right through to a highly diverse surface activity: interrelated levels that manipulate our perceptions of timescale. Any observation of a controlling framework remains distant, given the listener's experience of fluidity of expression. All of this is underpinned by a systematic use of harmonic gravity: focal pitch-classes are held in a balance between tension and resolution. That equilibrium creates a real sense of middleground. These pitch-centres subscribe to a large-scale abstract pattern, yet at strategic and audibly perceptible moments they have direct impact on the listening process. The polarity – but symmetry – of the C/F♯ tritone offers both tension and balance, fundamental principles set up in the translucence of the opening movement that (re)gain clarity here. Whereas the cello capitulated to a C♮ centre at the close of the first movement, the orchestra gives way to the soloist's F♯ here. The initial F♯ of the piece now stands at the heart of light, before fading into silence; its centrality offers a final sense of resolution.

Conflict and Complementation

Several of Saariaho's most characteristic compositional traits emerge from a consideration of her concerto writing. Something about the very nature of this genre suits this composer's desire to communicate with her audience. The concerto concept embraces abstract notions – of duality, struggle, dialogue and narrative – yet demands that they be fashioned into precisely imagined formal schemes, which embody those balanced oppositions in purely musical terms. Also, there is a strong sense of a personal voice within each of these pieces and this spills over into more general *concertante* instrumental writing in other works, underpinning their individuality and aiding their appeal. Deployment of both spatial duality and temporal dialogue through multi-level structures, especially in the interaction between architectural and organic formal impulses, is fundamental here. Indeed, the two distinctive definitions of '*concertare*', embracing conflict and complementation, are correspondingly synthesized as a result. That kind of structural discourse both emerges from and subscribes to the concerto principle: it acknowledges tradition yet offers renewal. Testament to this composer's creative ingenuity is the overriding sense that these distinctive examples contribute to an ongoing development of the form. (Indeed, at the time of writing, Saariaho's latest work is a clarinet concerto, *D'om le vrai sens*, to be premiered in September 2010.) The concerto remains one of the most enduring of all musical genres and Saariaho's highly imaginative contributions help to confirm and reinforce its continued relevance for music of today.

Chapter 8
Dichotomies, Relationships: Timbre and Harmony in Revolution

Vesa Kankaanpää

In her writings on music, Kaija Saariaho proposes a dichotomy between timbre and harmony, and explores the ways in which this interaction informs her ideas about musical structure.[1] In Saariaho's view, harmonic tensions traditionally function horizontally (that is, in succession) to shape musical form, while timbre constitutes the vertical (or simultaneous) matter that follows this movement (Saariaho, 1987: 94 and 132). One of her ambitions from early on in her compositional career has been to reverse this relationship: timbral processes come to generate musical form.

The idea of duality provides several fruitful analytical viewpoints into Saariaho's compositional thinking, not least because her theories of musical form are spurred by the timbre–harmony dichotomy. Oppositions of upheaval and continuity – of modernism and tradition – offer insights into Saariaho's musical ideology. On the one hand, she reinterprets the conventional roles of musical elements and creates form with previously unavailable technological tools. Progressive ideas are expounded, potential for form is seen where it has not been seen before, and instead of tonal form, we have timbral form. Yet on the other hand, there is a degree of continuity in the concepts describing the building blocks of music, with clear links to tradition. As such, Saariaho's more subversive ideas are placed in a conceptual musical world of tonality, harmonic functions and even sonata-form architecture. In this world, she applies familiar concepts in an unfamiliar fashion.

There is a further dichotomy in Saariaho's approach to composition: a duality between theory and practice. Saariaho's compositions are supported by innovative theoretical ideas that she explores in her writings. We thus see the concept of composer as theorist: to compose is to explore, create, discover, analyse. Commitment to the process of research is essential, and this is achieved by constructing systems and theories. But Saariaho is also a composer for whom that which is sensory – *what is actually heard* – is central. It is evident on several levels that her theories provide inspiration and a framework within which an intuitive approach can flourish. This is reflected in the titles of Saariaho's compositions, which hint at a number of associations and meanings, but fall short of full explanations. Perhaps it is this intuitive character of her music that makes

---

[1] See Saariaho, 1987, and its revised version, 1991.

it so approachable to the listener: the sounds that are heard are interesting in themselves; their sensory pleasure has as powerful immediacy.

This chapter considers three works in detail, each of which is based on a different approach to the timbre–harmony relationship. First, in *Im Traume* (1980) for cello and piano, Saariaho explores the idea of a stable backdrop of harmonic colour, against which timbral and melodic gestures are set. Second, *Jardin secret I* (1984–85) for tape, is a study in sound synthesis (Stockhausen's *Studie I* and *II* come to mind), in which the same abstract models are used for both timbre and harmony. This raises the question of whether it remains useful – or even possible – to differentiate between timbre and harmony when listening. Finally, in *Lichtbogen* (1985–86) for chamber ensemble, Saariaho uses many of the compositional methods introduced by French spectral composers, her computer-based analysis of several cello gestures generating materials for the pitch structures of the composition. Plans and drafts provided by the composer highlight the diverse aspects of her compositional process, and her application of the theoretical ideas of spectral analysis.

By writing texts and composing music, Saariaho has participated in various discourses on musical composition. But musical ideas and methods do not develop independently of history, as creative innovation is an ideological gesture, a comment on past and future music. A compositional technique or solution is therefore situated in a particular musical-historical context, and that context is important for the analysis of compositional process. Therefore, the goal here is not simply to illustrate Saariaho's techniques, but also to identify relevant musical-historical contexts for her discoveries.

Harmony as a General Sonority: *Im Traume*

Im Traume, for cello and piano, is a composition in which harmony acts as a stable ground: a static and relatively unchanging background against which the composer sets sudden changes in instrumental colour and texture. Saariaho's aim was to establish musical form by contrasting two kinds of texture. In the first group, she places sounds produced by traditional instrumental techniques, and these represent *stasis*; in the second group are textures that employ extended instrumental techniques, and these stand for *tension* (Saariaho, 1987: 97 and 104).[2] But, in practice, the division between traditional and extended techniques is often unambiguous: all piano textures that avoid use of the keyboard are presumably 'extended', and the cello hardly ever plays 'traditional' techniques. Further, Saariaho does not elaborate why she considers traditional means of sound production as representing *stasis*, or why extended techniques create *tension*. It is easy to accept that the process of *changing* techniques creates variation and contrast, and this is certainly significant for the structure of the composition. But it is more difficult to appreciate how *tension* could be created *per se* by extended techniques: it is far

---

[2]   See also Oskala, 2005.

from clear how this connection could spring from perception alone. However, an explanation could lie in the fact that different instrumental techniques emerged at different points in music history. Listeners are simply more familiar with traditional techniques, and, as the instrumental forces of a piece become evident, expectations begin to emerge as to how those instruments traditionally sound. But the sounds produced by non-traditional methods are surprising, and listeners on the whole have less capacity for expectation concerning how these techniques will sound, and what other techniques will be presented as the work unfolds. The contrast of *stasis* and *tension* thus hinges on musical-historical awareness, and on the expectations created by the instrumental ensemble.

What, then, of the textural contrasts in *Im Traume*? It is possible to divide the composition into five parts, each of which can be further subdivided. Taking Part I as an example, this can be subdivided into six sections – A B A B A C – whose differentiation results from specific kinds of instrumental technique:

A   a mixture of traditional and extended techniques;
B   only traditional techniques; only the piano;
C   only extended techniques.

A pattern therefore emerges wherein mixtures of traditional and extended techniques alternate with sections of extended techniques only, or traditional techniques only. This could be one aspect of the 'network of textures on several levels' that Saariaho sought to achieve (Saariaho, 1987: 104).

Given that many of Saariaho's extended techniques produce sounds with no definite pitch, textures that employ traditional techniques are responsible for generating harmony in the composition. But as unconventional sounds occupy more of the work than traditional sounds, most of *Im Traume* actually has no clear harmony. The harmony that does exist is very static, and all harmonic elements are presented in the opening few gestures of the work.[3] As such, harmony does not seem to play a strong structural role: differences in textural types are of primary importance. And in the absence of change in the harmonic character of specific textures, the timbral and gestural dimensions of the music take on a more dynamic, structural function.

But how perceptible is the dynamism between *stasis* and *tension*? The sounds produced by extended techniques dominate the sounding image to such an extent that the traditional piano and cello sounds are not easily perceptible as a separate sonic category. As a purely timbral device, the contrast of traditional and extended techniques thus remains more conceptual than perceptual. The dynamism between *stasis* and *tension* is, however, evident when we consider the contrasts of textural types. Textures in which the piano produces traditional sonorities represent *stasis*; gestures created by timbral, dynamic and rhythmic means represent *tension*. Crucially, these differentiations are achieved without recourse to harmonic content: harmonies are static, non-continuous.

---

[3]   See Oskala, 2005.

Combining Timbre and Harmony through Sound Synthesis: *Jardin secret I*

In *Jardin secret I*, for tape, Saariaho's goal was to use similar models for constructing timbral and pitch structures: in particular, she divided the octave into several different symmetrical scales, which she then used to synthesize timbre and to determine harmony (Saariaho, 1983: 271; Saariaho, 1987: 124). There are at least two different ways in which a scale can be symmetrical. A whole tone scale is symmetrical because all the intervals are similar, as are scales where the intervals repeat in some kind of pattern, for example the octatonic tone-semitone. A different kind of symmetry is axial symmetry: a particular pitch acts as an axis about which other pitches symmetrically align, below and above. The symmetry in *Jardin secret I* is of the first type.

Using computers, a composer can arbitrarily determine the pitch system with an unlimited number of symmetrical divisions of an octave. In seeking to distance herself from traditional harmonic tensions and create new kinds of pitch hierarchies, Saariaho created interpolations between different symmetrical scales, gradually moving each pitch in a scale towards a pitch in another scale (Saariaho, 1983: 271; Saariaho, 1985: 165).[4] Example 8.1 shows a spectrogram taken towards the end of *Jardin secret I* that reveals the resultant blocks of ascending and descending patterns.[5] Each of the dots on the spectrogram corresponds to a note, or an overtone of a note. Time progresses from left to right (hours : minutes : seconds), pitch is indicated vertically (Hz), loud sounds are bright, soft sounds dark. As can be seen, there seem to be similarities between the blocks: pairs of parallel lines descending, remaining static, or rising are characteristic. A device that probably is in use here is the expansion matrix: the blocks share the same internal interval relations, while the distances between the lowest and the highest notes vary.[6]

The use of symmetrical scales may at first seem to contradict Saariaho's broader aim of creating new pitch hierarchies. In symmetrical scales, all pitches tend to have equal importance and harmonic tensions subside, whereas hierarchy implies relations of dominance between elements: some pitches are central, others are meaningful in relation to them. So when Saariaho moves between two symmetrical scales, both of which are foreign to the listener, is hierarchy created? Perceptually, this is doubtful, but that is not to say pitch structures are any less significant. What we have here are group phenomena, like in Ligeti's cluster music from the late 1950s and early 1960s. Volume is important, louder sounds dominate; movement and changes in ambitus create a sense of direction.

---

[4]   Here interpolation is a mathematical operation where new numerical values are calculated between two known values.

[5]   The spectrogram is taken from the recording *A Portrait of Kaija Saariaho* (BIS CD-307). This and subsequent spectrograms are made using the software *Acousmographe*, version 3.4 (INA-GRM, 2003–07).

[6]   See Saariaho, 1987: 128, figure 17.

Example 8.1   *Jardin secret I* – spectrogram of 7:50–9:50

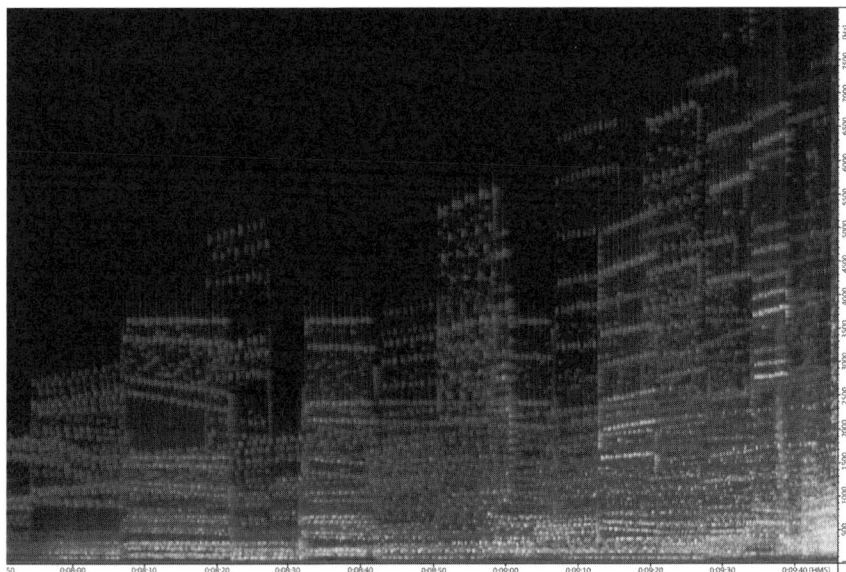

Saariaho realized *Jardin secret I* at IRCAM using the CHANT programme, originally devised for the synthesis of vocal sounds. An aspect of CHANT is its use of FOF-synthesis,[7] which can be used to simulate speech. There are several fundamental differences between conventional speech simulation programmes and FOF. In particular, speech synthesis is usually achieved by the filtering of voiced sound sources using a filter that simulates the resonances of the vocal tract. But in FOF-synthesis, these resonances are synthesized directly by using oscillators that produce the waveform of a formant;[8] if more formants are needed, the number of oscillators is increased. A particular strength of FOF-synthesis is the close connection between controllable variables and the perceptual, aural results. These variables include manipulation of the centre frequency of the formant, the amplitude, and the bandwidth of the formant.[9] The results of these processes can be seen clearly in *Jardin secret I*: Example 8.2 overleaf shows a spectrogram of the opening, wherein vertical lines show the different formants. Note also the slight changes in formant bandwidths (the vertical lines vary in width), and formant centre frequencies (some of the lines tilt).

---

[7]   FOF stands for *fonctions d'onde formantique* or formant wave function synthesis. See Rodet, 1984, or Dodge and Jerse, 1985: 216.

[8]   Formants are spectral peaks in the sound spectrum. Each vowel has a typical set of resonance frequencies (see Fant, 1960).

[9]   See Rodet, 1984: 9–10 and 14, or Dodge and Jerse, 1985: 216–17.

Example 8.2   *Jardin secret I* – spectrogram of 0:00–1:55

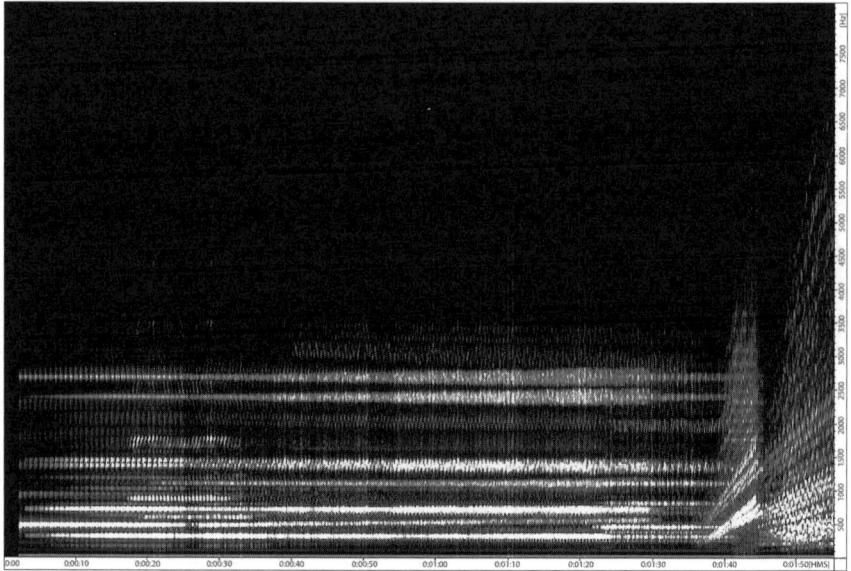

In sound synthesis, timbre and harmony are closely related: both involve identical interval structures in their construction. Using FOF-synthesis, the interval structures of harmonies can be transformed into timbres by taking each note as a centre frequency of a formant. The resulting timbres can be modified, for example, by changing the formant centre frequencies or by changing the bandwidths of the formants: when the bandwidths of formants are very narrow, we obtain the simplest timbres, as each formant becomes a partial (Saariaho, 1985: 165). According to Saariaho, symmetrical divisions of an octave underpin harmony at the beginning of *Jardin secret*; towards the end, these same symmetries form the foundation of inharmonic sound colours (Saariaho, 1987: 126–7).[10] So, there is hardly any difference between timbre and harmony in this kind of sound synthesis, for both concern pitch structures. Any virtues of their distinction are thus drawn into question.

However, there are times when this distinction remains useful. Timbre as a concept becomes relevant when a sound source can be identified, or, in this case, when all sounds are synthesized, imagined. Saariaho points out that

> In the first half of the piece the timbre itself follows an evolution which is largely its own, from clear, abstract sounds to sounds which are increasingly noisy and voiced. Here I used the identity or the referential capacity of the sounds as a means of providing a formal punctuation (Saariaho, 1987: 126).

---

[10]   Inharmonic sounds result from the presence of overtones that are not whole multiples of the fundamental frequency.

Example 8.3   *Jardin secret I* – spectrogram of entire work

There are two main timbral identities at play here: voice and bell. Vocal identity is created when the synthesized formants adhere, at least momentarily, to recognizable vowel formants. Bell sounds occur when the inharmonicity of the formant structure is connected with an attack–decay pattern characteristic of a bell. Example 8.3 shows where these groups come to dominate the sound-world: darker squares indicate the clearest vocal characteristics; the lighter square indicates bell sounds. Passages with distinct note identities constitute further cases wherein a timbre–harmony distinction remains relevant.

In *Jardin secret I*, it is quite difficult to determine aurally how many notes there are at any given moment. The spectrogram does not help, either: it only charts the distribution of energy in time and frequency space; it does not group the sonic phenomena into notes (with a fundamental frequency and overtones). Taking a section from the middle of the work as an example, a spectrogram shows descending pitches, raising pitches; figures moving up and down (see Example 8.4 overleaf). That some of the lines are in parallel motion is suggestive of overtones of a fundamental pitch, as would the simultaneity of onsets. We might expect to hear a descending line, a note in ascending and descending movement, or a static bass line. However, the listening experience is much more complex. The onsets do create aural images of notes, but the impression is soon diluted by the complex simultaneous movement of overtones. The fact that amplitudes change – overtones or notes fade out – does not help either: it remains difficult actually to determine how many different notes there are in this pattern. One notable exception is the last three minutes of the composition (see Example 8.1 above), where Saariaho creates

Example 8.4   *Jardin secret I* – spectrogram of 5:50–6:30

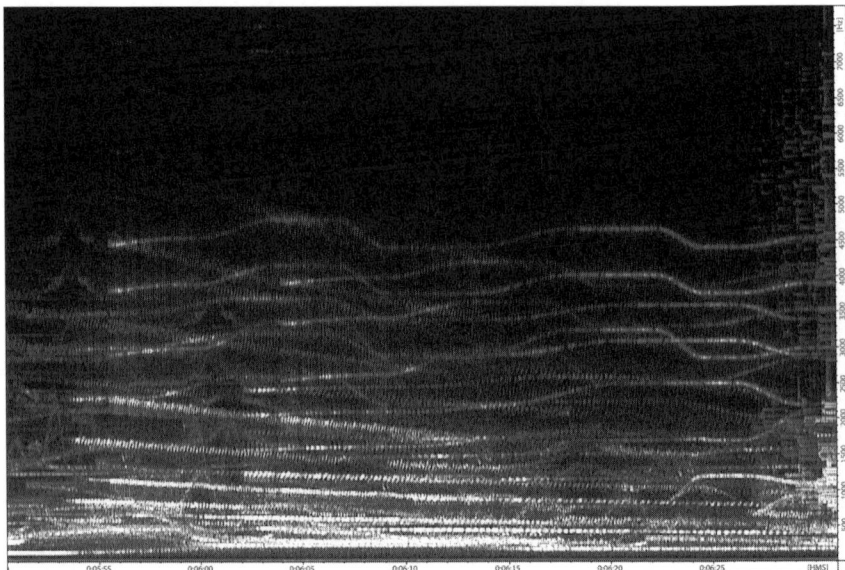

rather consistent note identities, resulting in a discernible contrapuntal movement. Here, timbre and harmony can be meaningfully discerned: we have bell sounds moving in polyphony.

However, for the most part, the aural image only hints at recognizable sound sources, bells and voices. How, then (or why), should the listener be able to decide whether a shimmering, bell-like sound is a complex inharmonic chord or a timbre made up of inharmonic partials? We are therefore forced into questioning whether the distinction between timbre and harmony is necessary or useful in this composition: they are identical in terms of the work's construction, and are practically indistinguishable in its aural image. *Jardin secret I* thus represents the kind of spectral composition wherein timbre as a distinctive musical concept begins to lose all relevance.

Timbre as a Model for Harmony: *Lichtbogen*

In *Im Traume*, Saariaho connects timbre and harmony through the idea of a *general sonority*, drawing parallels between harmonic colour and sound colour. In *Jardin secret I*, the synthetic timbres and harmonies share similar interval structures. But in *Lichtbogen*, for nine musicians and live electronics, Saariaho applied methods that in many ways resemble the techniques of instrumental synthesis (*synthèse instrumentale*), as developed by the French group, *l'Itinéraire*. The technique has two important phases: the spectral analysis of instrumental sounds, and the simulation of those sounds by an orchestra. While the analysis reveals the temporally changing spectral structure of a sound, the simulation can consist of translating the movements of partials into the individual instrumental parts of a score (Cohen-Levinas, 1991: 56). A vital aspect of instrumental synthesis is that the resulting orchestral texture reflects the temporal changes of the analysed spectra. Microscopic, transitory, sonic events expand temporally and become perceptible. Pitch structures in the spectra provide material for further manipulation: harmonic spectra transform into inharmonic spectra, for example (Wilson, 1988: 35 and 37).[11]

For the construction of harmonies in *Lichtbogen*, Saariaho analysed timbres with the IANA computer programme. In devising this programme, Gérard Assayag used Ernst Terhardt's algorithm, which mathematically models the perception of pitch.[12] Terhardt separated two kinds of pitch perception: analytic and holistic. An analytic perception focuses on the component pitches that shape timbre; a complex signal may result in the perception of several *spectral pitches*. A holistic perception focuses on determining a prevailing overall pitch, a *virtual pitch*; a complex signal produces several *virtual pitches*.

The analytical process begins with a Fourier transform of a recorded sound in order to establish its spectral components.[13] IANA then transfers these components into a tempered scale, the accuracy of which increases through numeric indications of the extent to which actual pitches deviate from the tempered scale (Terhardt, 1982: 679–80 and 686). One hundred cents is equal to a semitone, so the actual pitch of a spectral component can be 50 cents under or above a note from the tempered scale. The programme also specifies the amplitude of each component and provides an interpretation of the perceptual importance of each component.

Saariaho derived the harmonic material in *Lichtbogen* from analyses of several cello sounds. Example 8.5 shows Saariaho's spectral analysis of a cello F♯: the bottom row lists the perceptually important spectral components.[14] Saariaho was particularly interested in transitions between *pure* and *noisy* sounds. The first analysed transition begins with a pure harmonic flageolet sound, followed by the cellist gradually increasing pressure from the left hand while simultaneously moving the bow in the direction of the fingerboard. The second analysed transition was a glissando between two flageolet sounds (Saariaho, 1987: 129).

Changes in the spectral content of the sound during these transitions can be traced by performing several analyses upon different stages of the transition (Saariaho, 1991: 436). The analysis shown in Example 8.5 overleaf provided ten perceptually relevant pitches: under each note there are three numbers; if the bottom number is zero, the pitch is perceptually irrelevant. Saariaho proceeded to modify the

---

[11]   Additional information on such processes in Gérard Grisey's music can be found in Baillet, 2000: 67–74.

[12]   See Terhardt et al., 1982: 679–80 and 686, and Saariaho, 1991: 445.

[13]   A Fourier transform is a mathematical operation that produces a representation of a complex sound as a sum of sine waves, thus revealing its overtone structure.

[14]   Taken from Saariaho's sketches and notes, 1985.

Example 8.5   Sketch of *Lichtbogen* – analysis of cello F♯

Example 8.6 Sketch of *Lichtbogen* – rough draft of harmony

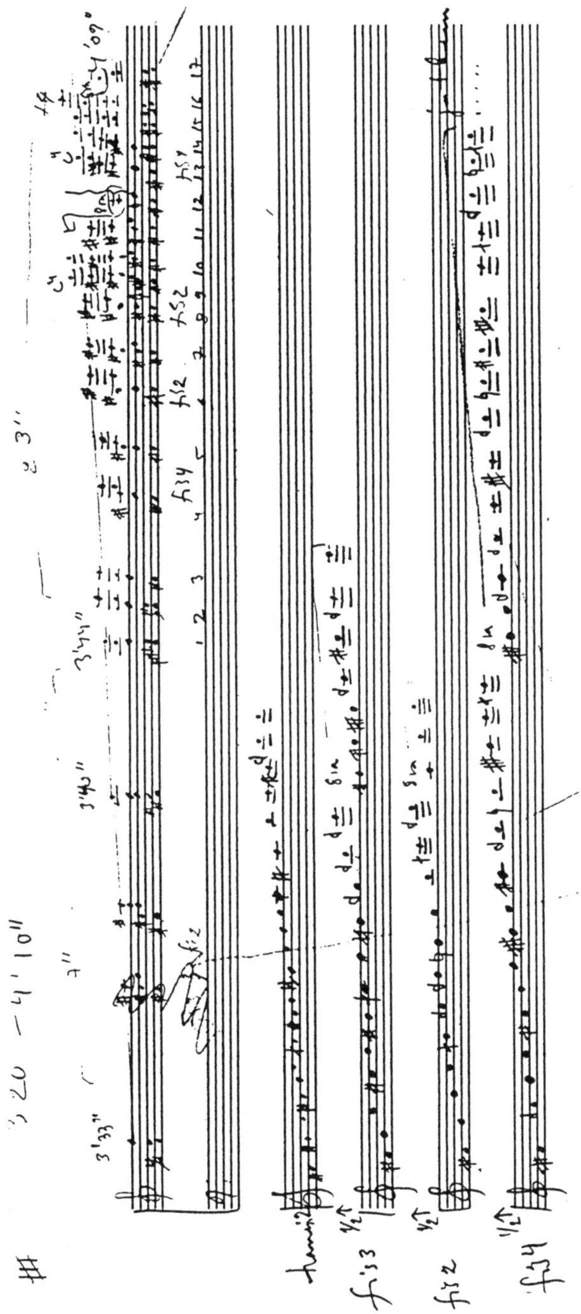

resulting pitch structures in many ways. First, she removed 'undesirable' intervals, in this case the octave (Saariaho, 1991: 436),[15] leaving pitch *classes*. Next, she converted these pitch classes (originally at the resolution of one cent) into notes of the tempered scale. The smallest change was the interpretation of F_1 (+43 cents) to $F\sharp_1$ (a change of 57 cents); the largest change was the interpretation of $A\sharp_2$ (-36 cents) to B_2 (a change of 136 cents). Following these adaptations, Saariaho arrived at a group of nine pitches – F, G♯, $F\sharp_1$, D_2, B_2, E_3, A_3, C_4, $A\sharp_4$ – which she used in chords, arpeggios and melodic lines. The harmonic constellations of the microtonally varied unison sequence at the beginning of the composition derive from analyses of the performed sound colour.

Chord patterns in Saariaho's sketches (see Example 8.6)[16] match the chords of the glockenspiel, grand piano and harp. The first chord ($F\sharp_1$, $A\sharp_2$, B_2, G_3 and D_4), for instance, is divided between these three instruments in bar 43, prior to further chord changes in bars 45, 47, 48 and 50. The section starting in bar 42 demonstrates Saariaho's idea of superimposing several textural levels. The strings and the flute form one level, the piano, harp and glockenspiel another (see Example 8.7). The qualities of these groups are opposed in several ways: the first group is capable of producing microtonal material, while the second can only sound notes of the tempered scale. In addition, their onset characteristics are dissimilar: the strings and the flute offer a great deal of control, whereas the glockenspiel, piano, and harp are in this sense rather more limited (Linjama, 1987: 112). Saariaho has also used the results of sound colour analysis in transitions, from glissandi, to arpeggios, to melodic phrases: an example can be seen in the string texture starting from bar 111. This texture, originally made up of microtonal glissandi, transforms towards an arpeggio chord. Similarities between the analytical material and the arpeggios are most evident from bar 127 onwards, as shown in Example 8.8.

Saariaho's sketches and notes do not indicate the use of such techniques as orchestral frequency modulation or phase shift, which are typical devices of composers from the *Itinéraire* group: Tristan Murail (b. 1947); Gérard Grisey (1946–98). Likewise, she has not been interested in the technique of orchestral sound colour modulation (*Klangmodulation mit einem Orchester*, LeNaour, 1991: 11). In frequency modulation, summation and difference tones are calculated between pitches. In phase shift, different parts of the spectrum are reinforced and attenuated over time. Both techniques simulate electronic sound generation and manipulation processes.[17] What Saariaho did instead was to determine the dynamic characteristics of instruments on the basis of the amplitude values of partials given by sound colour analysis (Saariaho, 1991: 445).

The unity of timbre and harmony manifests itself in *Lichtbogen* through their shared organizational principles. In particular, the sound colour transitions, which form the basis of harmonies, are instances of Saariaho's axis of *purity*

---

[15]   See also Linjama, 1987: 114.
[16]   Taken from Saariaho's sketches and notes, 1985.
[17]   See LeBaron and Bouliane, 1980/81: 433, or Wilson, 1988: 45.

Example 8.7 *Lichtbogen* – **superimposition of textural levels**

Example 8.8   *Lichtbogen* – texture-derived sound colour analysis

of sound: *pure* sound (a harmonic tone) and consonance are parallel; *noisy* sound (produced on the cello using excessive bow pressure) corresponds with dissonance. Further, Saariaho combines timbre and harmony by allocating to harmonic structures the same instrumental articulations from which she derived the harmonies in the first place: a 'tense' chord is played with a *noisy* sound colour (Saariaho, 1987: 130).

Musical Ideologies of Timbre and Harmony

Although Saariaho separates sound colour and harmony on a conceptual level, their organizational principles in *Lichtbogen* are quite similar. The aesthetic principle of unity of form and content is behind the search for the unity of timbre and harmony (Saariaho, 1987: 124). It is conceivable that this unity is achieved when the partial structure of a timbre – its internal harmony – corresponds with harmonic and melodic structures in the composition. In this sense, melodic and harmonic material is contained within the timbre. This conception of compositional process as a dialogue between form and content, whilst neither new nor limited to music, carried great significance as a modernist principle. Saariaho's specific source of inspiration for this type of structural thinking was Kandinsky, who formulated the idea of the unity of form and material in the following way: '*Form is the external manifestation of inner meaning*' (in Saariaho, 1987: 93).

It is rather surprising that Saariaho (writing in 1987) compares her thinking on timbre and harmony with the structures of functional harmony (see above). Why would she have felt the need to refer to musical principles so far removed from her own work? In 1987, there existed a catalogue of music stretching back almost a hundred years wherein the role of functional harmony had been called into question, and in which sound colour had taken on a structural function. One only has to consider the work of Stockhausen, Ligeti or *musique concrète*, for examples.

The explanation could lie in the aesthetic ideal of unity of form and content. Theories of harmony that are rooted in the overtone series go back as far as Pythagoras and his followers. In their system of thought, the numerical relationships present in harmonic overtones were analogous to the cosmic world order. In the latter half of the nineteenth century, Hermann von Helmholtz's work on sound colour established acoustical and physiological connections between tonal music theory and the overtones produced by musical sounds. More recently, the central argument in Charles Rosen's *The Classical Style* (1972) was that the formal structures of tonality were not just abstract schemes, but a consequence of the materials of tonal music (tonal melodies and harmonies). Saariaho's reference to functional harmony could therefore be understood as an attempt to situate her own compositional principles within the larger framework of Western musical composition. In functional harmony, Saariaho recognized ideals with which she felt familiar, but as a modernist, she also sought something new: the roles of harmony and timbre had to be reversed; a revolution. The reference to functional harmony is thus a reflection of Saariaho's compositional self-image. She places herself within the historical continuum of Western musical composition, but does this in a way that gives rise to a modernist interpretation of that tradition.

The issue of form and content also articulates Saariaho's affinity with spectral composers. Saariaho has never adopted the approaches of integral serialists and their version of form/content unification: for her, the expansion of serial organization to encompass musical parameters besides pitch leads to a pointless, musically meaningless organization; in her world, timbres have qualities that make them inherently dissonant or consonant (Linjama, 1987: 112). Yet while Saariaho wishes to distance herself from compositional procedures whose results are beyond perception, she regards herself as part of a tradition of parametric thinking: her music contains networks of simultaneous interpolation processes between musical parameters.[18]

Leonard B. Meyer has pointed out this characteristic in integral serial methods when criticizing Stockhausen's ideas on the isomorphism of pitch and time (Meyer, 1994: 246 and 270–73). Meyer censured the confusion of phenomena that are perceptually within different domains: rhythm (time) is a quantity, whereas pitch is a quality. Composers of the *Itinéraire* group have found fault with the parametric thinking of integral serialism, identifying discrepancies between compositional organization and listener perception. In his manifesto for spectral music, Grisey wanted to abandon all organizational models that were 'outside music' (Grisey, 1991: 298).[19] Musical structures should only be based on properties of sound, rather than taking inspiration from mathematical or physical models.

As such, it would be fair to expect the connections between timbre and harmonic structure in spectral techniques of instrumental synthesis to be readily perceptible: this is the crux of spectralist criticism levelled at integral serialism. However, there are at least two problems. The perception and understanding of timbre is subject to learning and cultural context: the nature of perception varies between individuals, and is contingent upon situation. To understand and interpret timbre is an acquired ability. Instrumental sounds are usually understood holistically, and the perception of overtones requires that attention is directed specifically to this property. In the case of harmony, the situation is different. At least for people raised within the sphere of Western music education, the obvious way of understanding harmony is rather analytical: harmonies consist of groups of notes (chords) and their successions (chord progressions). If we characterize different listening strategies by placing them on an axis from analytical listening to holistic listening, timbre and harmony seem to occupy opposite positions. To comprehend the connection between timbre and harmony implied by instrumental synthesis therefore requires a rather special listening strategy.

Tristan Murail, who has written on the relationship between timbre and harmony, argues that harmony can refer to any vertical structure of any sonic phenomenon (Murail, 1984: 158–9). A texture or a timbre that reveals its harmonic structure in computer analysis can constitute such a phenomenon. For Murail, timbre and harmony offer alternative descriptions of sonic events. 'Harmony' highlights the separateness of components within a sonic structure, whereas 'timbre' directs attention towards the sonic event as a whole. For his part,

---

[18]   Saariaho's letter to the author, 17 May 1995.

[19]   Grisey has crystallized the aesthetic principles of the *Itinéraire* group as follows: '*Nous sommes musiciens et notre modèle est le son et non la litérature, le son et non les mathématiques, le son et non le théatre, les arts plastiques, la physique des quantas, la géologie, l'astrologie ou l'acupuncture!*' ['We are musicians and our model is sound, not literature; sound, not mathematics; sound, not theatre, sculpture, quantum physics, geology, astrology or acupuncture!'] Grisey wished to abandon all 'non-musical' principles of organization. See also LeBaron and Bouliane, 1980/81: 426; and Baillet, 2000: 39–45.

Helmholtz contended that a sharp distinction between timbre and harmony was unnecessary, arguing that it is possible to learn to discern the overtone structure of musical sounds (Helmholtz, 1954: 24). The physical and physiological nature of timbre and harmony was, according to him, the same. The listener has access to two different listening strategies, and decides which to prioritize depending upon his or her intention in each particular case.

The connection between timbre and harmony in instrumental synthesis appears even more abstract when we consider the fact that the technique often begins with the observation of sonic events lasting only a few milliseconds. In the analysis of sound, a 'sonic microscope' is used to analyse such minute details; these events are then transferred to the macro level of harmonies by temporal extension. Also, the simulation by musical instruments of temporal arrangements of overtones yields sonic results that are far more complex than the original analysed sounds: each instrument comes with its own set of overtones. One could therefore argue that the criticism the *Itinéraire* group directed towards integral serialism applies equally to instrumental synthesis: in many ways, timbre is just as abstract when used to provide formal and aural models for harmony. In Stockhausen's music, abstract theoretical constructions are used; in instrumental synthesis, models are based on empirical observations of the microstructure of timbre. But in both cases, the principles of construction are beyond the perceptual capabilities of a listener.

Stockhausen's abstract parameterizations and instrumental synthesis offer two different solutions to the modernist aesthetic axiom of combining form and content. That both techniques provide musical results where the constructive principles of structure are not aurally verifiable is problematic only if such a connection is seen to be important from the point of view of compositional technique or musical aesthetics. Saariaho has never tried to bring about recognizable connections between a timbre and a harmony: the listener does not have to realize that harmonies are derived from timbres. In fact, there are significant differences between Saariaho's approach in *Lichtbogen* and the instrumental synthesis of the *Itinéraire* group. Saariaho approximated the results of sound colour analysis at several stages, especially in transferring the analytical results into notes from the tempered scale. Microstructures revealed in the analysis disappear in this process. The transposition of pitch structures, too, disconnects the resulting harmonies from the original analysis. Moreover, the results of sound colour analysis are dependent upon the particular way in which the cello resonates according to its own formant frequencies. Saariaho modified the analytical results by removing some intervals – particularly octaves – and by adjusting the octave transpositions of individual partials.

The connection between timbre and harmony in *Lichtbogen* is therefore highly abstract. Harmonic structures are the results of a process that begins with a sound colour analysis, but these harmonies do not exactly recreate the internal timbral complexities of the source sound. Saariaho has clearly not aimed at creating a psycho-acoustically verifiable connection between timbre and harmony, if, indeed, such a connection were possible in the first place. It would appear that techniques taken from instrumental synthesis are more a constructive principle, a particular way of producing and controlling musical material in a somewhat coherent fashion. The vistas opened up by the computerized sound analysis developed by the *Itinéraire* group function simply as a collection of tools and techniques to explore musical composition. In her writings, Saariaho never specifies whether it would be desirable for timbre to act as a model for large-scale harmonic structures.

The three compositions under consideration here were composed within a period of six years. During this time, Saariaho's compositional thinking evolved and developed in significant ways. *Im Traume* operates with traditional instruments, with the dichotomy between timbre and harmony played out in the contrast of articulations, textural definition and sound colour processes. Computerized sound synthesis and analysis extended Saariaho's compositional techniques considerably, also because sound colour analysis was for her a new tool in generating musical material. In *Jardin secret I*, she constructed sound colours and harmonies using similar technical methods. The connection between timbre and harmony is so fundamental that the conceptual dichotomy dissolves. Finally, the compositional tools applied in *Lichtbogen* – the methods of analysing sound and generating harmony – appear to have been central to many of Saariaho's subsequent compositions. The sonic imagery and formation of ensemble gestures, for example, in *Io* (1987), *Nymphéa* (1987), *Amers* (1992), *Solar* (1993) and *Graal théâtre* (1994) are clearly related to *Lichtbogen*. It would be an interesting topic for future study to categorize, or define the prototypes of ensemble gestures present in these compositions. A kind of impulse-resonance model would certainly be a possibility: a system in which an impulse, a shock, is followed by a slow decay; the resultant harmonic material is presented in the repetitive motions of different instruments. In her later works, the harmonic and rhythmic vocabulary is significantly different: pulsating rhythms and harmonic structures have their reference points in a much earlier kind of modernism.

The development of Saariaho's compositional technique within the six years considered here has been informed by two important ideas. One was a modernist-revolutionary way of thinking: the roles of fundamental musical elements in composition had to be rearranged. The other was the process of research into the details of sound, and the development and use of new tools and methods: a blend of theory and practice. Saariaho took part in this development through her writings and musical compositions. Her interest was not in the purity of methods or ideologies, but rather in the pursuit of techniques that allowed her to develop her own expressive language.

Chapter 9

Networks of Communication: (De)Crystallization and Perceptual Zoom in *Du cristal*

Jon Hargreaves

The idea of networks has obvious import for communication in the internet age. Central to it is the potential for expansion and flexibility: it is open to perpetual redefinition. Networks provide a means of conceptualizing, and understanding, music as communication; considering how networks might be manifest, the effects they have on perception, and their implications for meaning, can illuminate the visions, narratives and dialogues at play in Saariaho's output. One might consider 'network' simply to mean 'a set of connections' in the sense that it is used here; just as this composer's output never 'refer[s] to pre-established formal structures' (Saariaho, 1987: 93), no fixed theoretical model is applied. Discussion concerns the musical, semiotic and philosophical relationships – potential, imagined and realized – that might be perceived in the listening experience of *Du cristal* (1989–90). With a view to appreciating the broad range of meanings it offers listeners, and the many ways it facilitates communication, various aspects of the piece are considered in terms of how the composer's input might relate to what the listener is enabled to take away from the experience.

Saariaho quotes Kandinsky: '"Form is the external manifestation of inner meaning"' (ibid.). This is of general interest to those with a regard for her music, although it is particularly pertinent to a sound-mass piece such as *Du cristal* – the notion of 'tapping-in' to get at meaning is more than just a pun on the idea of composition as sculpture (or on telecommunications, for that matter). In this quotation, musical form is acknowledged as a medium for communication whilst meaning itself is located elsewhere, and further, that significance lies somehow 'inside' form seems to imply that this composer considers music to be meaningful at the level of content.

'What is *in* this piece?' is worth considering; it is an enormous question, of course, and may it never be fully answered. Earlier in her article the composer notes 'the *relationships* of harmony and timbre *in* musical form' (ibid.; emphasis my own). Regardless of the parameters in question, the point here is that this music is made up of *relationships*, rather than objects. Many of Saariaho's pre-compositional materials are dependent for their identity on perceptual synthesis. To hear them is to recognize a whole transformation rather than a plurality of attributes – take, for example, the glissando and multiphonic used as source materials for *Lichtbogen* and *Nymphéa* (*Jardin secret III*) (Pousset, 2000: 93–4), or indeed, the timbral trill that ends *Du cristal*. If pre-compositional decisions influence later 'notes-on-the-page' ones, as their name suggests, then connection is the very genesis of this music.

All of this is borne out: Saariaho frequently refers to the 'network' of interacting musical parameters within which her works exist (Saariaho, 1987: 94, 97, 104, 107, 124, 132). Note that the pieces themselves are not considered to be networks. Rather, they consist of superimposed curves of intensity in an external web of continua; listeners hear the products of networks. Fittingly, in discussing how form might be the external manifestation of inner meaning, the question 'what is in this piece?' leads to answers regarding 'what this piece is in'. As testament to its significance and value, *Du cristal* lies at the cusp of paradox; listeners are often presented with activity in one parameter, only to find that significance lies in another.

The idea that things might traverse perceptual domains seems very important to Saariaho. The childhood memories reported by Moisala at the start of her book involve the stimulation of multiple senses: hearing birdsong, experiencing the quietness of the house, feeling the warmth of the sun and the enjoying sunlight (see Moisala, 2009: 1–2, 9). Later in life, studying composition under Heininen was not merely musical training, but an experience which restored her confidence, and 'pulled [her] back to life … all those colours, seeing, hearing, and living in the intermingling dimensions of all the senses, zooming in and out, making great free associations; I had been there before' (ibid.: 6). Clearly this is a person for whom moments and periods of time can be characterized in multiple ways; the essence of these memories seems to lie in the combination of sensory experiences. Again, this evokes notions of internal and external: the senses are the channels through which the body and mind internalize the outside environment. Cross-modal and corporeal experiences are clearly of high importance to Saariaho as a composer, one who became frustrated during her studies at Freiburg because of the emphasis on intellectual pursuit, '"as if it were more important than other experiences, expressions and ways of life"' (ibid.: 9).

Embodiment, and the idea of what lies within and without, clearly played a major role in inspiring *Du cristal*:

> When she was writing *Du cristal* (From Crystal; 1989) for orchestra, she even felt the powerful, physical presence of the musicians. At the time, she was expecting her first child, and she became aware of having two hearts beating inside her body, at first one of them beating much faster than the other. Over the course of time, the heartbeat of the unborn child grows and slows down until the two hearts have almost the same beat. In *Du cristal* the fast heartbeats became the ticking pulse played by a triangle, accompanied by a much slower, low pulse played by a timpani or bass drum. Toward the end of the composition, the fast pulse becomes slower and eventually finds the same rhythm with the low pulse (Moisala, 2009: 35).

A narrative such as this is particularly interesting from the point of view of communication. The eventual coincidence of the crotale (in place of the triangle) and the bass drum at figure MM marks the end of the work, generating a feeling of closure: the instruments fall into phase with one another before the famous timbral trill in the cello leads into *...à la fumée*. This musical pattern is clearly appreciable, although surely only highly primed listeners would recognize its biographical connotations. The waves of the Pacific Ocean were another source of inspiration (ibid.: 35–6), although, again, this plays a rather mercurial role in communication. It is impossible to account for the listening history and knowledge of every person who hears this music. Therefore, the focus of this chapter is on considering the communication process from an analytical perspective: the subject for debate is the information offered by the listening experience called *Du cristal*.

The names of many of Saariaho's works bring together aesthetic beauty and empirical study; often, they evoke literary or poetic imagery, as well as fascinating phenomena for scientific study. The diptych *Du cristal ...à la fumée* is certainly no exception. Indeed, it is emblematic of this tendency: the title is an adaptation of the cellular biologist and philosopher Henri Atlan's essay, *Entre le cristal et la fumée* (1979). According to him, all living organisms lie between two forms of death, which correspond to smoke and crystal: *'entre le fantôme et le cadavre'* ['between the ghost and the corpse'] (Atlan, 1979: 5). The book itself examines how living cells self-organize, growing into complex systems as they multiply. Whereas from a Darwinian perspective this growth is directed towards an end product, Atlan argues that there are many more processes at play from the perspective of an individual cell; for every development contributing to the chain of events that results in the full organism, there are many other developments that do not. Thus, the internal redundancy, or the 'noise' within a system – those events that do not lead directly to the end goal – plays a huge part in the self-organization process (see Batt, 1994: 44–6).

Atlan's book in general, particularly the idea that noise might generate meaning, but also the implications of his thought for temporality (the blurring of linear cause and effect), resonates strongly with Saariaho's music. Indeed, the notion of a continuum with a solid and a gas at either end finds analogy with the sound/noise axis. More pertinently, however, the adaptation of Atlan's title suggests that this diptych presents a single musical process: notionally, there is a change from crystal (*Du cristal*, bar 1) to smoke (*...à la fumée*, double bar-line). Indeed there is a sense of dialogue between the two pieces: the same materials are subjected to contrasted formal processes, concerning integration (*Du cristal*) and disintegration (*...à la fumée*) (see Metzer, 2009: 182–95). The two works can be played separately, however, as well as forming a diptych. Nieminen quotes the composer: "'To my way of thinking, *Du cristal ...à la fumée* is a single work, two facets of the same image, but both fully drawn in, living, and independent.'"[1]

---

[1] CD liner notes for *Kaija Saariaho: Du cristal ...à la fumée, Sept Papillons, Nymphéa*, Ondine, ODE 1047–2.

Rather than discussing the nature of this contrasted pairing, the present chapter is focused on the first work of the diptych only, in an attempt to consider the communication process in depth. With that in mind, it is important not to forget that, in so many ways, this music has its origins in the living body. It is fitting therefore, to consider the immediate sensory impact of *Du cristal*.

From Crystal ...

The evocative power of 'crystal' enables a wealth of information to be communicated at the very opening moment of *Du cristal*. The network of associations facilitated by the first sound play a primarily important role in bringing about the immediacy with which this music communicates; instantly, for listeners primed by the title, this chord sounds like crystal is thought of. The semiosis is simple: for a long time, such 'washes' of sound as this have been associated with light and colour. However, as Adlington points out, there is subtlety at play here: the orchestral palette of *Du cristal* presents a spectrum of brightness, and the music occupies positions between its two extremes – the bright triangle and glockenspiel, and the dark bass drum (Adlington, 2003: 316). The simultaneous presence of different 'shades' within the palette enhances the visual metaphor: listeners are presented with a deconstruction of light, rather than a mere representation of it – a musical luminescence that transforms and evolves as the relative intensities of particular shades are altered. Alongside and within this, 'crystal' connotes clarity and purity, and the profile of this chord finds some analogy with those connotations in terms of pitch and orchestration.

In terms of orchestration, the overall timbre becomes blended as the energy of the initial impact fades. There are three bands of primary orchestral colour – woodwind, brass and strings, each supported by percussion – and although the high-pitched woodwind maintains its purity, the lower-register brass and strings are mixed together. Paradoxically, the dissolution of this momentarily clear division and homogeneity shows the composer's intention to communicate notions of clarity and purity; those ideas are expressed as points of departure, through the introduction of impurity and blurring.

Another striking characteristic of this sonority is its pitch content. In accordance with its banded orchestration, distinct and homogenous 'intervallic regions' can be identified, as shown in Example 9.1. Each of these regions radiates potential for tonal references, which are transitorily suggested, although not realized, as different parts of the chord intensify. The perceptual effect is that listeners can hear the chord 'rotating' in real time; various collectional affinities are hinted at as tonal colours emerge and fade. This facilitates proliferate and immediate musical communication. Given the historical importance of tonality in Western art music, Saariaho presents a wide range of listeners with a sound term with which they are in some sense well-acquainted, despite its novelty; paradoxically, this distinctive sound is a mechanism for experiencing

Example 9.1   *Du cristal* – opening chord

a) Orchestrational Characteristics

b) Tonal Reference

familiarity. Thus, at the outset, the piece presents an extremely clear, intriguing and accessible idea, which illuminates the ensuing musical process. Given the high regard this composer has for tonality (Saariaho, 1987: 94), tonal hearing is clearly something she intends and invites her listeners to experience. Even more information is transmitted by this distribution of pitches if it is considered from a spectral point of view, however.

Within a 'spectral chord', one of the notes is presented as the fundamental, implying that it projects a harmonic spectrum into which the other ones are subsumed. Thus, the non-fundamental pitches represent, or, put more positively, emphasize, different partials within that field of resonance. By implication, therefore, when listened to spectrally, Example 9.1 is experienced as a single composite sonority rather than as a vertical combination of intervals. Considering the levels at which these pitches intersect each other's harmonic spectra provides a particular point of interest.

Despite *notionally* being subsumed by the spectrum of the fundamental, D♭, in actual fact, each note of the chord projects its own field of resonance – the mind synthesizes these such that a single overall sound is heard. Thus, each pitch could be considered to embody a particular, numbered <fundamental : distinct partial> relationship with every other; C is the third partial of F, for example, where B♭ is the 45th partial of E.[2] In a sense, this sonority is a network of intersecting harmonic fields, because these relationships happen simultaneously. Notably, this is an all-interval, and thus by definition an 'all-overtone' chord, which implies that all 24 of these possible intersections are represented. In the first bar of the score, however, only 23 out of those 24 intersections are realized; it is not until B¼♯ is added in the second bar that the set is complete.

This kind of analysis reveals how the opening of *Du cristal* exploits the qualities of the harmonic series, although it does not, perhaps, directly clarify the communication process. Rare indeed is the listener who comments authoritatively on the distribution of partial relationships on hearing this work, and surely nobody would hear the first bar as incomplete, merely because a single intersection is not realized. However, at some point Saariaho must have taken a conscious decision to include the B¼♯; indeed, the special importance of that pitch is illustrated by its delayed entry. Notionally, the completion of the set of <fundamental : distinct partial> intersections ensures that the sonority is wholly integrated – a kind of spectral lattice. Evidently, despite the imperceptibility of some of its details, spectral technique plays a role in the communication process. The idea of integration seems to underpin the compositional thinking at this opening moment, as is borne out by the spectral characteristics and other manifestations of homogeneity explained above. It is surely significant that *Du cristal* starts with an intervallically and spectrally 'sealed' sonority, since this implies purity and clarity, qualities widely associated with crystals. By

---

[2]   Harmonic numbers refer to the spectrum within the 24-step octave used by Saariaho in *Du cristal*.

implication, as the work continues and the chord is transformed, things can only become less pure, less clear and less integrated – after all, this piece comes *from crystal*, and moves *towards smoke*. From a less poetic viewpoint, self-containment and 'fixedness' are central features of the physical structure of crystals, as explained below.

Crystals and (De)Crystallization

> Crystal. A solid with a regular polyhedral shape. All crystals of the same substance grow so that they have the same angles between their faces. However, they may not have the same external appearance because different faces can grow at different rates, depending on the conditions. The external form of the crystal is referred to as the *crystal habit*. The atoms, ions, or molecules forming the crystal have a regular arrangement and this is the *crystal structure*.[3]

> Crystal. Homogenous solid body of chemical element, compound or isomorphous mixture having a regular atomic lattice arrangement that may be shown by crystal faces.[4]

These definitions provide the same basic information, although there is a slight difference: in the first, externally observable form is emphasized to a greater extent than in the second. That subtle difference highlights their pertinence to this music-analytic chapter: the defining attributes of crystals regard their composition both at a large-scale, macro-level, and at the molecular micro-level. The analogy is particularly strong with spectrally conceived music: just as the eye sees the crystal habit rather than its underlying lattice structure, so the ear hears a sound rather than a differentiated distribution of partials. The idea that the first chord of *Du cristal* forms a kind of spectral lattice is hinted at above. Theoretically, an imperceptibly complete set of spectral bonds holds the chord together, just as the microscopic atoms in a crystal structure maintain fixed relative spatial positions. That regular arrangement of molecules arises as the unit-cell pattern repeats, generating symmetry in all dimensions, and in turn that replication implies a process of growth. This is of particular interest to the musically minded, because it suggests that crystal forms (as products) are determined by the growth of their content (a process).

Named for Atlan's essay on self-organization, *Du cristal* is not merely concerned with evolution of musical material, but with evolution itself; as different aspects of sounds intensify, different *kinds* of transformation are exposed. Thus, it presents

---

[3]   *Oxford Dictionary of Chemistry* (4th edn), ed. John Daintith, 2000: 158.

[4]   *Chambers Dictionary of Science and Technology*, ed. Peter Walker, 1999: 286. (Other definitions are offered in electronics, glass and botany, although this one is the most pertinent here.)

an ongoing relationship in which content emerges from formation, rather than merely a process in which form emerges from content. With a view to discussing how this is achieved, it is worth briefly considering the process in which crystals are formed.

Crystallization is a change in the state of matter ('phase') resulting in the formation of solid crystals, which occurs as the intensity of the energy applied to a liquid (or sometimes, a gas) is varied. However, the process is not quite as straightforwardly directed as this might suggest. 'Interfaces' – boundaries separating the two phases of the medium – develop, located at (and constituted by) the meeting points between solid crystal and the liquid solution in which it is growing. As this continues, of course, the interfaces become larger until the solution has yielded the maximum amount of crystal possible under the conditions. Two related processes occur at the interfaces: in one – *nucleation* – molecules cluster together, as the respective concentration levels of the solute and solvent settle; in the other, some of these clusters reach a point of critical mass, and become solid, as *crystal growth* occurs. Thus, in line with Atlan's explanation of the growth of living cells, dissolution is as inherent as solidification to this process, as many nuclei fail to crystallize. This means that there is an in-built resistance to the prevailing temporal momentum; overall, the process could be thought of as '(de)crystallization'.[5]

The purpose here is not to propose a programme for the unfolding of form in *Du cristal*, such that individual events relate to specific developments in the formation of a crystal; the metaphor is more general. Taken as a whole, *Du cristal* presents listeners with an uninterrupted 16-minute sound, different parts of which come to prominence at different times. This gives the impression that things emerge out of, and recede into, the composite sonority, just as molecules solidify and dissolve in a crystallizing medium. In accordance with Saariaho's predisposition towards cross-sensory experiences, a useful metaphor for the overall listening experience offered by *Du cristal* is that of watching crystallization. There are a number of potential points of interest for the observer, therefore, and as the eye follows activity in different parts of the medium, attention might be more or less focused on different levels of detail. At times, observers might attend to the evolution of small-scale clusters of molecules, which combine to form interfaces; alternatively, the focus might be on larger-scale shapes and patterns in the development of such an interface; and at other times, the observer might perceptually 'step back' from the microscopic focus to observe larger-scale patterns affecting the appearance of the medium as a whole. In considering the auditory perception of this music, one might consider analogies to that visual experience. As the eye can observe crystallization at a number of levels, so can the ear hear *Du cristal*.

---

[5]   See Rhodes, 2006: 38–9; and Callister and Rethwisch, 2010: 46–7 and 344–5, for more information on crystal structures.

Crystallizing Networks of Time and Space

The ideas above have important implications for the communication of notions of time and space, as they suggest that this piece is an environment within which listeners occupy different positions, and within which they might focus their attention in different 'directions'. This is quite distinct from imagining music to be an object moving across a temporal field as it progresses from its beginning to its end. To lend weight to this argument, it should be shown that the conventional narrative passage from start to finish is somehow broken down.

The notion of progression from one moment to the next is brought into question at the very outset of *Du cristal*, because, as mentioned above, different parts of the sustained opening chord intensify independently. As they do so, the various bodies within the overall sound can be perceived to infiltrate, to be subsumed by, and to emerge from one another – their timbral and harmonic similarities give rise to perceptual 'connections'. For example, in the passage shown in Example 9.1, the bass drum and timpani roll seems to protrude from the overall sound-mass, just as the repeated triangle strikes 'grow' out of the high-register woodwind; similarly, the horns' surge in bar 2 sets the harder-edged brass sound of the trumpets and trombones into relief. This obstructs any conventional sense that the music is moving; rather than the passage of time being marked by recognizably separate ideas, there is a single musical object here, which, in essence, remains static. Further, the points of connection between the constituent parts of the overall sonority can be manifest within different frameworks; a sound that initially brings about contrast in terms of pitch might find a close timbral relation with another sonority, to the extent that they might be perceptually grouped together. This can be made clearer in a simplistic, abstract example.

Each of the circles in Example 9.2 represents a distinct part of the composite sonority of *Du cristal* at a single point in time. As shown, they all have a timbral, and most have a harmonic, aspect, each of which may be perceived as the prevailing, identity-defining characteristic. Theoretically, therefore, either of those qualities might form the basis for a perceptible relationship with the surrounding parts of the work. Thus, listeners are enabled to perceive multiple narrative routes through the form; this is a perceptual *network*, rather than a linear, channelled progression (see Example 9.2). An example of the subtlety at play in *Du cristal* is that the distinctions between its parts are blurred, and not heard in so heavily structurally articulated a fashion as this diagram suggests. However, the underlying principle still stands. The behaviour and characteristics of particular parts of the overall sound-mass offer listeners multiple ways – harmonic, timbral, amplitudinal change, or a higher-order combination of these and others – of perceptually grouping the whole; just as, for molecules in a crystallizing medium, connections might be made in various dimensions.

The conception shown in Example 9.2 has two interrelated implications for perception, the first being the reining in of temporal momentum. Theoretically, the multiplicity of ways a listener can 'navigate' from one moment in time to the

Example 9.2   Perceptual network of harmony and timbre

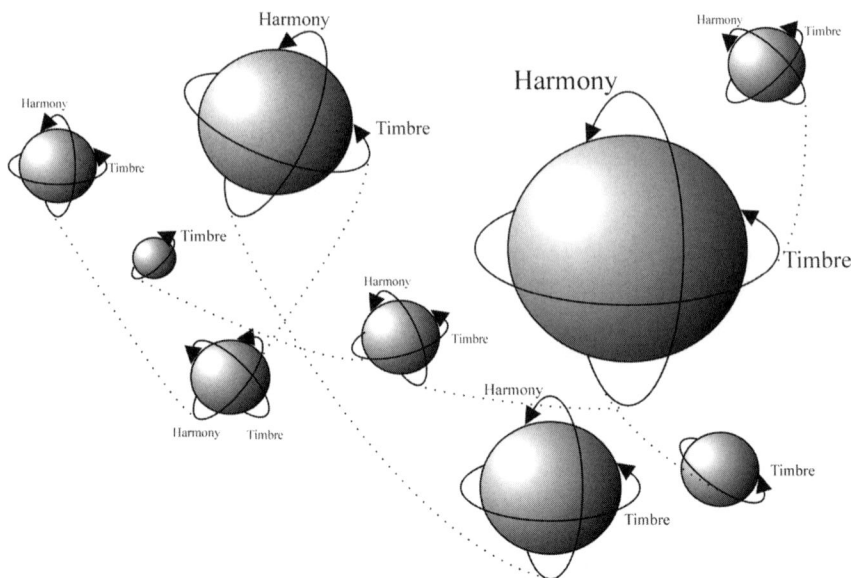

next breaks down the sense that there is a single, channelled narrative. Thus, the overall impetus is controlled by the composer, and drastically slowed down. The basic material of the piece is static: a gradually, albeit at times suddenly evolving sound-mass. Thus, the principal point of interest is located in the evolution of given *aspects* of that composite sonority, rather than in deeper-rooted changes to the mass itself. Saariaho's concern to imbue formal dynamism with significance (Saariaho, 1987: 94) ensures that such fundamental, global-level changes do occur, although because they are so severely protracted, listeners hear differences develop *within* an object rather than changes *of* object; the nature of perception is spatial, rather than temporal.

The second implication of this multi-directional conception of time, with its attendant lack of momentum, is that, metaphorically, *Du cristal* invites listeners to mediate between changeable spatial 'positions' in relation to the musical surface. As Example 9.2 shows, there is an emphasis on changes in the perceptual frame in which sounds are perceived, be it harmonic, timbral or otherwise. The fluid connections between different parts of the texture give rise to a situation in which a single sound might be related to its surroundings because of its pitch at one moment, and its timbre at the next. Thus, as transformations of the identity of sounds are perceived, it is the frame in which listeners place information that is altered, rather than the sounds themselves; notionally, the viewpoint of the observer has changed, rather than the observed. Arguably, as the form progresses, listeners mediate between different perceptual positions relative to the musical material.

Perceptual Zoom

Textural Hierarchy and Orchestrational Relief

The manipulation of listener perspective arises because the blurring of structural hierarchy plays so intrinsic a role in how *Du cristal* communicates. As the identities of sounds are continually recast, the perceptual unit is in constant flux, shifting from one structural level to another. Indeed, insofar as a basis for constancy in perceiving this work is possible, it consists of a flexible framework, which changes alongside the relationship between what is texturally fundamental and ornamental. At any given point in time, the composite sonority of *Du cristal* might be broken down on three levels:

1. Details arising from single instrumental parts
2. Mid-level groups of sounds, which together subscribe to a single composite identity
3. Sustained, background sonority.

Necessarily, this framework is loosely defined in order that it can be re-contextualized and realized in diverse ways; effectively, it merely spells out the notion that there is low-, mid- and high-level activity. However, such approximation lies at the core of *Du cristal*. The list above implies a fluid continuum through which materials move, rather than a rigid hierarchical framework in which all materials have a fixed place: repeatedly, textural details multiply, forming mid-level groups that may or may not grow to infiltrate and pervade the background sonority. In fact, the smoothing over of these divisions is the very process that constitutes *Du cristal*. Thus, the continual breaking down of the distinctions named above is the mechanism through which this piece communicates: just as molecules cluster together as interfaces in a crystallizing medium, so minute musical changes might affect the behaviour of, or indeed grow to become, larger-scale materials.

An implication of this disintegration of textural hierarchy is that not every level may be apparent at all times. For example, the seemingly empty soundscape at figure H seems initially to consist only of a background (see Example 9.3 overleaf). On closer inspection, it is clear that this is not merely a static sonority. There are foreground details: the harmonic glissandi create undulations in the composite sound, which are perceptible as a mid-level group. Thus, even at this point, the hierarchy is not completely flat, although the perceptual levels are clearly closer together than in the preceding environment, where the distinction between foreground events and the more slowly evolving background state can be heard. By implication therefore, the composer can manipulate the perception of textural depth by controlling the extent to which the various parts of the texture differ (be it in terms of rate of change, amplitude, timbre, pitch/register and so on).

Example 9.3　*Du cristal* – 'empty soundscape', figure H

Subject Position and Perceptual Zoom

When listening to Renaissance choral music of, say, Victoria or Palestrina, it is common for individuals to switch between two types of hearing in the course of a performance: some of the time, they follow the counterpoint, and at other times, they allow themselves to be absorbed by the musical aura as it fills the acoustic space. The difference concerns listeners' notional 'position' relative to the musical surface. Hearing an aura, they might be considered to be *inside* the music, as it flows around them.[6] By contrast, when tracking contrapuntal voices, the situation is more akin to their being located *outside* a musical object, observing the relationships between its parts: to perceive lines moving together through musical time and space is unintentionally to negotiate for oneself a position which is not on any of the paths they follow. The distinction between these two 'subject positions' (Clarke, 2005: 91–125) lies in the extent to which listeners differentiate between parts of the composite sonority. Arguably, this also applies to the perception of noise as opposed to delineated harmony. Despite stylistic differences, contrapuntal and 'aural' hearings of sixteenth-century counterpoint are related to the conflation of harmony and timbre.

Perceptions of *Du cristal* might be considered to tend towards two kinds: 'harmonic listening', which is akin to tracing counterpoint, as listeners actively discern concurrent parts of the sonority; and 'timbral listening', in which they do not. These labels, of course, represent the extremes of a continuum; rarely is perception purely of one kind or the other. To contend that particular textures lead to particular kinds of hearing would be a failure to recognize the sophistication at play in musical perception, on two counts. First, listeners might *elect* to hear something as harmonic rather than timbral, or vice versa (for example, the pitch content and the orchestration of the first chord of *Du cristal* are discussed separately); the identifying characteristics of a given sonority are the product of subjective judgement. Second, musical materials might invite (rather than require) a particular kind of hearing. For example, the imitative entries in Palestrina invite comparison based on the similarities of their pitch organization; other, less-imitative passages of the same music might invite a timbral hearing more readily. The way musical textures are heard is the product of an interaction between the disposition of the listener and the characteristics of the material in question. Resultantly, the very same sonority might be heard from either perspective.

The graph in Example 9.4 overleaf shows how listeners might perceive texture in Saariaho's music. It is not intended as an index for perception, but merely as an expression of the ideas discussed above. The horizontal axis shows hypothetical musical textures, ordered according to how they present the relationship between background sonority and foreground detail: in the middle, there is parity between what is fundamental and what is ornamental (in a solo melody, every note counts

---

[6]   Indeed, the etymological roots of 'aura' lie in the Latin and Greek for 'wind' or 'breeze'.

Example 9.4   Orchestrational relief 'graph'

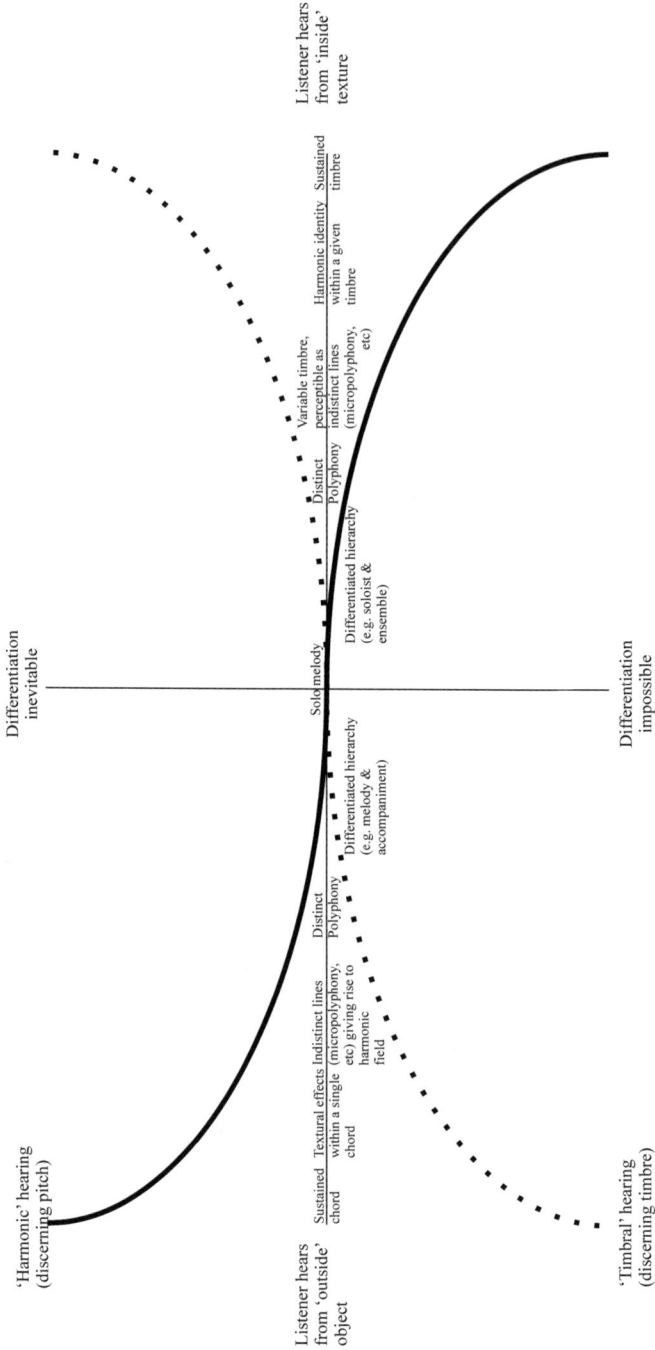

as it constitutes the entire sonority until the next note takes its place); further out in either direction, the named textures are more readily divisible into detail and underlying substance. Thus, at either end, the background is further back, and the foreground is closer to the front. Notice also the circularity: 'sustained chord' and 'sustained timbre' could well refer to the same musical material, heard from a different perspective.

The curves populating the graph exist simultaneously, representing timbral and harmonic perceptions of the same musical environment (or, in the latter case, harmonic material). Depending on the conditions, the sounds heard might prompt a listener's perception to jump vertically (or to skip horizontally across) to the equivalent position on the other curve. For example, an individual might be attending to the relative smoothness of a micropolyphonic texture, before suddenly focusing on its pitch content due to a change elsewhere in the overall sonority; on this graph, that listener would have 'switched' from the dotted to the unbroken curve.

There are two more things to note here, relating to the perception of textural depth, which in turn gives rise to the impression that things protrude from, or sink back into, the musical surface. First, the composite sonority invites varying levels of differentiation at separate times. For example, the texture might consist of sustained string harmonics and bass drones, less sustained mid-register chords played by brass, and an oscillating texture arising out of scalar figures in the woodwind. These three 'layers' of sound correspond to background, middleground and foreground, each one implying a different subject position. Elsewhere in the score, there may be no background sonority, and elsewhere still there may only be a foreground melody. Thus, the texture is invested with variable depth. This is certainly not unique to *Du cristal*, although, arguably, the textural manipulation here turns the metamorphoses between these 'auditory scenes' into meaningful processes. One might think of the (fluid) textural hierarchy as being inflated and deflated.

Second, as musical materials grow from timbral detail to textural characteristic or sustained chord, theoretically, listeners' perceptions move from left to right along the curves on the graph. Thus, subject position can be manipulated: as the status of detail changes, listeners are invited to zoom in, or to zoom out and survey things occurring over longer time spans at the background.[7] Speculative though all this may seem it is clear at first hearing that the process by which materials emerge into the foreground and/or recede back again plays an important part in *Du cristal* as a whole.

---

[7]   Herein lies the relationship between tonal background structures and the kind of textural background discussed here – in both cases the allusion to depth represents the observation that certain patterns and cycles move more slowly than those around them; listeners have to stand back (or zoom out) to take in all of the information. Just as sentences are read from left to right, pages from top to bottom and books from front to back, so (in essence) melodic movement is horizontal, harmony is vertical, and tonality implies a third spatial dimension – depth.

Observing Form; Forming Observation

To perceive musical form is to take a fixed perspective on sound events, such that they can be understood to belong to a single pattern. Thus, it may seem paradoxical to consider global unity, having discussed the continual renegotiation of subject position in (or by) *Du cristal*. However, changes in the viewpoint of the observer do not necessarily imply a lack of large-scale changes within the observed. The perception of form usually implies the division of a stream of information into large-, mid-, and small-scale sections and units, such that lower-level events are contained on the next level up. The process of perceiving such global order is deliberately confused in *Du cristal*, in two important ways. First, because listeners are presented with a number of independent routes through the piece concurrently, there is no single, form-defining narrative; the music is different for different people. Second, the grouping together of discrete low-level events into units is disrupted; listeners can easily perceive the growth of textural details as they pervade the background sonority. Thus, the outlines of the underlying patterns are masked.

The problem of form boils down to the sheer volume of transformations occurring at any one time in *Du cristal*. As Metzer puts it, 'when sound incessantly changes and music zips back and forth across a broad continuum, it becomes impossible to insist upon specific positions and roles' (Metzer, 2009: 185). Commentators have taken different approaches to addressing this problem. Brech (1999) separates out structural levels and explains activity on each one in minute detail, although this leads her continually to qualify exceptions to that structural index. Pousset (2000) takes the opposite approach, citing an introduction-plus-ternary shape at the highest level. Rather than discussing details, he simply cites Stoïanova, who explains that the piece 'already contains an entire network of internal relations and temporal equilibria of sonic materials and processes' (Stoïanova, 1994, cited in Pousset, 2000: 100). The section divisions given by Metzer and Pousset are shown in Example 9.5.[8]

In all music, form is constituted by interactions between different parameters, and this is made aurally apparent here; there is an ongoing competition for prevalence. Clearly, Metzer and Pousset consider different aspects of the sonority to predominate at different times within the form, given their section divisions; overall, activity in no single domain holds any more significance than that in any other. There are many ways of 'measuring' *Du cristal* besides those shown in the table, although it suffices here to consider tempo, pitch and textural patterns. Tempo is the most easily quantifiable of the three, and is discussed first.

---

[8]   In the table, 'M' and 'P' refer to Metzer's and Pousset's analyses. Metzer identifies his sections with bar numbers, whereas Pousset divides the score at 3', 8' and 14'. These are allocated to the nearest rehearsal figure. Timings are taken from Esa-Pekka Salonen's recording (on CD *Kaija Saariaho: Du cristal ...à la fumée, Sept Papillons, Nymphéa*, Ondine, ODE 1047–2). 'Infinite melodies' describes pointillistic, register-traversing melodic figurations scored for 'clear metallic timbres' (synthesizer, glockenspiel, vibraphone and piano); this label originates from the composer herself (see Metzer, 2009: 189).

Example 9.5 *Du cristal* – formal outlines

Fig	Bar	Time	Analyses M	Analyses P	Tempo (bpm)	'Bass Pitch'	Section	Description of Events (Texture)
–	1	0:00			50	D♭		Opening chord melts on repetition
A	12	0:48			60	D♭		Opening chord has melted
B	19	1:02				C♯		Solo violin breaks away from chord
C	27	1:26		INTRO		C♯ (&C)	Decay of first chord	W-wind lines join violin
D	35	1:47				C♯ (&C)		Hiatus: violins trill
E	39	2:01				C¼♯		Oscillating w-wind texture
F	49	2:20				C¼♯–G♯		'Infinite melodies' enter
G	59	2:38	A		(rit.)	D		Percussion throbs form aftermath of chord
H	65	3:01			48	D♭–D¼♭		'Empty' string harmonic sound-scape
I	78	4:00				D¼♭		'Infinite melodies' enter
J	88	4:22				B¼♯	Occupation of abyss	W-wind occupy sound-scape, picc. solo
K	94	4:39		A	(accel.)	A		Piano & low strings enter: wide intervals
L	101	5:01	A		60 (rit.)	A♭–D		Strings 'noise' intensifies as flutes enter
M	108	5:19			48	D♭		Chords alternate in hns and tpts/tbns
N	122	6:06				D♭	Hn./tpt. antiphony	Cresc. as w-wind join strings' trills
O	131	6:36	bar 126		(accel.)	C¼♯		'Pointillist' synth. interjections begin
P	142	7:11			60	C	Division of *tutti*	Timps erupt into solo material
Q	155	7:33				n/a		Fls gliss. announces block-like texture
R	169	7:58				n/a		*fff* strings herald new section of timp. solo
S	183	8:26			48; 72	G♭	Timp. solo	Vast strings chord; gliss. clears pitch space
T	191	8:53			60	C♯–A–F♯		Hiatus: oboes feature
U	201	9:16				G♭		W-wind trilling & scalar oscillations
V	209	9:30				F♯		Timps & percussion intensify
W	218	9:50	B			F	*Tutti* pulsations and rhythmic cycles	Trills & pulsations intensify behind perc.
X	227	10:02			74	A		*Tutti* pulsation (full chromatic chord)
Y	237	10:15			(rit.)	A–C¼♯		Pulsations recede into strings gliss.
Z	250	10:39		B	60	C¼♯		Repeating mobiles come to fore
AA	261	11:02				C¼♯		Drums at apex of *cresc.* as flutes enter
BB	268	11:14				C¼♯		Drums cease; muted horn pulsations
CC	278	11:35			44	B¼♭–A♯		Hiatus: vl. solo & w-wind scalar lines
DD	283	11:52				A¼♯–A		Stasis: flute 'leads' new chords
EE	291	12:16				B¼♭–A♯		Flute-led stasis (harp & piano enter)
FF	300	12:45				D♭	Alterations to *tutti* 'medium'	*Tutti* chord (prominent minor triad; stasis)
GG	308	13:12				D–G		Bell texture comes to foreground
HH	315	13:38			74	D♭		Chord repeated; w-wind texture pulsates
II	323	13:58				D		W-wind pulsations become lines
JJ	330	14:12	A		60	D♭		Percussion eruption
KK	342	14:35			44	D♭		Hiatus: 'empty' string sound-scape
LL	348	15:04		A¹		D♭		Pulsations within string sound-scape
MM	354	15:32				D♭	Occupation of abyss	Bass drum & crotale enter
NN	364	16:16				D♭		Crotale and bass drum coincide, vc. trill
End	368	16:36				D♭–(E♭)		Vc. timbral trill fades/leads to ...*à la fumée*

Tempo: Pulse Paths

The metronome marks given in the score form a network, consisting of three 'pulse paths', through 60 bpm, which functions as a connecting hub (see Example 9.6). This is not merely a convenient arrangement of numbers – it bears relation to the compositional decisions taken by Saariaho. As shown in Example 9.5, there are three clearly defined sections corresponding to these pulse paths. This would seem to support Pousset's introduction-plus-ternary-form assertion, since the first three minutes of the form follow the 50:60 pulse path, and are thus set apart. However, there is no recurrence of the 48:60:72 path to provide closure for the ternary shape. Instead, the 44:60:74 path is engaged at figure T. Thus, purely in terms of tempo, this is an expanding, open form: not only is there a lack of large-scale recurrence, but, as time goes on, the difference between slow, medium and fast tempi grows.

Example 9.6   *Du cristal* – tempo network

44 (c.45) bpm   74 (c.75)bpm

50 bpm ⟶ 60 bpm ⟵

48 bpm   72 bpm

45:60:75 = 3:4:5
48:60:72 = 4:5:6
50:60 = 5:6

Changes between pulse paths occur at points of rest or stability in other parameters: at the onset of 48 bpm at figure H, the musical texture is made up of an empty soundscape, and although D♭ itself does not return, its approximate recurrence (D¼♭) is surely significant. Similarly, the switch to the 44:60:74 path (figure T) is marked by relative stasis: a feature is made of the oboes within an overall hiatus. It could be argued that this third pulse path is not actually engaged until figure X, where it peaks at 74 bpm (60 bpm is common to all three paths). However, the tutti pulsations suggest significant interaction between parameters at that point.

Within each of the three tempo-defined sections of the work, there are two peaks, which, with their attendant troughs, seem to coincide with other significant events. As a rule, the high points in the tempo curve correspond to those in other parameters, that correlation being strongest towards the middle of the form: figures L, P, and X all mark increases in tempo as well as points of textural intensification. At either end of the work however, such structural markers do not coincide. For example, the woodwind pulsations at figure HH are characterized by relaxation rather than arousal, which is eventually provided by the sudden percussion eruption at JJ, the mid-point in an overall slowing down. The troughs within the tempo curve seem to concur with points of repose overall, for example at figures H, S, CC and KK. There are exceptions again, however; for example, with the return of 48 bpm at figure M comes a more intense sonority. In addition to these textural effects, it is notable that decreases in tempo seem to mark points of both activity and inactivity in pitch patterns: the 'bass pitch' is stable at figures H, M, Z, JJ and KK, for instance.

Pitch: Shifting Grounds and Figures

'[T]he tonal system is, in [Saariaho's] own experience, the most effective means of using harmony to construct and control dynamic musical forms' (Saariaho, 1987: 94), and indeed the large-scale pitch pattern in *Du cristal* extends this reference; this piece could be thought of as being 'about' the return to D♭ (or one of its microtonal approximates, D¼♭ or C¼♯). A number of features contribute to the feeling of tonal centricity in general, and particularly on that pitch:

1. *Du cristal* begins and ends with D♭ as the spectral fundamental.
2. The first two instances that the 'bass pitch' departs D♭, A♭ (V of D♭) is used as a staging point before returning.
3. D♭ (or its equivalent), is by far the most 'stable', or sustained, pitch to be used as a fundamental.
4. The most significant departure from D♭ comes at figure S, where the tonally related G♭ has prominence.
5. The significance of G♭ is established within 30 seconds of its establishment as the bass note, as it is departed from, and returned to, passing through an F♯-minor triad.

It is no great surprise that there is more than a hint of tonal reference in this post-spectral work, given the basic characteristics of the harmonic series (together, the fundamental and partials two to six form a major chord). Therefore, regarding communication between composer and listeners, it is all the more crucial to consider the extent to which this is intentionally played upon. As well as intimations of large-scale tonal shape, there are more direct, smaller-scale allusions. Soon after the start of the 'G♭ episode' there are clear references to functional chords in that key (see Example 9.7 overleaf).

Such 'tonal' sonorities can sometimes be heard on the surface, although to consider small-scale tension and release as a structurally bonding force is to deny a great deal of the sophistication of pitch organization in *Du cristal*. An important difference between the functionality of tonal centres and the implications arising from spectral fundamentals is that where the former divide and direct *time*, the latter are primarily *spatial*, serving to reconfigure the harmonic environment as they project fields of resonance. At the background, movement between pitches forms a shape; at more immediately perceptible levels, the manner in which pitch space is occupied shapes the form.

Dynamic patterns of tension and release are brought about in *Du cristal* because of patterns of distribution and density in pitch organization. Example 9.8

Example 9.7   *Du cristal* – 'tonal' sonorities at figure U

Example 9.8 *Du cristal* – reduction of pitch content, opening to figure E

*This B♭, an artificial harmonic, sounds two octaves higher than written here.

shows a reduction of the pitch content from the opening as far as figure E. Overall, the process is one of thinning out to the sparsely accompanied trill after figure D, although prior to that moment, the space is populated more densely, peaking at figure B. The analogy with crystallization and changes in the state of matter is fairly obvious: as microtones are added, pitches cluster together; the corollary is that the clear outline and spatial distribution of the opening chord gradually melts.

Example 9.8 shows how the occupation of pitch space shapes moment-to-moment continuity at the outset of *Du cristal*; evidence that this kind of thinking is influential at higher structural levels can be seen in the passage between figures R and Y. Example 9.9 overleaf shows the vertical sonority heard at each rehearsal figure between those points; note that the absence of microtones allows for a cumulative process which culminates in the presentation of the total chromatic at figure X. The theoretical implication is that filters alter the 'resolution' – the size of gradation – according to which the octave is divided; only certain pitches are allowed through onto the score. A hypothetical list of these is given below:

1. Overtone-rich noise
2. Microtonal aggregates
3. The chromatic scale
4. Aggregates from other collections (diatonic, pentatonic, etc.)
5. Single fundamentals.

Example 9.9   *Du cristal* – vertical sonorities at figures R to Y

If the 16-minute sound of *Du cristal* is considered to be a figure, then its pitch content is perceived against the grounds named above. The list in itself implies levels of zoom, naming a set of frames in which the sounds of the piece might be perceived to be contained. To hear the 'bass notes' themselves as moving on one hand implies a more zoomed-out frame still, in which harmonic, (referentially tonal) centres move around. On the other hand, a change of spectral fundamental implies not movement but change – that the texture is resonating in a different way, rather than that a new step has been taken. Thus, pitch organization contributes to the fusion of harmonic and timbral hearings of *Du cristal* even at the highest level: in the former, the musical object moves through time; in the latter, the configuration of acoustic space appears to change, as the perspective from which it is perceived shifts from one spectral 'viewpoint' to the next.

Example 9.10   *Du cristal* – 'background' pitch structure

Should this discussion appear to avoid the role played by pitch organization in the form of *Du cristal*, there is a clear background structure at play (Example 9.10 shows the pitch centres shown in Example 9.5). This pattern underpins the form, although the nature and extent of the influence it exerts is brought into question in the listening experience. Indeed, as it projects spectral resonances it provides a platform for the transformation of pitch motion into timbral activity, rather than dictating harmonic implications. Rather than *containing* events, this pattern provides points from which the environments inhabited by the form can grow, enabling various perspectives on the product of that process: at different times it is a back-, further-back-, and still-further-background structure.

Texture: Open and Closed, Inside and Out

Traditionally, orchestration and texture have been seen as the dressing for musical substance, itself defined by patterns of pitch or rhythm. There are inharmonic and arhythmic elements in Saariaho's music, however, and this could give rise to the argument that timbre is actually its most important unifying feature. Without entering that debate, it is clear from the outset that timbral–textural patterns play a role that is at least equal to those of other parameters in the form of *Du cristal*. Nonetheless, discussing the use of this parameter as a structural force is problematic on account of its multi-dimensionality: it is difficult to assign a definitive high and low point to orchestral texture, because it is the product of numerous intensities. A large-scale textural shape can be perceived, however, considering this work in terms of orchestral relief.

Example 9.11 *Du cristal* – **textural narratives**

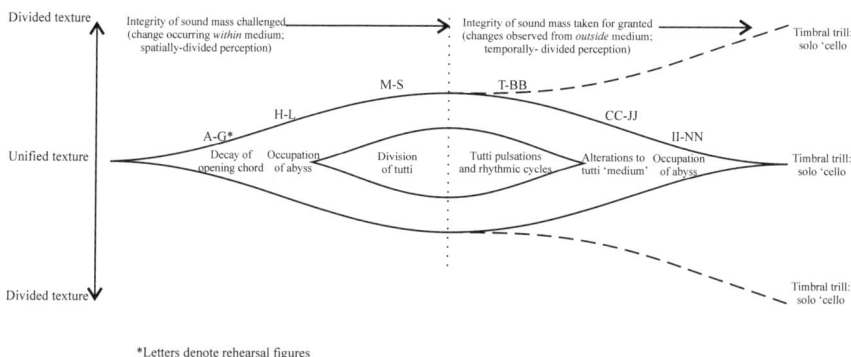

*Letters denote rehearsal figures

Metzer holds the view that the act of expression in this diptych is intimately connected with the 'raising of a voice' (Metzer, 2009: 186ff), a process that comes to fruition in *...à la fumée*, as the soloists provide a concerto element. To perceive a voice is to be able to separate it out from the rest of the texture, and, as the graph in Example 9.4 shows, there are a number of intermediate textural gradations between the single sound-mass at say, figure H, and the highly differentiated texture at figure P, where the timpani solo is accompanied by distinct blocks of colour. There is a large-scale shape at play here, which provides both a sense of return and progression (see Example 9.11). The integration of the sound-mass is brought into question in the first half of the form; it is threatened in numerous ways, as the orchestral texture is continually regrouped (see Example 9.5). The clear, distinct features of the opening chord melt to become 'melodic' lines (figure B), which become concentrated on a semitonal trill at figure D, before that energy disperses into an intertwined woodwind texture that in turn melts to a smooth, blended though gently oscillating sound-mass (figure H). Eventually, those oscillations grow and protrude from the background texture, to the point that two foreground entities are placed in antiphony with one another; the horns and trumpets (and trombones) answer each other's chords from figure M. Other groups of instruments are used to reinforce those two bodies, for example the woodwind and string trills at letter N and the rhythmic synth interjections at O. Eventually, what originated as a horn-trumpet dialogue becomes over-populated, and the timpani emerge as a solo instrument, supported – or even obstructed – by single, block chords in distinct sections of the orchestra (figure Q). All this activity dies down, as a vast chord is sounded, heralding the end of the first half of the form, at figure S (bar 183 in a 368-bar score).

If the first half of the work concerns disintegration – the cohesion of the opening chord is challenged time and again – then in the second, by contrast, the integration of the sound-mass is taken for granted. At figure X, the entire orchestra comes together in the most uniform texture in the score; in a work with many climaxes, these *furioso* semiquaver pulsations surely mark one of the, if not *the*, most significant point(s) of arousal. Eventually, they are replaced by cyclic ostinati (figures Y to Z) as percussion mobiles emerge from within the sonority, stopping at figure BB. Following this, the sound-mass itself is continually modified: at figure DD, the flute leads changes in the pitch profile of the chord, before the opening sonority returns, its decay leading to a different texture with each reiteration. Finally, the oscillating sound-mass of figure H returns at KK, providing an environment for soft pulsations within the strings (at figure LL) and the meeting of the crotale and bass drum to close the work (figure NN);this disintegrates into the solo cello trill that leads into ...*à la fumée*.

Texturally, on one hand, a composite sonority becomes divided and is then reunified, closing a large-scale formal arch; on the other, the subject position gradually moves from the inside to the outside of the sonority, forming an open shape as changes occur at increasingly high levels within the textural hierarchy. Perhaps this provides grounds for the simultaneous independence and interdependence of the works in this diptych. At the end of *Du cristal*, listeners can both experience completion and anticipate continuation.

Looking at Looking: Embodied Communication and Perceptual Zoom

Consideration of the network of visual imagery, empirical fact and musical form evoked by *Du cristal* illuminates how the work communicates. Semiotic associations with light are facilitated by features of its musical organization, which in turn resonate with crystals: notions of clarity, purity and integration. Most immediately, this is communicated through the orchestration and pitch content of the opening sonority. Following that moment, larger-scale patterns of textural organization bring about a shifting balance between divided hierarchies and more consistent, fluid relationships between ornamental detail and fundamental substance. The relation to crystallization is clear: the composite sonority perpetually changes state as boundaries – textural interfaces – develop within the musical medium; these either remain intact or melt as they either contain or are traversed by musical materials. Further, this metaphor plays an important role within the diptych as a whole, as it sets the conditions for, and is extended in the form of, ...*à la fumée*, where discontinuity mirrors the unpredictability of smoke.

The process of textural inflation and deflation manipulates certain elemental features of temporal and spatial perception: as timbral and harmonic aspects of sounds intensify to the extent that they characterize perceptual identity, multiple narratives arise within the form. Visual imagery – indeed the notion of vision itself – is also evoked: the continually changing nature of textural division obstructs listeners' ability to perceive 'edges', according to which the evolving sound-mass might be subdivided. In this way, subject position is manipulated, particularly in terms of proximity, which in turn invokes the notion of perceptual zoom. Metaphorically, on hearing so vast a sound-mass as this, listeners are sometimes so close to the musical surface that its perceptual 'outlines' (the outer extremes in terms of pitch, and oppositions within its timbre) are imperceptible, and at other times they are allowed to perceive relations between its parts. Consider, for example, the outer wall of a building: at a distance of 25 metres or so, the observer can perceive the building and its surroundings; from very close-up, say 10–30 centimetres away, visual perception is saturated, and it is nigh on impossible to grasp any sense of scale – although the observer is outside the building, his or her vision is wholly contained by the wall.

As her quotation of Kandinsky suggests, notions of inner and outer play a significant role in Saariaho's music, although it can be difficult to see how 'zoom' relates to any kind of dialogue between composer and audience. However, listeners lie at the heart of her approach to composition, unlike that of the traditionally isolated, model 'Composer' (see Moisala, 2009: 4). Her 'sound laboratory' experiments (see ibid.: 26–7) are genuinely pertinent to her music, which manipulates auditory perception, offering experiences that are at least as sensory as they are intellectual. Indeed, her output appeals to the most fundamental point of connection between this composer and her listeners: both have bodies that inhabit (and constitute) physical environments. Considered thus, it is inconceivable that notions of internal and external – the basis of perceptual zoom – could not be meaningful.

It is all too easy to forget that the concept of zooming has its roots in the eye, rather than in the camera, and in accordance with Saariaho's cross-sensory disposition, the fact that significance in her music arises principally from patterns of sound rather than light is easily overlooked. The ears, in addition to being instruments of temporal perception (used for hearing vertical synchronies within horizontal counterpoint, for example, and of course for fundamental, survival-related purposes), also have an evolutionary function as spatial locators (for surviving in the dangerous outside world; *Du cristal* exploits this in a safe, aesthetic one). Indeed, if aural perception is a means of gaining knowledge of the surroundings – in this case, of the musical *aura* – it is easy to understand how the oppositions between space and time posited in this piece can give the impression that listeners mediate between being inside an environment, or outside an object. Ultimately, the interactions between spectral timbre and tonal harmony engage an internal dialogue in listeners, between physical sensation and perceptual synthesis; in a sense (or in multiple senses), *Du cristal* facilitates the integration of body and mind. In doing so, necessarily, it also invokes the separation of the two. Paradoxically, and in line with Atlan, disintegration plays an important part in this musical passage from crystal …

Bibliography

Adlington, Robert, 'Moving beyond Motion: Metaphors for Changing Sound', *Journal of the Royal Musical Association*, 128/2 (2003): 297–318.

Agawu, Kofi, *Playing with Signs: A Semiotic Interpretation of Classical Music* (Princeton: Princeton University Press, 1991).

Allanbrook, Wye Jamison, *Rhythmic Gesture in Mozart: Le Nozze di Figaro and Don Giovanni* (Chicago and London: University of Chicago Press, 1983).

Anderson, Julian, 'A Provisional History of Spectral Music', *Contemporary Music Review*, 19/2 (2000): 7–22.

—— and Kaija Saariaho, 'Seductive Solitary: Julian Anderson Introduces the Work of Kaija Saariaho', *The Musical Times*, 133/1798 (1992): 616–19.

Anderson, Martin, 'London, Barbican: Saariaho's *L'Amour de loin*', *Tempo*, 57/224 (2003): 42–3.

Atlan, Henri, 'Creativity in Nature and in the Mind: Novelty in Biology and in the Biologist's Brain', *SubStance*, 19/2–3 (1990): 55–71.

——, *Entre le cristal et la fumée: Essai sur l'organisation du vivant* [*Between Crystal and Smoke: Essay on the Organization of the Living*] (Editions du Seuil: France, 1979).

—— and Carl R. Lovett, 'Metaphysical Postulates and Methods of Research', *SubStance*, 12/3 (1983): 43–7.

Attali, Jacques, *Noise: The Political Economy of Music* (Oxford: Manchester University Press, 1985).

Bachelard, Gaston, *The Poetics of Space*, trans. Maria Jolas (Boston: Beacon Press, 1964 [1958]).

Baillet, Jérôme, *Gérard Grisey. Fondaments d'une écriture* [*Gérard Grisey. Foundations of a Style*] (Paris: L'Harmattan, 2000).

Balzac, H. de, *Séraphîta* [1835], at <http://www.biblisem.net/narratio/balzsera. htm> (accessed 25 August 2010).

Barker, Francis, *The Tremulous Private Body: Essays on Subjection* (Ann Arbor: University of Michigan Press, 1995).

Bartel, Dietrich, *Musica Poetica: Musical-Rhetorical Figures in German Baroque Music* (Lincoln, NE and London: University of Nebraska Press, 1997).

Bartolozzi, Bruno, *New Sounds for Woodwind* (Oxford: Oxford University Press, 1982 [1967]).

Batt, Noëlle, '"L'Entre-deux", A Bridging Concept for Literature, Philosophy, and Science', *SubStance*, 23/2, Issue 74: Special Issue: Between Science and Literature: 38–48.

Batta, András, *Ooppera: Säveltäjät – Teokset – Esittäjät* [*Opera: Composers – Works – Performers*], trans. Elli Ainola et al. (Köln: Könemann, 2001).

Battier, Marc, and Gilbert Nouno, 'L'Electronique dans l'opera de Kaija Saariaho, *L'Amour de loin*' ['The Electronic in Kaija Saariaho's Opera, *L'Amour de loin*'], *Musurgia*, 10/2 (2003): 51–9.

Beck, Stephen David, 'Review [untitled]', *Computer Music Journal*, 16/4 (1992): 92–3.

Benestad, Finn, *Musik och tanke. Huvudlinjer i musikestetikens historia från antiken till vår egen tid* [*Music and Thinking: Approaches to Musical Aesthetics from Antiquity to Present Day*] (Ystad: Rabén & Sjögren, 1978).

Beyer, Anders, *The Voice of Music: Conversations with Composers of our Time* (Aldershot: Ashgate, 2000a).

——, 'Till Death Do Us Part – A Portrait of the Finnish Composer, Kaija Saariaho', *Nordic Sounds*, 1 (2000b): 3–9.

Blacking, John, *How Musical Is Man?* (Seattle: Washington University Press, 1973).

Bösche, Thomas, 'Zwischen Opazität und Klarheit: Einige abschweifende Bemerkungen zu Dérive 1' ['Between Opacity and Clarity: Some Digressive Remarks on Dérive 1'], *Musik-Konzepte* [Music-Concepts], 96 (1997): 62–92.

Bradshaw, Susan, 'The Instrumental and Vocal Music', in William Glock (ed.), *Pierre Boulez: A Symposium* (London: Eulenberg, 1986).

Brech, Martha, 'Kaija Saariaho's Diptych *Du cristal* and *A la fumée*: An Analytical Approach', in Tomi Mäkelä (ed.), *Topics. Texts. Tensions: Essays in Music Theory on Paavo Heininen, Joonas Kokkonen, Magnus Lindberg, Usko Meriläinen, Einojuhani Rautavaara, Kaija Saariaho and Aulis Sallinen* (Magdeburg: Otto-von-Guericke-Universität, 1999), pp. 26–50.

Burkitt, Ian, *Bodies of Thought. Embodiment, Identity and Modernity* (London: Sage, 1999).

Callister, William D., and David G. Rethwisch, *Materials Science and Engineering*, 8th edn (Hoboken NJ: Wiley, 2010).

Chanter, Tina, *Ethics of Eros: Irigaray's Re-Writing of the Philosophers* (New York: Routledge, 1995).

Chion, Michael, *Audio-Vision: Sound on Screen*, trans. Claudia Gorbman (New York: Columbia University Press, 1994).

Clarke, Eric F., *Ways of Listening* (New York: Oxford University Press, 2005).

Clifton, Thomas, *Music as Heard: A Study in Applied Phenomenology* (New Haven: Yale University Press, 1983).

Cohen-Levinas, Danielle, 'Gérard Grisey: Du spectralisme formalisé au spectralisme historicisé' ['Gérard Grisey: From Formalized Spectralism to Historical Spectralism'], *La Revue musicale: L'Itinéraire*, 421–4 (1991): 51–65.

Cumming, Naomi, 'The Horrors of Identification: Reich's *Different Trains*', *Perspectives of New Music*, 35 (1997): 129–52.

Cusick, Suzanne G., 'Feminist Theory, Music Theory and the Mind/Body Problem', *Perspectives of New Music*, 32/1 (1994): 8–27.

Davis, Kathy, *Embodied Practices: Feminist Perspectives on the Body* (London: Sage, 1997).

Derrida, Jacques, *Sovereignties in Question: The Poetics of Paul Celan*, ed. Thomas Dutoit and Outi Pasanen (New York: Fordham University Press, 2005).

——, *Specters of Marx: The State of the Debt, the Work of Mourning, and the New International*, trans. Peggy Kamuf (London: Routledge, 1994).

——, *Cinders*, trans. Ned Lukacher (London: University of Nebraska, 1991).

——, *Of Grammatology*, trans. Gayatri Chakravorty Spivak (London: Johns Hopkins University Press, 1976).

Dodge, Charles, and Thomas A. Jerse, *Computer Music. Synthesis, Composition, and Performance* (New York: Schirmer Books, 1985).

Dolar, Mladen, *A Voice and Nothing More* (Cambridge MA: MIT Press, 2006).

Dusman, Linda, 'No Bodies There: The Absence and Presence in Acousmatic Performance', in Pirkko Moisala and Beverly Diamond (eds), *Music and Gender* (Urbana and Chicago: University of Illinois Press, 2000).

Ehrenzweig, Anton, *The Hidden Order of Art* (London: Phoenix Press, 2000 [1967]).

Eluard, Paul, *Oeuvres complètes* [*Complete Works*], eds Marcelle Dumas and Lucien Scheler (Paris: Gallimard, 1968).

Emmerson, Simon, 'Acoustic/Electroacoustic: The Relationship with Instruments', *Journal of New Music*, 27/1–2 (1998): 146–64.

Fant, Gunnar, *Acoustic Theory of Speech Production* (The Hague: Mouton & Co., 1960).

Fineberg, Joshua, 'Spectral Music', *Contemporary Music Review*, 19/2 (2000a): 1–5.

——, 'Guide to the Basic Concepts and Techniques of Spectral Music', *Contemporary Music Review*, 19/2 (2000b): 81–113.

Fisher, George, and Judith Lochhead, 'Analyzing from the Body', *Theory and Practice*, 27 (2002): 37–67.

Floros, Constantin, *György Ligeti: Jenseits von Avantgarde und Postmoderne* [*Beyond Avant-Garde and Postmodern*] (Vienna: Verlag Lafite, 1996).

Forge, Andrew, 'Monet at Giverny', in Claire Joyes (ed.) *Monet at Giverny* (London: Mathews Miller Dunbar, 1975).

Foulkes, David, *A Grammar of Dreams* (Hassocks: Harvester Press, 1978).

Freud, Sigmund, *The Interpretation of Dreams*, trans. Joyce Crick (Oxford: Oxford University Press, 1999 [1900]).

——, *The Interpretation of Dreams*, 3rd edn (1911), trans. A.A. Brill, at <http://books.google.co.uk/books?id=M1afft7NY3AC> (accessed 25 August 2010).

Friedman, Stanley M., 'One Aspect of the Structure of Music. A Study of Regressive Transformations of Musical Themes', *Journal of the American Psychoanalytic Association*, 8 (1960): 427–99.

Frith, Simon, *Performing Rites. On the Value of Popular Music* (Oxford: Oxford University Press, 1996).

Fruss, Diana, *Essentially Speaking* (New York: Routledge, 1989).

Gadamer, Hans-Georg, *Truth and Method*, trans. Joel Weinsheimer and Donald G. Marshall (London and New York: Continuum, 2004).

Gauguin, Paul, *Noa Noa*, trans. O.F. Theis (New York: Nicholas L. Brown, 1919).

Gaunt, Simon, and Sarah Kay (eds), *The Troubadours: An Introduction* (Cambridge: Cambridge University Press, 1999).

Goehr, Lydia, *The Quest for Voice: On Music, Politics, and the Limits of Philosophy* (Oxford: Clarendon Press, 1998).

——, *The Imaginary Museum of Musical Works: An Essay in the Philosophy of Music* (Oxford: Clarendon Press, 1992).

Grabócz, Martha (Márta), 'La Musique contemporaine finlandaise: Conception gesturelle de la macrostructure. Kaija Saariaho et Magnus Lindberg' ['Gestural Conceptions of Macrostructure'], *Les Cahiers du Cirem. Centre International de Recherches en Esthétique Musicale*, 26–7 (1993): 155–68.

Griffiths, Paul, *Modern Music: The Avant Garde since 1945* (London: Dent, 1981).

Grisey, Gérard, 'Did you say Spectral?', trans. Joshua Fineberg, *Contemporary Music Review*, 19/3 (2000): 1–3.

——, 'La Musique: Le Devenir de sons' ['Music: The Growth of Sounds'], *La Revue musicale: L'Itinéraire*, 421–4 (1991): 291–300.

Haapanen-Tallgren, Tyyni, *Trubaduureja* [*Troubadours*] (Porvoo: WSOY, [1925]).

Hall, Nancy Abraham, 'Multiple Times and Distant Spaces: Thomas Hardy, Henri Atlan, and Carlos Fuentes's *Instinto de Inez*', *Bulletin of Hispanic Studies*, 86 (2009): 417–32.

Hargreaves, Jon, 'Music as Communication: Networks of Composition', doctoral thesis, University of York, 2008.

Hatten, Robert S., *Interpreting Musical Gesture, Topics, and Tropes: Mozart, Beethoven, Schubert* (Bloomington: Indiana University Press, 2004).

——, *Musical Meaning in Beethoven: Markedness, Correlation, and Interpretation* (Bloomington and Indianapolis: Indiana University Press, 1994).

Hautsalo, Liisamaija, 'Kehtolaulutopos neljässä suomalaisessa oopperateoksessa' ['The Topic of Cradle-Song in the Four Finnish Operas'], in *The Yearbook of Ethnomusicology* (Helsinki: Finnish Society for Ethnomusicology, 2010).

——, *Adriana Mater* (Helsinki: Finnish National Opera, 2008a).

——, '*Kaukainen rakkaus* – Saavuttamattomuuden semantiikka Kaija Saariahon oopperassa' ['*L'Amour de loin*: The Semantics of the Unattainable in Kaija Saariaho's Opera'], Acta Musicologica Fennica, 27 (Helsinki: Finnish Musicological Society and Helsinki University Press, 2008b).

——, 'Transelementit Kaija Saariahon oopperassa *Kaukainen rakkaus*' ['Transcendental Elements in Kaija Saariaho's Opera *Love from Afar*'], in Anne Sivuoja-Gunaratnam (ed.), *Elektronisia unelmia. Kirjoituksia Kaija Saariahon musiikista* [*Electronic Dreams. Writings on the Music of Kaija Saariaho*] (Helsinki: Helsinki University Press, 2005), pp. 231–56.

——, 'Kaipausta yliaistilliseen. Kaukainen rakkaus on modernismistaan huolimatta romanttinen ooppera' ['Longing for the Transcendental. Despite its Modernism, Love from Afar is a Romantic Opera'], *Rondo/Classica*, 42 (2004): 22–3.

——, 'Kaipuu, rakkaus, kuolema. Kaija Saariahon esikoisooppera kypsyi vuosikymmenen, mutta valmistui vuodessa' ['Longing, Love, Death. Kaija Saariaho's Ripened for a Decade but was Finished in a Year'], *Rondo*, 38 (2000): 16–20.

Heiniö, Mikko, *Karvalakki kansakunnan kaapin päällä: kansalliset attribuutit Joonas Kokkosen ja Aulis Sallisen julkisuuskuvassa* [*A Fur Hat on the Nation's Cupboard: National Attributes in the Joonas Kokkonen's and Aulis Sallinen's Reception*] (Helsinki: SKS, 1999).

——, *Suomen musiikin historia 4: Aikamme musiikki* [*The History of Finnish Music 4: Contemporary Music*] (Helsinki: WSOY, 1995).

——, 'Lähtökohtia oopperatutkimukseen' ['Starting Points for Opera Research], *Musiikkitiede* [*Musicology*], 2 (1989): 66–94.

Helmholtz, Hermann L.F. von, *On the Sensations of Tone as a Physiological Basis for the Theory of Music* (New York: Dover Publications, 1954).

Hennion, Antoine, and Line Grenier, 'Sociology of Art: New Stakes in a Postcritical Time', in Stella Quah and Arnaud Sales (eds), *The International Handbook of Sociology* (London: Sage, 2000).

Hinkle-Turner, Elizabeth, 'Review [untitled]', *Computer Music Journal*, 23/3 (1999): 117–18.

House, John, 'Monet's Water Garden and the Second Water Lily Series (1903–1909)', in Jacqueline and Maurice Guillaud (eds), *Claude Monet at the Time of Giverny* (Paris: J.M.G., 1983).

Howell, Tim, 'A Shadow, An Aura and Some Notes on Light: Re-Defining the Sibelius Legacy', *Proceedings of the Fifth International Sibelius Conference*, Oxford, September 2010 (forthcoming).

——, *After Sibelius: Studies in Finnish Music* (Aldershot: Ashgate, 2006).

Huter, Bettina, '*L'Amour de loin* – "The Story Has Chosen Me". Interview mit Kaija Saariaho', in Bettina Huter (ed.), *Oper im Kontext. Musiktheater bei den Salzburger Festspielen* [*Opera in Context. Musical Theatre in the Salzburg Festival*] (Innsbruck: Studien Verlag, 2003), pp. 80–88.

Iitti, Sanna, 'Sukupuolen merkitys Kaija Saariahon taiteessa' ['The Meaning of Gender in Kaija Saariaho's Art'], in Anne Sivuoja-Gunaratnam (ed.), *Elektronisia unelmia. Kirjoituksia Kaija Saariahon musiikista* [*Electronic Dreams. Writings on the Music of Kaija Saariaho*] (Helsinki: Helsinki University Press, 2005), pp. 125–50.

——, '*L'Amour de loin*: Kaija Saariaho's First Opera', *IAWM Journal*, 8/1–2 (2002): 9–14.

——, 'Kaija Saariaho: Stylistic Development and Artistic Principles', *IAWM Journal*, 3 (2001): 17–20.

——, '"Mutta tämähän on maisema, Madame Saariaho!" – Kaija Saariahon *Lichtbogen*' ['"But This is a Landscape, Madame Saariaho" – Saariaho's *Lichtbogen*'], master's thesis, Sibelius Academy, Helsinki, 1993.

Iliescu, Mihu, 'Kaija Saariaho, *L'Amour de loin:* Une approche lyrique postmoderne' ['Kaija Saariaho, *Love from Afar*: A Postmodern Lyrical Approach'], *Analyse Musicale* [*Musical Analysis*], 39 (2003): 33–43.

Irigaray, Luce, *An Ethics of Sexual Difference*, trans. Carolyn Burke and Gillian C. Gill (London and New York: Continuum, 2004 [1984]).

——, *This Sex Which is Not One*, trans. Carolyn Burke (Ithaca, NY: Cornell University Press, 1985 [1977]).

Johnson, Julian, 'The Status of the Subject in Mahler's Ninth Symphony', *Nineteenth-Century Music*, 18 (1994): 108–20.

Kahn, Douglas, *Noise Water Meat. A History of the Sound in the Arts* (Cambridge MA: MIT Press, 1999).

Kallberg, Jeffrey, *Chopin at the Boundaries. Sex, History and Musical Genre* (Cambridge MA and London: Harvard University Press, 1996).

Kankaanpää, Vesa, 'Rollentausch. Das Verhältnis von Klangfarbe und Harmonik in Saariahos Frühwerk' ['Role-Reversal. The Relationship between Timbre and Harmony in Saariaho's Early Works'], *MusikTexte* [*Music-Texts*], 110 (2006): 61–71.

——, 'Displaced Time: Transcontextual References to Time in Kaija Saariaho's *Stilleben*', *Organised Sound*, 1/2 (1996): 87–92.

——, 'Sointivärin käsite musiikin kuvaajana. Kaija Saariahon sointivärikäsitykset ja niiden ilmeneminen soolohuiluteoksessa *Laconisme de l'aile*' ['The Concept of Sound Colour. Kaija Saariaho's Conceptions of Sound Colour and their Application in the Solo Flute Work *Laconisme de l'aile*'], *Musiikki*, 3 (1995): 218–48.

Karbusicky, Vladimir, *Grundriss der musikalischen Semantik* [*Outline of Musical Semantics*] (Darmstadt: Wissenschafliche Buchgesellschaft, 1986).

Karttunen, Anssi, 'Notes on Light', programme note (Chester Music, 2007).

Kimberley, Nick, 'Kaija Saariaho: The Sound of Dreams (And a Few Nightmares)', *The Independent*, 19 November 2001, at <http://www.independent.co.uk/arts-entertainment/music/features/kaija-saariaho-the-sound-of-dreams-and-a-few-nightmares-663736.html> (accessed 25 August 2010).

Kirk, Ross, and Andy Hunt, *Digital Sound Processing for Music and Multimedia* (Oxford: Focal Press, 1999).

Komsi, Piia, 'From the Grammar of Dreams: *Kaija Saariahon sävellys Sylvia Plathin tekstiin*' ['*From the Grammar of Dreams*: Kaija Saariaho's Setting of Text by Sylvia Plath'], dissertation, Sibelius Academy, 2001.

Korhonen, Kimmo, *Inventing Finnish Music: Contemporary Composers from Medieval to Modern* (Helsinki: Finnish Music Information Centre, 2007).

——, *Finnish Concertos*, trans. Timothy Binham (Helsinki: Finnish Music Information Centre, 1995a).

——, *Finnish Orchestral Music 2*, trans. Timothy Binham (Helsinki: Finnish Music Information Centre, 1995b).

——, *Finnish Piano Music*, trans. Timothy Binham (Helsinki: Finnish Music Information Centre, 1997).

Koskelin, Olli, Radio interview with Saariaho, YLE Radio 1, 7 September 2002.

Kramer, Jonathan, *The Time of Music: New Meanings, New Temporalities, New Listening Strategies* (New York: Macmillan, 1988).

——, 'New Temporalities in Music', *Critical Inquiry*, 7/3 (1981): 539–56.

Kramer, Lawrence, *Musical Meaning: Toward a Critical History* (Berkeley: University of California Press, 2001).

——, *Classical Music and Postmodern Knowledge* (London: University of California Press, 1995).

——, *Music as Cultural Practice, 1800–1900* (Berkeley: University of California Press, 1990).

Lampila, Hannu-Ilari, 'Kaija Saariaholla ei ole ollut Suomessa sävellyskonserttia kymmeneen vuoteen' ['It has been Ten Years since the Last Concert of Kaija Saariaho's Compositions in Finland'], *Helsingin Sanomat* [Helsinki's main daily newspaper], 14 September 1997.

Langlois, Frank, 'Un nouvel amour' ['A New Love'], *Opéra International*, 3 (2000): 24.

Lauretis, Theresa de, 'Rebirth in *The Bell Jar*', in Linda Wagner-Martin (ed.), *Sylvia Plath: The Critical Heritage* (London: Routledge, 1988), pp. 124–34.

LeBaron, Anne, and Denys Bouliane, 'Darmstadt 1980', *Perspectives of New Music*, 19/1–2 (1980/81): 420–41.

Leeuwen, Theo van, *Speech, Music, Sound* (Basingstoke: Macmillan, 1999).

Lefebvre, Henri, *The Production of Space*, trans. Donald Nicholson-Smith (Oxford: Blackwell, 1991) (orig. French publ. 1974).

Lehtonen, Tiina-Maija, 'Kaija Saariaho: Värien säveltäjä' ['Kaija Saariaho: The Composer of Colours'], *Synkooppi*, 2 (1984): 40–42.

LeNaour, Anne, 'Kaija Saariaho, eine finnische Komponistin in Paris' ['Kaija Saariaho, a Finnish Composer in Paris'], in Susanne Winterfeldt (ed.), *Kaija Saariaho: Klangportraits*, 4 (1991): 9–13.

Leppert, Richard, *The Sight of Sound. Music, Representation, and the History of the Body* (Berkeley: University of California Press, 1993).

Levinas, Emmanuel, *Time and the Other*, trans. Richard A. Cohen (Pittsburgh: Duquesne University Press, 2000).

Linjama, Jyrki, 'Kaija Saariaho – säveltäjä värien, valon, visuaalisuuden voimakentässä' ['Kaija Saariaho – composing in the power field of colours, light, and vision', *Synteesi*, 1–2 (1987): 110–17.

Lorieux, Grégoire, 'Une analyse d'*Amers* de Kaija Saariaho' ['An Analysis of *Amers* by Kaija Saariaho'], *Déméter* (November 2004), at <www.univ-lille3.fr/revues/demeter/analyse/lorieux.pdf>.

Lyotard, Jean-François, 'A Few Words to Sing', in Adam Krims (ed.), *Music/Ideology. Resisting the Aesthetic* (Amsterdam: G+B Arts International, 1998), pp. 15–36.

Maalouf, Amin, *L'Amour de loin*, trans. George Hall, at <http://www.tripoli-city.org/amour/index.html> (accessed 25 August 2010).

——, *Adriana Mater* (Paris: Bernard Grasset, 2006).

Mäkelä, Tomi, 'Kaija Saariaho und Finnland', in Hans-Klaus Jungheinrich (ed.), *Woher? Wohin? Die Komponistin Kaija Saariaho* [*From Where? To Where? The Composer Kaija Saariaho*] (Mainz: Schott Music, 2007).

Malherbe, Claudy, 'Seeing Light as Colour; Hearing Sound as Timbre', trans. Joshua Fineberg and Berry Hayward, *Contemporary Music Review*, 19/3 (2000): 15–27.

Maycock, Robert, 'Finnish Whispers', *Classical Music* (14 January 1989).

Metzer, David, *Musical Modernism at the Turn of the Twenty-First Century* (Cambridge University Press: Cambridge, 2009).

Meyer, Leonard B., *Music, the Arts, and Ideas. Patterns and Predictions in Twentieth-Century Culture* (Chicago: University of Chicago Press, 1994).

Michel, Pierre, 'Entretien avec Kaija Saariaho' ['Interview with Kaija Saariaho'], in Risto Nieminen (ed.), *Kaija Saariaho* (Les Cahiers de l'Ircam, Compositeurs d'aujourdhui, no. 6) [in the series Ircam Journals, Composers of Today, no. 6] (Paris: Ircam, Centre Georges Pompidou, 1994), pp. 7–23.

Minkkinen, Marja, 'Kaija Saariahon vokaalinen kirjoitus teoksissa *Du gick, flög* ja *From the Grammar of Dreams*' ['Kaija Saariaho's Vocal Writing in *You Went, Flew* and *From the Grammar of Dreams*'], in Anne Sivuoja-Gunaratnam (ed.), *Elektronisia unelmia. Kirjoituksia Kaija Saariahon musiikista* [*Electronic Dreams. Writings on the Music of Kaija Saariaho*] (Helsinki: Helsinki University Press, 2005), pp. 49–84.

Moisala, Pirkko, *Kaija Saariaho* (Woman Composers series, no. 1) (Chicago: University of Illinois, 2009).

——, and Beverley Diamond (eds), *Music and Gender* (Urbana and Chicago: University of Illinois Press, 2000).

Monelle, Raymond, *The Musical Topic: Hunt, Military and Pastoral* (Bloomington: Indiana University Press, 2006).

——, *The Sense of Music: Semiotic Essays* (Princeton and Oxford: Princeton University Press, 2000).

Morgan, Robert P., *Twentieth-Century Music: A History of Musical Style in Modern Europe and America* (New York and London: Norton, 1991).

Murail, Tristan, 'After-Thoughts', *Contemporary Music Review*, 19/3 (2000): 5–9.

——, 'Spectra and Pixies', trans. Tod Machover, *Contemporary Music Review*, 1/1 (1984): 157–70.

Nieminen, Risto, *Kaija Saariaho* (Paris: Editions Ircam, Centre Georges Pompidou, 1994).

——, 'At the Moment the Computer and I Belong Together', trans. Susan Sinisalo, *Finnish Music Quarterly*, 3/4 (1985): 22–7.

Niiranen, Susanna, 'Veijareita ja pyhimyksiä, lörppöjä ja kaunokaisia: Trubaduurien suhtautumistapoja runojensa naisiin' ['Rogues and Saints, Chatters and Belles: Attitudes of Troubadours towards Women'], in Susanna Niiranen and Marko Lamberg (eds), *Ihmeiden peili: keskiajan ihmisen maailmankuva* [*The Mirror of Miracles: Worldview of Medieval People*] (Jyväskylä: Atena, 1998), pp. 113–32.

Noske, Frits, *The Signifier and Signified: Studies in the Operas of Mozart and Verdi* (The Hague: Martinus Nijhoff, 1977).

Oskala, Anni, *The Voice in Kaija Saariaho's Music, 1977–2000*, D.Phil. dissertation, University of Oxford, 2007.

——, 'Unta musiikista, musiikia unista: Kaija Saariahon uniaiheisista teoksista' ['Dreams about Music, Music about Dreams: On the Theme of Dreams in Kaija Saariaho's Works'], in Anne Sivuoja-Gunaratnam (ed.), *Elektronisia unelmia. Kirjoituksia Kaija Saariahon musiikista* [*Electronic Dreams. Writings on the Music of Kaija Saariaho*] (Helsinki: Helsinki University Press, 2005), pp. 257–93. Also available in German: 'Träumen über Musik, Musik über Träume: Traummotive in Kaija Saariahos Werken', trans. Ekhart Georgi, in *MusikTexte* [*Music-Texts*], 110 (2006): 46–60.

Otonkoski, Lauri, 'The Grammar of Dreams – Kaija Saariaho, Composer', *Finnish Music Quarterly*, 5 (1989): 2–7.

Paynter, John, 'Music and People: The Import of Structure and Form', in John Paynter, Tim Howell, Richard Orton and Peter Seymour (eds), *Companion to Contemporary Musical Thought* (London: Routledge, 1992).

Peirce, Charles Sanders, *The Philosophy of Peirce, Selected Writings*, ed. Justus Buchler (London: Kegan Paul, 1940).

Pennanen, Ainomaija, *Ennen ensi-iltaa* [*Before the Première*], radio programme on YLE Radio 1, 19 August 2000.

Pentikäinen, Juha, *Suomalaisen lähtö. Kirjoituksia pohjoisesta kuolemankulttuurista* [*Passing of a Finn: Writing on the Northern Death Culture*] (Helsinki: SKS, 1990).

Pickens, Rupert T. (ed.), *The Songs of Jaufré Rudel* (Toronto: Pontifical Institute of Medieval Studies, 1978).

Plath, Sylvia, *Ariel: The Restored Edition*, ed. Frieda Hughes (London: Faber & Faber, 2004).

——, *The Bell Jar* (London: Faber & Faber, 2001).

——, *Ariel*, ed. Ted Hughes (London: Faber & Faber, 1965).

Pousset, Damien, The Works of Kaija Saariaho, Philippe Hurel and Marc-André Dalbavie: Stile Concertato, Stile Concitato, Stile Rappresentativo', trans. Joshua Fineberg and Roman Hyacinthe, *Contemporary Music Review*, 19/3 (2000): 67–110.

——, 'La transparence du signe' ['The Transparency of the Sign'], in Risto Nieminen (ed.), *Kaija Saariaho* (Les Cahiers de l'Ircam, Compositeurs d'aujordhui, no. 6) [in the series Ircam Journals, Composers of Today, no. 6] (Paris: Ircam, Centre Georges Pompidou, 1994).

Ratner, Leonard G., *Classic Music, Expression, Form, and Style* (New York: Schirmer Books, 1980).

Rawnsley, Andrew C., 'A Situated or a Metaphysical Body? Problematics of Body as Mediation or as Site of Inscription', *Janus Head*, 9/2 (2007): 625–47.

Rebelo, Pedro, 'Haptic Sensation and Instrumental Transgression', *Contemporary Music Review*, 25/1–2 (2006): 27–35.

Rhodes, Gale, *Crystallography Made Crystal Clear: A Guide for Users of Macromolecular Models*, 3rd edn (Burlington VT, San Diego and London: Academic Press, 2006).

Rickards, Guy, 'Review [untitled]', *Tempo*, 192 (1995): 45–7.

——, 'Review: Paavo Heininen and the Finnish Scene', *Tempo*, 174 (1990): 47–51.

Ricoeur, Paul, 'Narrative Time', *Critical Inquiry*, 7/1 (1980): 169–90.

Riikonen, Taina, 'Tarinoita suusta: puhumisen ja kuiskimisen asuttamia huilisti-identiteettejä' ['Stories from the Mouth: Flautist Identities inhabited by Speaking and Whispering'], in Anne Sivuoja-Gunaratnam (ed.), *Elektronisia unelmia. Kirjoituksia Kaija Saariahon musiikista* [*Electronic Dreams. Writings on the Music of Kaija Saariaho*] (Helsinki: Helsinki University Press, 2005), pp. 295–323.

Rodet, Xavier, 'Time-Domain Formant-Wave-Function Synthesis', *Computer Music Journal*, 8/3 (1984): 9–14.

Rosen, Charles, *The Classical Style – Haydn, Mozart, Beethoven* (London: Faber & Faber, 1971).

Roubaud, Jacques, *Echanges de la lumière* [*Conversations on Light*] (Paris: Editions A.M. Métailié, 1990).

Rowell, Lewis, 'Stasis in Music', *Semiotica*, 66/1–3 (1987): 181–95.

Saariaho, Kaija, *Grammaire des rêves* (score notes) (n.d.), at <http://www.chesternovello.com/default.aspx?TabId=2432&State_3041=2&Work Id_3041=7860> (accessed 25 August 2010).

——, *Terra Memoria* (score notes), at <http://www.chesternovello.com/default.as px?TabId=2432&State_3041=2&workId_3041=19140> (accessed 2 February 2010).

——, *Cendres* (score notes), at <http://www.chesternovello.com/Default.aspx ?TabId=2432&State_3041=2&workId_3041=11095> (accessed 2 February 2010).

——, 'Musiikissa, musiikista, musiikkiin' ['In Music, on Music, into Music'], in Pekka Hako and Risto Nieminen (eds), *Ammatti: säveltäjä* [*Composing as a Profession*] (Helsinki: Like, 2006), pp. 124–32.

——, 'Some Thoughts on my Concertos', in Anne Sivuoja-Gunaratnam (ed.), *Elektronisia unelmia. Kirjoituksia Kaija Saariahon musiikista* [*Electronic Dreams. Writings on the Music of Kaija Saariaho*] (Helsinki: Helsinki University Press, 2005).

——, *Amers*, CD-liner note; interview with Martin Anderson (Sony: SK 60817, 2001).

——, 'Matter and Mind in Music', in Pirkko Tuukkanen (ed.), *Matter and Mind in Architecture*, (Helsinki: Alvar Aalto Foundation, 2000).

——, 'Kielen ja äänen synteesit' ['The Syntheses of Language and Sound'], in Kaija Saariaho et al., *Prisma CD-ROM. Aspects of Contemporary Music Seen Through the Work of Kaija Saariaho* (Helsinki: WSOY, 1999) (originally published in *Helsingin Sanomat* [Helsinki's main daily newspaper], 14 June 1987).

———, *Mirrors* (score notes) (London: Chester Music, 1997).

———, 'Timbre et harmonie' ['Timbre and Harmony'], in Jean-Baptiste Barrière (ed.), *Le Timbre, métaphore pour la composition* [*Timbre, a Metaphor for Composition*] (Paris: Christian Bourgois Editeur & IRCAM, 1991).

———, 'Timbre and Harmony: Interpolations of Timbral Structures', *Contemporary Music Review*, 2/1 (1987): 93–133.

———, 'Shaping a Compositional Network with Computer', *Proceedings of the 1984 International Computer Music Conference, Paris* (San Francisco: International Computer Music Association, 1985), pp. 163–5.

———, 'Using the Computer in Search of Timbral Organization and Composition', *Proceedings of the Rochester 1983 International Computer Music Conference* (San Francisco: International Computer Music Association, 1983), pp. 269–73.

———, 'Kirkua saat, mutta lennä!' ['It's alright to scream, but (for goodness' sake) Fly!'], in Pekka Hako and Risto Nieminen (eds), *Ammatti: säveltäjä. Yhdentoista suomalaisen säveltäjän puheenvuoro aikamme musiikista* [*Profession: Composer. The Address of Eleven Finnish Composers on Contemporary Music*] (Helsinki: Synkooppi ry, 1981): 115–19.

Salonen, Esa-Pekka, 'Näky' ['Seeing things'], in Pekka Hako and Risto Nieminen (eds), *Ammatti: säveltäjä* [*Composing as a Profession*] (Helsinki: Like, 2006), pp. 133–9).

Saussure, Ferdinand de, *Course in General Linguistics*, ed. Charles Bally and Albert Sechehaye, trans. Wade Baskin (Glasgow: Collins, 1974).

Schwandt, Erich, 'Tarantella', Grove Music Online, at <http://www.oxfordmusiconline.com> (accessed 18 August 2010).

Schwarz, David, 'Listening Subjects: Semiotics, Psychoanalysis, and the Music of John Adams and Steve Reich', *Perspectives of New Music*, 31 (1993): 24–56.

———, *Listening Subjects. Music, Psychoanalysis, Culture* (Durham, NC: Duke University Press, 1997).

Shanon, Benny, 'Novelty in Thinking', *SubStance*, 19/2–3 (1990): 48–54.

Shilling, Chris, 'Embodiment, Experience and Theory: In Defence of the Sociological Tradition', *The Sociological Review*, 49/3 (2001): 327–44.

Siltanen, J., 'Valosta, lasista ja säveltämisestä' ['Of Light, Glass and Composing'], *Kulttuurivihkot* [*Cultural Notebooks*], 10 (1982): 44–9.

Sivuoja-Gunaratnam, Anne, 'Gestures of Desire in Kaija Saariaho's Music', *Music and Gesture Conference*, Norwich, 27–31 August 2003, unpublished paper script (2003a).

———, 'Desire and Distance in Kaija Saariaho's *Lonh*', *Organised Sound*, 8 (2003b): 71–84.

——— (ed.), *Elektronisia unelmia. Kirjoituksia Kaija Saariahon musiikista* [*Electronic Dreams. Writings on the Music of Kaija Saariaho*] (Helsinki: Helsinki University Press, 2005).

Small, Christopher, *Musicking. The Meaning of Performance and Listening* (Hanover NH and London: Wesleyan University Press, 1998).

Spitz, Ellen, *Art and Psyche. A Study in Psychoanalysis and Aesthetics* (New Haven: Yale University Press, 1985).

Stearns, David, 'Kaija Saariaho', at <andante.com>, accessed September 2002.

Stoïanova, Ivanka, 'Alchemie der Klänge: Kaija Saariaho – ein Porträt' ['Alchemy of Timbre: Kaija Saariaho – A Portrait'], *MusikTexte*, 110 (2006): 21–9.

——, 'Kaija Saariaho. Spektrale Komposition und symphonisches Denken' ['Kaija Saariaho. Spectral Composition and Symphonic Thinking'], in Martina Homma (ed.), *Frau Musica (nova): Komponieren Heute* [*Women of (New) Music: Composition Today*] (Sinzing: Studio, 2000).

——, 'Une oeuvre de synthèse: Analyse d'*Amers*' ['A Work of Synthesis: Analysis of *Amers*'], in Risto Nieminen (ed.), *Kaija Saariaho* (Les Cahiers de l'Ircam, Compositeurs d'aujordhui, no. 6) [Ircam Journals, Composers of Today, no. 6] (Paris: Ircam, Centre Georges Pompidou, 1994).

——, 'Kaija Saariaho. Im Inneren des Klangs: Die Wege des Bewuβtseins' ['Kaija Saariaho. Inside the Sound: The Paths of Consciousness'], in Susanne Winterfeldt (ed.), *Kaija Saariaho* [Klangportraits, vol. 4] (Kassel: Furore Verlag, 1991).

Stone, Alison, *Luce Irigaray and the Philosophy of Sexual Difference* (Cambridge: Cambridge University Press, 2006).

Tarasti, Eero, *A Theory of Musical Semiotics* (Bloomington and Indianapolis: Indiana University Press, 1994).

——, *Myth and Music: A Semiotic Approach to the Aesthetics of Myth in Music, Especially that of Wagner, Sibelius and Stravinsky*, Acta Musicologica Fennica, 11 (Helsinki: Finnish Musicological Society, 1978).

Terhardt, Ernst, Gerhard Stoll and Manfred Seewan, 'Algorithm for the Extraction of Pitch and Pitch Salience from Complex Tonal Signals', *Journal of the Acoustical Society of America*, 71/3 (1982): 679–88.

The Ensemble Sospeso – Pierre Boulez (1993), at <http://www.sospeso.com/contents/articles/boulez_p2.html> (accessed 2 February 2010).

Torvinen, Juha, *Musiikki ahdistuksen taitona: filosofinen tutkimus musiikin eksistentiaalis-ontologisesta merkityksestä* [*Music as the Art of Anxiety: A Philosophical Approach to the Existential-Ontological Meaning of Music*], Acta Musicologica Fennica, 26 (Helsinki: Finnish Musicological Society, 2007).

Välimäki, Susanna, *Subject Strategies in Music: A Psychoanalytic Approach to Musical Signification*, Acta Semiotica Fennica, 22; Approaches to Musical Semiotics, 9 (Imatra and Helsinki: International Semiotics Institute, 2005).

——, 'Psykoanalyyttinen lähestymistapa musiikintutkimuksessa II: Psykoanalyyttisen musiikintutkimuksen suuntauksista ja tutkimustyypeistä' ['Psychoanalytic Approach to the Study of Music II: On the Trends and Categories in the Psychoanalytic Study of Music'], *Musiikki* [*Music*] (2003): 52–99.

——, 'Psykoanalyyttinen lähestymistapa musiikintutkimuksessa I: Psykoanalyyttisen teorian ja musiikkitieteen suhteesta' ['Psychoanalytic Approach to the

Study of Music I: On the Relationship between Psychoanalytic Theory and Musicology'], *Musiikki* [*Music*] (2002): 5–35.

——, 'Subjektistrategioita Sibeliuksen *Kyllikissä*' ['Subject Strategies in Sibelius's *Kyllikki*'], *Musiikki* [*Music*] (2001): 5–50.

Weiss, Albert Paul, *A Theoretical Basis of Human Behaviour* (Oxford: Adams, 1929).

Welton, Donn, 'Introduction: Situating the Body', in Donn Welton (ed.), *Body and Flesh. A Philosophical Reader* (Oxford: Blackwell, 1998).

Werf, Hendrik van der, 'The Music of Jaufré Rudel', in George Wolf and Roy Rosenstein (eds and trans.), *The Poetry of Cercamon and Jaufré Rudel* (New York and London: Garland Publishing, 1983), pp. 177–94.

Whiteley, Sheila (ed.), *Sexing the Groove: Popular Music and Gender* (New York: Routledge, 1997).

Whitford, Margaret, *Luce Irigaray: Philosophy in the Feminine* (London: Routledge, 1991).

Whittall, Arnold, *Exploring Twentieth-Century Music: Tradition and Innovation* (Cambridge: Cambridge University Press, 2003).

Wilson, Peter Niklas, 'Unterwegs zu einer "Ökologie der Klänge". Gérard Grisey's *Partiels* und die Ästhetik der Groupe de L'Itinéraire' ['Towards an "Ecology of Sounds". Gérard Grisey's *Partiels* and the Aesthetic of the *Itinérarie* Group'], *MELOS*, 2 (1988): 33–55.

Wolf, George, and Roy S. Rosenstein (eds), *The Poetry of Cercamon and Jaufré Rudel* (New York and London: Garland Publishing, 1983).

Index